The
Truth
About
Angels

And
Near-Death
Experiences

Michael D. Fortner

Trumpet Press, Lawton, OK

Abbreviations & Volumes Used:

ESV – English Standard Version
KJV – King James Version
MEV – Modern English Version (Based on the Textus Receptus)
Strong's numbering is in parentheses ( ).

Library of Congress Catalog-in-Publication Data: 2013930119

Author: Fortner, Michael D.
Title: The Truth About Angels and Near Death Experiences
1. Angels 2. Life After Death 3. Heaven 4. Hell 5. NDEs

ISBN: 979-8-8689-1956-5

Learn about other books by the author at
www.usbibleprophecy.com and www.michaelfortner.com

Trumpet Press is a member of the *Christian Indie Publishing Association* (CIPA).

Table of Contents

Introduction 9

Chapter 1: Angels: The Early Years 11

Chapter 2: Angels in The New Testament and Beyond...............23

Chapter 3: The Angel of the Lord 28

Chapter 4: Historical Opinions About Angels 43

Chapter 5: Angels in Christian History 53

Chapter 6: Angels and War 77

Chapter 7: Angels of the Modern Era 103

Chapter 8: Angels that Heal or Comfort or Direct.....................151

Chapter 9: Angels in Dreams and Visions 161

Chapter 10: Angels at Death and After 168

Chapter 11: Near Death Experiences 177

Bibliography...218

A Note From the Author

You will notice that in this book there are no "end notes" at the end of the chapter or the end of the book. This is because it is very troublesome for a reader to look up a note which may have some important information that will go unread, or may only be "Ibid." It is especially difficult to have end notes with an ebook; therefore, the print and ebook editions of this book have been formatted exactly the same, with notes within the text. For book references, I often only provide the author's last name and the title, which may be shortened. The full reference can be found by looking in the Bibliography.

I use the Modern English Version (MEV) as the main scripture text because it does not have any verses removed or shortened like other modern translations, but I do use other versions when they are better in a particular passage. Sometimes it takes reading a verse in several translations to see clearly what it actually says in the original Greek or Hebrew. Also, all underlining or other emphasis in this book is my own, and is never found in the original quotes. Now a word about quotes. Because of the misuse of source material in other books, from science to religion, some people will suspect that I have taken passages out of context or that I have misrepresented what someone or a prophecy actually says, so I include the actual quotes so you can read them for yourself, at least most of the time. Where necessary, I cite references and tell you where I get information and interpretation; other than that, you can assume that the interpretation is my own. Even when I quote others, I often will make observations related to the quote which are not found in the original information.

And it is important that you read the quotes to get the most out of this book; I assume that you will read the Scripture passages, but more importantly, there may come a time when your Bible has been taken from you, so I include most of the verses I reference.

Other Books by the Author:

At The End
The Fall of Babylon the Great and The Final Antichrist
The Return of Christ and The Three Days of Darkness
Satan's False Prophets Exposed
Editing God: Textual Criticism and Modern Bibles Analyzed
The Last Great Spiritual Conflict: A Vision and Two Prophecies

8

Introduction

There is no actual teaching concerning angels in the Bible, except that we should not worship them (**); but we can learn a lot about angels by what is recorded in the Bible. But why stop there? Angels have continued their work right up to the present day, therefore, this book will examine the appearances of angels <u>from Genesis through today</u> in an effort to learn, not only a correct doctrine of angels, but also what exactly guardian angels do, or don't do; how, why, etc.

In this book, I will examine a vast amount of evidence about angels in an effort to learn as much about them as possible. I also expose the stories of fallen angels who have appeared, pretending to be good angels. And I do the same with Near Death Experiences; some are from God, some are from a being of light that I show is actually Satan, the "Shining One."

People tend to like books that do not challenge their ideas and opinions, but that agree with, or at least confirm, their beliefs. Books about angels are no different. Some angel books hold a New Age point of view, others are theologically Catholic or Protestant. Authors normally do not include information that contradicts widely held beliefs about angels.

This book takes a non-denominational point of view, in that, it includes <u>a little theology, and some general teaching</u> and angel stories from an <u>independent-thinker point of view</u>. So this book does more than just include lots of angels stories, but I provide my own analysis to determine if it is a real, believable story or, if it could be an appearance of a fallen angel. For example, there is a commonly belief that "The Angel of the Lord" in the Old Testament is the Pre-incarnate Jesus, but I have a chapter that <u>proves,</u> it is NOT.

Sometimes the stories in this book support Catholic doctrine, other times Protestant, and other times neither. I consider myself knowledgeable and wise enough to be able to recognize truth from error, so I include theological information and commentary, and angel stories that are believable to me personally, based on my decades of Bible study and having a God-given insight and ability to figure things out, which I have had from a young age (except perhaps during my puberty years). And finally, I have a chapter that examines Near Death Experiences (NDEs). This is a topic of growing importance because so many people have had them; and many do not show heaven or hell, but support a New Age after-life. I discuss this and provide a Biblically based, solid answer, with new insights.

And so, this book is only for those who are <u>open-minded, truth seekers</u>. If you believe that everyone who are not members of your denomination are going to hell, then this book is NOT for you. If you believe that the only truth that exists is found inside the Bible, and none is found in other books such as Enoch, or Tobit, etc., then this book is not for you. If you believe the Earth is flat, this book not for you! Don't buy a book you know you will not like just so you can give it a 1-star rating. That is fraud.

Chapter 1

Angels: The Early Years

Angelology . . . is not a doctrine which we are justified in ignoring. (Rev. John Balcom Shaw, D.D.) (Fowler, *Our Angel Friends*, page 64)

Angels are found in the Bible, from Genesis to Revelation. The word "angel" means messenger, but they are much more than that. They also carry out God's judgment, engage in war against earthly armies, and perform seen and unseen acts here on earth to carry out God's desires for humanity, and bring about answers to our prayers.

Biblical evidence indicates that angels existed before the physical universe. According to the book of Hebrews, humankind was *"made a little lower than the angels"* (2:7). This passage suggests that humanity was created after the angels, as does Job 38:4–7, which says that when God created the physical universe, *"the morning stars sang together, and all the sons of God shouted for joy."* The morning stars and the sons of God are believed to be angels. This means that angels were the first of God's created beings, and this is likely why they are referred to as "sons of God."

The ancient Greeks, such as Plato, Socrates, and Aristotle believed in angels. Socrates claimed to have one that *"forbade the philosopher from doing certain things and encouraged him to undertake others"* (Lewis, *Angels A to Z*, page 115). You may ask, why God would send a guardian angel to assist a pagan; one who did not believe in the true God? You have to see the big picture; he wrote many things that have been a great benefit to the entire world, including those who believe in Yahweh (Jehovah). Perhaps God wanted those things written, and he knew Socrates was the best person to write them.

This is an example of how angels help God and humanity; they don't merely deliver messages to humans, as seen in the Bible, but they also help shape history. Angels help God in all that he does, and has ever done. Angels do not merely help administer the world and human affairs in this present age; they also helped God during the creation process. If a rib was literally taken from Adam and used to create Eve, then it was angels who did it.

Genesis 1:26 says that humans were made in the likeness of God. But what does that mean?

Dr. Michael Heiser said:

> The plurals in Genesis 1:26 mean that, in some way, we share something with them [the angels] when it comes to bearing God's image. (*The Unseen Realm*, page 41)

Does God have two eyes, two ears, a nose, and a mouth? Do we look like God or the angels? The Bible *does* say that we are made in the image of God, yet virtually all people who study this subject believe that God and the angels have no physical features at all like humans, because they are spirits, sometimes literally appearing as orbs of light with no features. They believe that angels merely take on the shape and appearance of humans when they appear on Earth, including being male or female. The Eastern Orthodox Church even frequently refers to angels as the "*bodiless ones*."

At one time I disagreed, but I have changed my mind and now agree. I believe that in their original state, they are more likely to be just balls of light. There are actually reports of people saying that an angel appeared to them, but it was just a ball of light. But they most often appear in human form, because they can take on any bodily form or shape they desire. And appearing to humans in human form is what makes us the most comfortable.

I believe human spirits also have no shape before we are born. When people have died and gone to heaven and returned, or just been out of their bodies, they report that they have the same appearance as their physical bodies; so it seems that once a human spirit is born into a physical body, it permanently takes on that shape, even when no longer in that body. And the Apostle Paul said that when we get to heaven, we will be known as we are known on Earth (1 Cor. 13:12).

Because the existence of angels has been deeply embedded in the history of humanity, knowledge of angels likely goes back as far

as the origins of civilization. It appears that other nations also believed in angel-like beings. A. C. Gaebelein, in *What the Bible Says
About Angels,* said:

> The mythologies of nearly all the ancient nations speak of such
> brings. Babylonian mythology pictured them as gods who con-
> veyed messages from gods to men. Roman and Greek mythology
> had its genii, semi-gods, fauns, nymphs and naiads, who visited
> the earth. . . . Egypt and Eastern nations believed in such super-
> natural, unseen creatures. The belief is well-nigh universal. My-
> thologies are the faint and distorted echoes of a common prime-
> val knowledge possessed by the race. If such beings of a higher
> rank than man did not exist we would not find them in the tradi-
> tional beliefs of the nations of old. (p. 14)

Of course, there is no clear proof that these other beings in ancient cultures and religions were angels. Just because there is a simi-
larity, it may not mean a common origin. It is understandable that if
an ancient people were to see angels, they would worship them as
gods and develop myths around them.

In Assyria, the Lamassu were female gods with wings, or were
they angels (?), while their male counterparts were called Shedu
(King, *Enuma Elish*: *The Seven Tablets of Creation*).

If this is merely a god-
dess, why does it have
wings? (Lamma, God-
dess, Iraq, 2000-1800
BC, bronze, baked clay-
Oriental Institute Muse-
um, University of Chica-
go, Wikimedia.org.)

Belief in angels also existed in the Zoroastrian religion of Persia, which still has some followers. There are three classes of angelic beings in Zoroastrianism: Amesha Spentas (literally means "Beneficient Immortals"), Yazatas (Guardian Angels), and Fravashis (Angels).

Zoroastrians pick a patron angel for their protection, and throughout their lives are careful to observe prayers dedicated to that angel. (http://www.avesta.org/angels.html)

Illustrated Manuscript, rawpixel.com

The word "angel(s)" appears almost 300 times in the Bible, with 15 times in the book of Genesis. But angels are actually referenced more times than that, sometimes called *"sons of God,"* or Cherubim, or Seraphim, or just "men," as in Gen. 18.

It appears that the first recorded account of an angel saving someone is found in Genesis 16, when Abraham's servant flees into the desert and an angel appears to tell her that she should return to Abraham. If she had stayed in the desert, she would either have died or been forced to marry some shepherd or Bedouin just to survive. Then, only two chapters later, two angels warn Lot and his family to leave town before the destruction of Sodom and Gomorrah.

Abraham's grandson, Jacob's, first encounter with angels was when he had a dream of a ladder with angels descending and ascending (Genesis 28:12). Angels do not need to use a ladder, but dreams are symbolic and need interpretation. This is a message from God to Jacob and us, telling us that angels are coming to earth and back to heaven on a continual basis.

An angel of God appeared to Abraham, Jacob, and Moses, and an angel went before the Hebrews through the desert in the form of a pillar of fire. The Bible does not directly tell us that while Moses was on Mt. Sinai, there were many thousands of angels, but the psalmist tells us about it:

> The chariots of God are twice ten thousand, even thousands of thousands; the Lord is among them, as in Sinai, in the holy place. (Psalm 68:17)

In Exodus, God tells Moses that he is going to send an angel to protect and guide the Hebrews into the Promised Land:

> "Behold, I send an angel before you to guard you on the way and to bring you to the place that I have prepared. Pay careful attention to him and obey his voice; do not rebel against him, for he will not pardon your transgression, for my name is in him." (2:20 -21)

God also told the Hebrews that he would send his angel to help them drive out the Canaanites, Amorites, and Hittites. This means that angels were fighting with the Hebrews in their battles, which allowed them to be victorious. Later, an angel appeared to Gideon and commissioned him to wage war (Judges 6). Then an angel appeared to a barren woman to tell her she would have a child named

Samson. Sometime later, an angel appeared to Elijah several times to give him instructions and food.

When Hezekiah was king, the Assyrians had surrounded Jerusalem, and God sent an angel to kill 185,000 of the troops in one night (1 Chronicles 21:15). But before that happened, the Assyrians had successfully attacked and killed many Jews in the surrounding region; Jerusalem being the last city not yet conquered. So why did God wait so long before delivering the people? We can only surmise that they had not yet humbled themselves before God and begged his mercy, the way King Hezekiah finally did.

The book of Daniel tells us that angels appeared to Daniel several times to tell him about the future of Israel. Then some jealous, hateful men conspired against Daniel because he was a godly, praying man, and had him thrown into a pit of hungry lions. But God sent an angel to shut the mouths of those lions, and he was totally unharmed after spending all night in the pit with them.

During one appearance, the angel said to Daniel, *"in the first year of Darius the Mede, I stood up to encourage and to strengthen him"* [Darius] (11:1) (Jubilee Bible 2000). God was with this pagan king because God wanted Darius to win the war against Babylon. In this way, God delivered the Jews from Babylonian captivity. Angels also appeared to Ezekiel, Isaiah, and many others, no doubt.

Since the word "angel" means "messenger," every time you see the word "angel" in the Bible, you should actually read "messenger." Rabbi Mordecai Finley of Bel Air, California is quoted as saying:

> "The Hebrew word for angel, 'malakh,' comes from 'malakha,' which means 'toil,' or 'work.' And a malakh, an angel, really means an agent of God, a worker for God, and emissary of God, as it were, or a messenger." (*In Search of Angels*, David Connelly, page 138).

There was no detailed teaching about angels in the Law of Moses; the Israelites learned about them through experience. Angels appeared so often that they entered the common knowledge and language of the Hebrew people, as can be seen in these references:

> And Achish answered and said to David, I know that you are good in my sight, like an angel of God. (1 Samuel 29:9)

> For as an angel of God, so is my lord the king, to see what is good and bad. (2 Samuel 14:17)

In 1 Kings 13:18, an old prophet lied to a young prophet and said, *"An angel spoke to me by Yahweh's word, saying"* that the young prophet should return to the old prophet's home to eat and stay the night. He lied, but it shows how common and believable it was for angels to appear and give messages, or they would not have made such casual references to them.

God did not allow graven images to represent Him, yet he *did allow images of angels*, and <u>even commanded it</u>. When the Hebrews built their Temple, Cherubim were depicted on the walls of the Temple in Jerusalem (2 Chron. 3), and two were on the Ark of the Covenant.

One representation of the Ark of the Covenant. (Creative Commons license.)

But what is truly shocking, is that <u>two giant Cherubim stood inside the Most Holy Place</u>; also called the Holy of Holies in the Temple, that were 10 cubits tall (2 Chron. 3:10-13) with wings stretched out. Each wing was 5 cubits, which means the wings were likely attached at the center of the back, not the side, or the 4 wings and Cherubim would have been longer than the room, which was 20 cubits.

(Some translations say they were carved of wood and overlaid with gold, while others say they were made of cast metal and overlaid with gold; this is because the meanings of the original Hebrew words in this passage are not fully understood.)

Some people want to claim that Cherubim were winged lions, which is absurd; there is no reference to winged lions in the Bible or in any other Jewish writing that I know of. And none has ever ap-

peared to anyone to do or say anything! But there are references to Cherubim guarding the way to the Tree of Life with flaming swords. Should we believe that a winged lion could wield a sword?! No, the Bible is not *The Chronicles of Narnia.*

Because winged lions have long bodies and are not upright like humans, they would have taken up most of the entire Holy of Holies! Therefore, the evidence indicates that they were winged angels. One of the reasons for believing they were winged lions, is the known ancient sculptures in Assyria, which depict winged lions with human heads, and have a similar name:

In Assyrian, they are called *kirubu*. In Hebrew, they are called *Kerub*. In Akkadian, karibu/kuribu means, "protecting spirit" or "divine spirit." The same can be said for the Assyrian *kirubu* and the Hebrew *kerub*. (www.ancient-origins. net, *Flaming Swords and Winged Beasts: What Were These Ancient Creatures? The Origins of Cherubim – Part II*, by Cam Rea)

Humans tend to turn reality into myths, and so with stories of winged angels appearing and disappearing, it is not a surprise that humans made them into winged lions with human faces. But they are not described as such in the Bible or by any known eyewitness report throughout history. Creatures that do not exist would not be represented in the Temple in Jerusalem.

The Bible gives us progressive revelation from Genesis through Revelation, and so we learn more about angels the farther along we get in the Bible and on through to today. Even though the Bible does not describe the appearance of Michael or Gabriel, we know that many of them have wings because they were seen on the Temple walls and in the Holy of Holies with wings. Therefore, it is a totally false claim that angels were never believed to have wings until the time of Constantine, as some writers and documentaries have said. And Psalm 18:10 and Isaiah 6:2 say that angels have wings and fly! And because some of them do have wings, it is highly likely that there were times when an angel appeared that it had wings, even though it is not stated to have wings in the Bible. Because the Bible never describes one.

In the book of 2 Enoch, he describes how he was asleep when two angels showed up with a message from God that he would be going to heaven with them, and to tell his family about it before he leaves. He described those angels as having wings:

> And there appeared to me two very large men, so big that I never saw such on earth. Their faces were shining like the sun, their eyes were like a burning light, and from their lips fire was coming out. They were singing. Their clothing was of various kinds in appearance and was purple. Their wings were brighter than gold, and their hands whiter than snow. (1:6)

But why would they ever appear with wings? Spirit-beings do not need wings to fly; so why the wings? Just as they use spiritual swords and ride spiritual horses, they could certainly also have wings. It seems that there are similarities between the physical and spiritual dimensions that we cannot currently explain. For example, there is spiritual grass, flowers, and trees in Paradise and heaven, and even a massive wall around the great city where everyone lives in heaven (many sources, including *Flight to Heaven*, Dale Black, page 105).

Some researchers believe that Cherubim are a different form of angel from the messengers who appear to humans, or of a different rank. Because we now have literally thousands of eyewitnesses to angels, we have many reports of angels with and without wings. Many people who have also died, gone to heaven, and returned report seeing angels as we see them here on earth with human features; some with and without wings.

According to Roland Buck, that is in fact true. He reported in *Angels on Assignment* back in 1979 that there are four types of angels; only the worship angels have wings, and Lucifer was an archangel of the worship angels. Another group lives permanently here on earth because they minister full-time to humanity. He also said there are the warring angels, of which Michael is the archangel. And Gabriel is the archangel of the messenger angels who deliver messages from God.

Angels appeared frequently in the Old Testament, and they continued their work between the Testaments. In 2 Maccabees 3, we learn how a traitor went and told the Greek King Seleucus about all the wealth in the Temple treasury, so he ordered Heliodorus to confiscate it. After Heliodorus arrived in Jerusalem, the people and the priests called upon God to save the offerings that were made to him there. When Heliodorus was attempting to confiscate the gold and silver, a mighty warrior wearing gold armor on a horse *"adorned with beautiful trappings"* suddenly appeared, then rushed at him and struck him. Then two warriors,

> "young men notable in their strength, and beautiful in their glory, and splendid in their apparel, who stood by him on either side, and scourged him unceasingly, inflicting on him many sore stripes" (3:26).

Heliodorus was picked up off the ground by his men, put in a litter, and carried away, near death. The people were afraid that the King would think that they attacked and killed Heliodorus, so the High Priest made a sacrifice to God and asked him to spare his life:

> While the high priest was making an atonement, the same young men appeared again to Heliodorus dressed in the same clothing, and they stood and said, "Be very grateful to the high priest Onias, since for his sake the Lord has granted you your life. 34 And see that you, who have been flogged by heaven, report to all people the majestic power of God." Having said this they vanished. (3:33-34) (NRSV)

Clearly, these were angels who came in answer to the prayers of the people. Again in the war of the Maccabees, the Jewish General Judas Maccabeus called upon God before a major battle. He prayed:

> "O Lord, you sent your angel in the time of King Hezekiah of Judea, and he killed fully one hundred eighty-five thousand in the camp of Sennacherib. 23 So now, O Sovereign of the heavens, send a good angel to spread terror and trembling before us. 24 By the might of your arm may these blasphemers who come

against your holy people be struck down." (2 Mac. 15:22-24) (NRSV)

God answered that prayer when 6,000 Jewish men defeated an army of 10s of thousands.

> When the battle became fierce, there appeared to the enemy from heaven five resplendent men on horses with golden bridles, and they were leading the Jews. Two of them took Maccabeus between them, and shielding him with their own armor and weapons, they kept him from being wounded. They showered arrows and thunderbolts on the enemy, so that, confused and blinded, they were thrown into disorder and cut to pieces. Twenty thousand five hundred were slaughtered, besides six hundred cavalry. (2 Maccabees 10:29-31) (NRSV)

In the Old Testament, angels often appeared even though they were not specifically called upon for help, but the above example shows that God does send angelic help when requested, and genuinely needed. The New Testament also contains clear evidence that angels come to our aid when requested. Jesus said, *"Do you think that I cannot now pray to My Father, and He will at once give Me more than twelve legions of angels?"* (Matthew 26:53). But Jesus did not call for them, and he was murdered.

In spite of two giant angels standing in the Most Holy Place, and all of the angels that were said to have appeared during the centuries of the Old Testament, and between the Testaments, by the time of Jesus, the Sadducees did not believe in angels! It is sad the way humans can develop such unbelief while ignoring large amounts of evidence that should actually cause belief. But that is just human nature. Perhaps the reason the angels announced the birth of Christ to simple shepherds rather than religious authorities was because the shepherds were able to believe the message, whereas the authorities were not.

We still have these modern-day Sadducees within Christianity today who refuse to believe in the appearance of angels, the working of miracles, and even NDEs by Christians. A book was published in 1843 titled, *Modern Miracles Condemned by Reason and Scripture*. In this little book, the author spoke against those who claimed to have seen visions and dreams. One person was in a state of near death; upon recovery, she claimed to have seen angels and heaven and knew about individuals who had died, which was proven correct

once word reached the community about those who had just died;
yet people refused to believe it. The author appears to have made up
his mind even before examining the evidence:

> All such publications as the *Entranced Female* assume that this
> system of revealed truth [the Bible] is incomplete, and that its
> deficiency, both as to matter and mode of communication, re-
> quires to be supplied by supplementary and improved revela-
> tions! (page 18)

Isn't that always the argument? *We have the Bible, therefore,
God no longer communicates with his people or performs miracles
for them, or anything!* The *Entranced Female* is not New Revelation, it merely shows that God did not go to sleep once the Bible
was written! He has continued working the same way among his
people as he always has.

There is Nothing New about it! As will be shown, God never
stopped interacting with his people, even after the Bible was written.
Unbelieving churches eventually become compromised with worldli-
ness and lukewarmness, or they become very legalistic with every jot
and tittle explained in such detail that any variation from their view
is called heresy.

But not everyone is so closed-minded. Even back in 1875,
Charles D. Bell had a wise and insightful opinion on the subject:

> The Bible lays open to us a universe peopled with spirits inter-
> mediate between God and man. If it assigns no time to their crea-
> tion; if it makes no distinct revelation of their nature, their attrib-
> utes, their number, their character, yet is it explicit on the point
> of their existence, and their gracious ministry. Again and again
> they appear in the Old and New Testaments as "God's messen-
> gers;" His "ministers;" as "spirits;" and as "flames of fire;" "the
> holy ones;" "watchers;" and "the hosts," or "armies of God."
> They encamp about the righteous, comfort the sorrowful, fight
> for the good, oppose the wicked, smite the ungodly, and perform
> the Redeemer's behests of grace and love on behalf of His pur-
> chased people.

> Nor have they ever withdrawn from this world. The services they
> once undertook on behalf of God's children they still perform.
> We shall do well to realize this truth, and welcome heartily, and
> suitably reverence (not idolatrously worship) these our angelic
> friends. (*Angelic Beings: Their Nature and Ministry*, p. 175-176)

Chapter 2

Angels in The New Testament
and Beyond

We reject the Bible when we reject angels, for they are woven into the very warp and woof of the revered pages. (Alfred Fowler) (Fowler, *Our Angel Friends*, page 198)

Even though Gabriel and Michael are both mentioned in the Old Testament, the word "archangel" does not appear until 1 Thessalonians, and again in Jude. There is no way to know just when the term began use, or how it became known that the rank of *archangel* even exists. It is highly probable that many appearances of angels were never written down.

Gabriel appeared to Zachariah in Luke 1 to tell him that his wife was going to have a son who became John the Baptist; then Gabriel appeared again to Mary to inform her that she would give birth to Jesus. Angels appeared to shepherds to announce the birth of Jesus; an angel appeared in a dream to Joseph and told him to flee to Egypt. Angels even ministered to Jesus after he was tempted by Satan in the desert and on the Mount of Transfiguration. An angel rolled away the stone that covered the tomb of Christ and then announced that he had risen to Mary and Martha. And an angel spoke to the Apostles when Jesus was taken up into the clouds, and told them He will return in the same manner.

Even after the Holy Spirit was poured out, angels continued all their activities. An angel told Cornelius to send for Peter, and in Acts 8, Philip was having a revival when an angel told him to travel south, where he met with an Ethiopian, whom Philip converted and baptized; then the man took the gospel back to Ethiopia. I suspect, that some times when we believe that God spoke to us, it was really an angel. They can also put thoughts into our minds to do this or that or look into this or that subject, without actually using words in sentence form. The more we pray for guidance from God, the more we will receive it.

> Augustine accepted the theology of St. Paul; but he could not break away from his sins. He withdrew to his garden, reclined under a fig-tree, and gave vent to bitter tears. He wrestled with the angel, and his deliverance was at hand. It was under the fig-tree of his garden that he fancied he heard the voice of an angel chanting and often repeating, "Tolle, lege; tolle, lege" -- "Take up and read; take up and read!" He opened the Scriptures, and his eyes alighted on the text in Romans 13:13. His conversion was accomplished. (John Lord) (Fowler, *Our Angel Friends*, page 104)

In Acts 12:7, an angel appeared to Peter, released him of his shackles, and led him out of prison. In this, and other similar accounts found in history, the prison doors opened by the will of the angel. But when something like an automobile needs to be lifted, it does not just rise up or levitate, angels literally lift up the vehicle (see later in this book).

Later in Acts 16:25-26, Paul and Silas were shackled in prison when an earthquake hit, and the chains of all the prisoners were loosed. I do not believe that a normal earthquake can cause shackles to become unlocked, which means it was no doubt brought about by an unseen angel.

In Acts 27, Paul was on his way to Rome by ship when they were caught in a storm and were in danger of sinking. An angel appeared to Paul and told him that everyone on the ship would be saved if they stayed with the ship. Paul, no doubt, had been praying hard for the safety of the ship and those on board.

And in the book of Revelation, angels are seen bringing about God's judgments upon the world. Therefore, it is clear that the coming of the Holy Spirit has not replaced the work of the angels. And certainly not the Bible. How can written words replace the actual intervention that angels bring? They cannot! It was likely Paul who said about angels, "*Are they not all ministering spirits, being sent forth to minister to those who are about to inherit salva-*

tion?" (Hebrews 1:14) (AFV). Do people still need miracle interventions today? Yes!

These are <u>not</u> all of the angelic interventions and appearances in the Bible, just most of them. There were so many appearances of angels within the early church, (which were not written down), that a false teaching arose that resulted in people worshiping angels, which Paul spoke against in Colossians 2:18. It seems many of the Jews in former centuries also developed an adoration of angels (from Tobit, 12:15; Philo, in *lib. de Somn.*; Josephus, War. lib. 2, cap. 8, sec. 7); which is understandable considering the extent to which angels were doing God's work.

There is an actual term for the worship of angels, called angelolatry. The Council of Nicaea in A.D. 325 declared belief in angels an official part of Church dogma, which apparently caused an outbreak of angelolatry, so the Synod of Laodicea in 343 condemned the worship of angels as idolatry. Many churches today have gone to the other extreme and act as if angels are now asleep.

The Apostle Paul frequently made reference to angels, such as in this passage:

> I command you in the sight of God, and the Lord Jesus Christ, and the chosen angels, that you observe these things without prejudice, doing nothing by partiality. (1 Timothy 5:21)

So, it appears that angels were very important to some of the Jews, and certainly to all of the early Christians. But most "modern" Jews do not believe in angels, <u>even the Orthodox Jews</u>. It is *"only the most traditional sects, such as the Hasidim,"* that believe in literal angels (Lewis, *Angels A-Z*, page 237).

As you have likely been able to conclude from the material thus far, the idea of guardian angels comes to us from the Bible. Not only because of what actually took place, but also from what is written in Psalm 91:

> Because you have made Yahweh your refuge, and the Most High your dwelling place, no evil shall happen to you, neither shall any plague come near your dwelling. For he will put his angels in charge of you, to guard you in all your ways. (9-12) (WEB)

Barnes Notes on the Bible says the word "charge" means that God will "command" angels to come to our aid. The passage is best understood as saying that if you put your trust in God, he will not allow evil to attack you, by sending angels when needed. It does not mean you have an angel walking by your side all day, every day! It also means you will not receive any judgment from God. The passage in question is merely a general promise of what can happen if we pray for angelic protection, not what will absolutely happen to all Christians in all circumstances. Where was Stephen's guardian angel? He was stoned to death and became the first Christian martyr.

The New Age Movement takes that same verse, and a few others, and teaches that we all have several guardian angels. Jane Howard claims she can see her guardian angel sitting beside her as she drives a car. Really? Since God AND ANGELS know the future, why would an angel need to waste years to literally be right beside someone who is not in any actual danger? Should there be a time of danger for you, the angel can travel hundreds, perhaps thousands, of miles in a split second to come to your aid. So there is no need for one to literally be by your side 24/7 on a continuous basis; it is nonsense. I am sure there are times when angels are needed 24/7, but only during times of extreme danger. She also claims to commune with angels daily, and teaches other people to engage in the same New Age wizardry:

> "I run workshops worldwide, and I do personal readings for people – one-on-one, or by mail or phone. During that reading I introduce people to their own guardian angel, allowing them to experience the sensation of the presence of the angel and of receiving messages for themselves." (*In Search of Angels*, David Connolly, page 146)

This, of course, is a totally false teaching, and the spirits these people interact with are not angels, but "familiar spirits," or even demons. Eileen Freeman, author of *Touched by Angels,* was one of the people responsible for a modern resurgence in belief in angels. It is almost a Christian-based book, which I do not recommend, but she did say some good things in it:

> Some people think they can use angels for mediumistic purposes to contact the dead or give them lucky numbers for the week to come. (I strongly doubt that anyone who is reading this book is in this category.) The only angels such people will "conjure" are fallen spirits, the absolute zeros on the love scale; and it is far better to have nothing to do with them under any circumstances. (page 146-147)

And in another place, she said of angels:

> They don't want people to gather in a circle and spend an hour exclusively trying to communicate with any of them, to focus on them alone, as though they were ends in themselves. (Ibid., page 189)

The best evidence tells me that not only must we trust in God on a day-to-day basis, but we should specifically pray for angelic protection should the need arise. By doing so, we increase the likelihood of receiving angelic help, but it is not guaranteed.

One reason many people have a wrong view of guardian angels is because of what Jesus said in Matthew 18:10:

> See that you don't despise one of these little ones, for I tell you that in heaven their angels always see the face of my Father who is in heaven. (WEB)

Notice that it says the little children's angels were in heaven. They are not here on Earth sitting by each child to protect them from all harm, as many people dreamily like to believe. There is no more information to use on this subject than this one passage, and since the angels are not said to guard or protect them in any way, we can only guess that perhaps each child has an angel in heaven to watch and report on how the child is doing in all its various areas of growth, and perhaps even as it goes into adulthood and chooses a path in life. No one can really say for sure, but it does NOT prove that every child or human has a guardian angel!

A theology of angels gradually developed within the early Church concerning their mission, different categories of angels, their nature, etc., but it was and still is largely speculation. Dionysius wrote that there were nine orders of angels subdivided into three groups:

     * Seraphim, Cherubim, and Thrones.
     * Dominions, Virtues, and Powers.
     * Principalities, Archangels, and angels.

This, of course, is wrong because Seraphim and Cherubim are clearly angels, as are archangels. But Dominions, Virtues, Powers, and Principalities, no one knows for sure, we can only speculate that they might be offices, functions, and territories over which they have authority.

Chapter 3

The Angel of the Lord

The termination "el" of their names (angel) implies power, strength, and is synonymous with that by which we call the Almighty, God. (M) (Fowler, *Our Angel Friends*, page 124)

In the Old Testament, the term *"the angel of the Lord"* appears many times, which of course refers to an angel of Yahweh. But because of the word "the" before "angel," Christian theologians expect us to believe that this does not refer to an ordinary angel but to the pre-incarnate Messiah, the Son of God. But this is a mistaken viewpoint.

We know that "angel" means *messenger* because, many times when an angel showed up, he came with a message from God. There was a time when, if a king wanted to send a message to another king, the first king would send a man to travel to that other country and personally deliver the message. He was, of course, referred to as the messenger of the king. There were other uses of the term messenger:

> Prideaux observes, that the minister of the Synagogue, who officiated in offering the public prayers, being the mouth of the congregation, delegated them as their representative, messenger or angel to address God in prayer for them, was in Hebrew named Sheliack-Zibbor, that is, the angel of the church; and that from hence the chief of the ministers of the seven churches in Asia, in the apocalypse are, by a title borrowed from the Synagogue, called the angels of the churches. (Clayton, *Angelology*, page 114)

I will translate the above into normal language: A man would stand up and give a public prayer to God on behalf of the entire congregation. Since this person delivered a message, or prayer, to God, he was called the *messenger of the synagogue*. Jesus made use of this and called the pastors of the Seven Churches of Asia in the book of Revelation, messengers of the churches. But the word "angel" is not translated into "messenger" in Revelation, as the use of the word should indicate; so our English translations, and likely others as well, have Jesus saying, *"To the angel of the church in Ephesus write"* (2:1).

But long before there were messengers of synagogues, and messengers of the churches, there were also messengers of God to the Hebrew nation. The Bible uses the phrase, *"the angel of the Lord."* It literally says, *"the messenger of Yahweh"* (Jehovah). Therefore, to say *"the angel of the Lord,"* is like saying *"the messenger of God,"* rather than the messenger of the king; or the messenger of some other god worshiped by the surrounding nations.

The belief in angels existed from the earliest times, and so this belief likely also existed among surrounding people and in connection to their gods. Dr. Michael Heiser says:

> In the ancient Near East, the term *shedu* was neutral; it could speak of a good or malevolent spirit being. These Akkadian figures were often cast as guardians or protective entities. (*The Unseen Realm*, page 33)

In another place, Dr. Heiser said that Ugarit, a city-state in Syria, worshiped a god named El, who was similar to Yahweh, with his own *"the 'sons of El,' and messenger gods (mal'akim)"* (Ibid., page 46). The ancient Sumerians and Akkadians (4500-1800 B.C.) had winged beings called the apkallu. The *Dictionary of Deities and Demons in the Bible* says of the ancient Sumerians and Akkadians:

> . . . clay figures of seven apkallu were used with an apotropaic function. . . . placed at the head of the bed of the sick person, the seven bird-apkallu buried against the wall . . . and the seven fish-apkallu, who guard the threshold of the bedroom . . . (page 74)

The word "apotropaic" means they ward off evil spirits, so these *apkallu* functioned as guardian spirits. Another ancient religion in particular believed in guardian angels, that being Zoroastrianism in Persia. They were called *amesha spenta*, literally meaning *"beneficent immortals."*

The ministry of angels, and their supervision over human affairs, was a favorite and firmly believed in doctrine of the ancient Persians. They supposed that the eternal throne was situated in the sun, which, for that reason, became the chief object of their adoration; and that through the stars were distributed the various orders of angels that encircled it. In common with different other orientals, they held that the stars are either themselves spirits, or vehicles of spirits, and that the falling stars are the firebrands, which the good angels hurl after the bad who dare to encroach upon their territories. They considered that, in the direction of human affairs particular angels had different provinces and posts assigned them, with which their brethren interfered not; and in honor of them they bestowed their names upon the months and days. (Edward I. Sears, A.M.) (Fowler, *Our Angel Friends*, page 120)

<u>Moses and the Hebrews doubtless knew about these guardian spirits of other nations</u>; therefore, it is no surprise that the first several times that an angel is mentioned in the Bible, he is called *"the Angel of Yahweh,"* <u>to distinguish him from any of the other guardian spirits that other people believed existed</u>.

It is believed that the Hebrews did not yet know about fallen angels, but they knew that other nations believed in guardian spirits. Even though we know today that other gods do not actually exist, fallen angels do exist and still appear with the intent to deceive people. Even today, if an angel appears, we need to know if it is an angel of Yahweh or a fallen angel impersonating a good angel. Examples are given in other chapters.

In Hinduism, there are two different groups of spirit beings that are similar to angels. The Maruts, also called Marutagana, are considered storm deities who are aggressive warriors, armed with "golden weapons," and ride golden chariots pulled by strong horses. There are also the Devas, who are the guardians of Earth and manage the daily affairs of the universe.

The above information should be enough to cause Bible students to understand the truth, but sadly, it is not. Those who are handicapped by theological training believe the phrase refers to the preincarnate Son of God because it says "the" rather than "an" angel of the Lord. But if this is true, then God is his own messenger! (FYI, like most theologians, Dr. Heiser believes the angel of the Lord was Messiah.)

Apparently, there is such a shortage of angels in heaven that God must send the second member of the Godhead to deliver messages to people and do many other things, numerous times throughout the Old Testament period! But theologians use faulty reasoning to come to that conclusion. I will examine several instances.

Here is what one preacher wrote:

> It is noteworthy and of great interest that the ancient Jews in their traditions regarded the Angel of the Lord, in every instance, not as an ordinary angel, but as the only mediator between God and the world, the author of all revelations, to whom they have the name *Metatron*. They called him "the angel of the countenance" (see Is. 63:9), because he always sees and beholds God's countenance, and they speak of him as the highest revelation of the unseen God, a partaker of His nature and of His majesty. They speak of him as the Schechinah. A Talmudical statement declares "the Metatron, the Angel of the Lord, is united with the most high God by oneness of nature", while another source speaks of him as "having dominion over all created things."

> The very ancient Midrash known as *Otiot de Rabbi Akiba* makes the following declaration about the Angel of the Lord, "The Metatron is the angel, the prince of the face, the prince of the law, the prince of wisdom, the prince of strength, the prince of glory, the prince of the temple, the prince of the kings, the prince of the rulers and the high and exalted."

> These ancient Jewish sources identify, therefore, the Angel of the Lord, whom they call Metatron, with the Messiah and as one with God. This was also the view of later Jews. . . . (Gaebelein, *What the Bible Says About Angels*. p. 20)

What he says about ancient Jewish belief may well be accurate, but that does not mean their belief is correct. Gaebelein may also not have been well informed on this subject, because the Jews also believed that Metatron was Enoch. This would make the pre-incarnate Son of God having been Enoch! No, sorry, that is nowhere near correct.

> Just prior to the Flood, the prophet Enoch was transported — while still alive — directly to heaven and transformed, first into an angel, and then into the angel-prince Metatron. In 3 Enoch he describes his transformation: . . .

> The Jewish prophet Elijah was transformed into the great angel Sandalphon, who exceeds the height of all other angels "by the length of a journey of five hundred years." Sandalphon is an angel-prince — the twin brother of Metatron and a master of heavenly song. (Connolly, *In Search of Angels*, page 98)

Is this the origin of the belief that humans can become angels? And another reference says:

> The angel Metraton is the king of angels. Metraton distributes among all princes or angels of the nations their necessaries. . . . Metraton, by some of the Rabbins, is considered as the great personage mentioned in the Old Testament, under the term of "The angel of the Lord," or "The Angel-Jehovah." "The Messenger of the Covenant," specified in Malachi, chap. 3:1. (Clayton, *Angelology*, p. 199)

But, of course, they have other reasons just as bad for believing that *the Angel of the Lord* is the pre-incarnate Son of God; I will just use the title Messiah. Let's begin with the account of Hagar, Abraham's servant who fled into the wilderness:

> 9 Then the angel of the Lord said to her, "Return to your mistress, and submit yourself to her authority." 10 The angel of the Lord also said to her, "I will multiply your descendants exceedingly so that they will be too many to count." . . .
>
> 13 Then she called the name of the Lord that spoke to her, "<u>You are the God who sees</u>," for she said, "<u>Have I now looked on Him who sees me</u>?" 14 Therefore the well was called Beer Lahai Roi. It is between Kadesh and Bered. (Genesis 16:9-10, 13-14)

Here is what a highly respected commentary said:

> The angel of Jehovah. This phrase is especially employed to denote the Lord himself in that form in which he condescends to make himself manifest to man. (Barnes Notes)

And here is what *The Wycliffe Bible Commentary* says:

> This "angel" was not a created being, but Jehovah himself, manifesting himself to Hagar. . . . He identifies himself with Jehovah; he speaks and acts with God's authority; he is spoken of as God, or as Jehovah. (Pfeiffer, 1962)

After the mention of Cherubim guarding the way to the Garden of Eden, this is the first mention of an angel in the Bible. Though, as mentioned above, the belief in angels is very ancient and likely dates back before the time of Noah, Hagar did not have a full knowledge or concept of God and his angels. So it is understandable that any divine-like being would be mistaken for God. She is out in the desert, and a bright and shining spirit-being appears to her; it is natural that she thought it was God. This is probably the reason that during several other appearances of angels, the angels refused to give their names because the people would have thought it was God's name.

We must realize that the Bible merely reported what Hagar said and what she believed, that she believed she had seen God. Just because she believed that she saw God, does not mean that she actually did see God. We will see another, even better example of this shortly.

All angels speak with the authority of God because that is what they do; they are God's messengers, and as a consequence, most of the time they don't say, *"God sent me with this message for you,"* though once or twice an angel does say something similar in the Bible. In Luke, an angel appeared to Zechariah, the priest (1:18), and told him that he would have a son, John the Baptist. But the angel did not say, *God told me to tell you*, but merely said:

> "Do not fear, Zechariah, for your prayer has been heard, and your wife Elizabeth will bear you a son, and you shall call his name John . . . He will turn many of the sons of Israel to the Lord their God. . . ." (Luke 1:13, 16)

Zechariah had doubts and asked the angel how he could be sure this would happen. The angel was not happy and scolded Zechariah for not believing him:

> "I am Gabriel, who stands in the presence of God. And I was sent to speak to you and to bring you this good news. And now you will be silent and unable to speak until the day that these things happen, because you did not believe my words, which will be fulfilled in their season. (1:19-20).

Wow! I detect, at the very least, impatience because of Zechariah's doubt, *"How could he possibly doubt my word; I am a high-ranking angel!"* Then Gabriel identifies himself and gives the source of his authority, which is that he stands in the very presence of God. He still did not say, *God told me to tell you*, or even *I have come with a message from God*. He merely spoke with authority; then he told Zechariah where he got his authority.

When an angel speaks, it is as if God were speaking, because they speak for God. Doubting an angel is almost as bad as doubting God (though we know that Satan can appear as an angel, so we should be careful about believing any spirit that shows up). Also, not only did he speak with God's authority, but when Zechariah doubted, Gabriel had the power to pronounce judgment, apparently without even consulting God on the matter. So angels have the power and authority to not only speak for God, but also to take action based on that authority. This incident also reveals to us that angels have personalities and emotions, with independent thought and free will. Just the same as humans.

Many people today have this same kind of authority to act on behalf of someone else. They can buy and sell real estate and sign contracts, all without asking permission from their boss; this is called *Power of Attorney*. It is a legal document that gives power to another person to act on his or her behalf.

Bob is a real estate tycoon and gives Mary the *Power of Attorney*. Then Bob discovers that Mary has sold a huge office building for $1000.00. He cannot legally do anything to her, except fire her, because she had full legal right to sell the building that Bob owned. If you have *Power of Attorney*, then you can act in ALL ways and in ALL circumstances as though you are that other person. In the same way, angels have God's power and authority to act.

In like manner, we Christians have been given authority by Jesus to cast out demons; but we are commanded to exercise this authority in *"the name of Jesus."* The angels just speak and act by the authority God has given them, without needing to say, "In the name of Yahweh" or "Jesus."

The messengers of God deliver the words of God in the same way that a prophet does. Prophets do not always preface their words with *"Thus says the Lord;"* sometimes they just begin to prophesy as if God were speaking, "My people . . ." No one would mistake a prophet for God, so we should not mistake an angel for God.

Gabriel let Zechariah know that he was not an ordinary angel, but one who stands in the presence of God, which is why he is called an Archangel. The book of Tobit was written by an Israelite after they were taken captive by Assyria. It tells us about the angel

Raphael, who came to heal Tobit. When he finally identified himself, he said, *"I am Raphael, one of the seven holy angels, which present the prayers of the saints, and which go in and out before the glory of the Holy One"* (12:15).

Zechariah 4:10 says, *"These seven are the eyes of Jehovah which run to and fro through the whole earth"* (MKJV). And the book of Revelation, chapter 4:5, says: *"Seven lamps of fire were burning before the throne, which are the seven Spirits of God."* Then in chapter five, Jesus is seen symbolically as a slain lamb (yet standing) with *"seven horns and seven eyes, which are the seven Spirits of God, sent out into all the earth"* (5:6). These seven spirits of God appear to be seven angels of authority and power that rule over other angels throughout the world. They are helping God fulfill his plan for the world. And <u>since they are called the seven spirits of God</u>, that makes the angels more than mere created beings, but it makes them in a certain sense, *"sons of God"* (a phrase that appears 11 times in the Bible and refers to angels).

So we know that Raphael and Gabriel are two of those seven spirits of God. The Book of Enoch names Raguel, Saraqael, Remiel, Raphael, Uriel, Gabriel, and Michael. The *Apocalypse of Peter* names, Barakiel, Ramiel, Uriel, Samiel, and Azael. The book called the *Word and Revelation of Esdras* [Ezra] *the Holy Prophet*, names, Michael, Gabriel, Uriel, Raphael, Gabuthelon, Aker, Arphugitonos, Beburos, and Zeuleon. Then, in the Parables of Enoch, Phanuel is mentioned.

The book of Isaiah says, *"the angel of His presence saved them"* (63:9). But as we just saw, there are actually seven of these angels that stand in the presence of God, not just one.

The book of Hebrews says several times, making a clear point, that the Messiah was NEVER an angel!

> 5 For to which of the angels did He at any time say: "You are My Son; today I have become Your Father"? . . . 6 And again, when He brings the firstborn into the world, He says: "Let all the angels of God worship Him." 7 Of the angels He says: "He makes His angels spirits, and His servants a flame of fire." 8 But to the Son He says: "Your throne, O God, lasts forever and ever; a scepter of righteousness is the scepter of Your kingdom." (1:5-8)

Messiah did NOT need to function as an angel in the Old Testament period, because there are seven high-ranking angels that have the authority of God to act on God's behalf.

The encounters of Gabriel with Zechariah show that angels are not all sugar and spice, or brimming with love. They can also pronounce judgment upon you, but as a general rule, those who fear God do not have to fear being struck down by an angel:

> . . . in the apocalyptic representations of St. John, we behold them controlling evil spirits; wielding the elements of this world; producing, directing, and bringing to a termination the great convulsions of time; conveying the souls of the just to the paradise of God, and severing the wicked from the good at the day of judgment. (Clayton, *Angelology*, page 192-193)

In another encounter in Genesis, Jacob wrestled with an angel who did not appear as a bright, shining angel but as a man, but afterwards he thinks it was God. The text says,

> a man wrestled with him there until daybreak. . . . Then the man said, "Your name will no more be called Jacob, but Israel. For you have fought with God and with men, and have prevailed." . . . Jacob called the name of the place Peniel, saying, "I have seen God face to face, and my life has been preserved." (Gen. 32:24, 28, 30)

I will make this argument short. Hosea 12:4 tells us that Jacob wrestled with an angel, *mal'âk*. The Hebrew of "God" in verse 28 is not Yahweh, but *elohiym*, which is the plural of elohim. So why would this word here be used for God? Hosea knew the reason, because it actually refers to an angel.

And if he actually saw the face of God, then the Bible is <u>boldly in error</u>. Exodus gives us the words of God himself telling Moses: "*You cannot see My face, for no man can see Me and live*" (33:20). Yet, in 33:11, it says, "*The Lord spoke to Moses face to face, just as a man speaks to his friend.*" This means God was personally there speaking with Moses, not through an angel, but Moses was not allowed to see his literal face, and neither did Jacob, nor Hagar who fled from Abraham into the desert.

Using the excuse that it was not the Father, but the Messiah is not sufficient, since the Messiah was and is the second person of the Trinity; God is three in One. So the Messiah is God. But someone might ask, if Jesus is God, how did the Apostles see his face? Only because he was inside a human body; <u>we were only allowed to see his human flesh</u>. But in his pre-incarnate state, no one could see his face, because he is God. This one point alone is enough to NOT believe he was The angel of the Lord.

This leads us to the most difficult verse, because it appears to call God himself an angel. When Jacob was on his deathbed, he was pronouncing a blessing on his children:

> He blessed Joseph and said, "God, before whom my fathers Abraham and Isaac walked, the God who fed me all my life long to this day, 16 <u>the angel who redeemed me</u> from all evil, bless the boys; . . . (Genesis 48:15-16)

In the above passage, Jacob was merely recounting the times and ways in which he had encountered God, and one was through the angel he wrestled with. He was NOT saying that the angel was God! We know that God is not a created being, right? Then it must refer to the Messiah, except that he is NOT a created being either!

There are many statements in the Bible that cannot be taken at 100% literal face value (more on this later). The Promised Land was not literally flowing with milk and honey, and the *"whole world"* of the Bible does not refer to the entire planet.

I will only give a few more references to *the angel of the Lord*, which should be sufficient. In Exodus 2, God tells the Hebrews that he will send an angel to protect and guide them into the Promised Land:

> 20 Indeed, I am going to send <u>an angel</u> before you <u>to guard you along the way</u> . . . Be on guard before him and obey his voice. Do not provoke him, for he will not pardon your transgressions, for <u>My name is in him</u>. . . . 23 <u>For My angel</u> will go before you and bring you to the Amorites, and the Hittites, and the Perizzites, and the Canaanites, the Hivites, and the Jebusites, and I will completely destroy them. (v 21, 23)

Take notice that it says, "<u>an</u>" angel, not "the" angel, yet we are still expected to believe that he is the pre-incarnate Messiah because it says *"My name is in him."* A Bible commentary says:

> "<u>The name of Jehovah was in this angel</u>; that is to say, Jehovah revealed Himself in Him; and hence he is called in 33:15, 16 the face of Jehovah, because the essential nature of Jehovah was

manifested in him. This angel was not a created spirit, therefore, but the manifestation of Jehovah Himself." (Keil and Delitzsch, *Commentary on the OT*)

Yet, these theologians will argue that Jesus was NOT an angel, like the Jehovah's Witnesses claim. Since Jesus was never "an angel," then this cannot be the pre-incarnate Son of God. And if this refers to the second person of the Godhead, then this passage has God speaking of himself in the third person. It would be like you saying to your son, "Do as dad said, son. Or dad will not be happy."

While doing research for this book, I learned that there are, in fact, some Trinitarian theologians who do NOT believe that the Angel of the Lord is Messiah. Such as Rev. V.S.S. Coles, of Oxford, who wrote about the above passage in Exodus 2, in *A Book of Angels*. He quotes Dr. Pusey, who says:

"It seems to me most probable that he was a created Angel ... of this Angel God says 'My name is in him.' [2] In him were manifested the Divine Attributes: he was the minister of God's justice, who would not pardon their transgressions; to him God required obedience to be paid. His speaking was God speaking in him . . . Since God was present in him, God uses as equivalent terms the words 'the angel of his presence' [3] or 'My presence,' [4] the same angel, I think, was meant by Elihu, the 'angel interpreter.'"[5] (page 55)

Footnotes: 2] Ex. 23:21. 3] Is. 63:9. 4] Ex. 33:14. 5] Job 33:23.

It bears repeating that angels have the authority of God; this is basically what God was saying in Exodus 2, that this angel has His authority to act on behalf of God.

Another clear example of my assertion that the phrase *"the Angel of the Lord"* is merely a way to say an angel of Yahweh, instead of some other god, is found in the Book of Jasher. Though not in the Bible, it shows what the Jews of that era believed concerning this issue:

13. And on that night the Lord sent one of his ministering angels, and he came into the land of Egypt unto Joseph, and the angel of the Lord stood over Joseph, and behold Joseph was lying in the bed at night in his master's house in the dungeon, for his master had put him back into the dungeon on account of his wife.

14. And the angel roused him from his sleep, and Joseph rose up and stood upon his legs, and behold the angel of the Lord was standing opposite to him; and the angel of the Lord spoke with Joseph, and he taught him all the languages of man in that night, and he called his name Jehoseph. (49:13-14) (from an 1840 translation; eSword software)

This passage calls the angel of the Lord, *"one of his ministering angels."* Now for an especially interesting account; in Judges 13:3,9,13, 15-18, 20-21 it says *"the angel of the Lord"* appeared to the wife of Manoah to tell her that she would have a son, Samson. As the custom was, Manoah and his wife prepared a meal for the stranger:

> And the Angel of Jehovah said to Manoah, If you keep Me, I will not eat of your bread. And if you prepare a burnt offering, you shall offer it to Jehovah. (v.16) (LITV)

Manoah then asked what his name was, but he refused to give it. Some translations say he said it was "secret," others say that it was "wonderful," which is one of the names of Christ (Isa. 9:6). It does not actually say what happened, but Josephus said the angel touched the flesh with his rod, and fire shot up and consumed it, just the same as what took place on a visit with Gideon (Judges 6:21). We only know that when the flame shot up, then the angel *"went up in the flames from the altar"* (v. 20). When Manoah and his wife saw this, they fell down with their faces to the ground.

So there is some evidence, since he accepted the sacrifice and his name may have been *wonderful*; I can see how they believe that this was a Christiophany, an appearance of the pre-incarnate Christ. However, they are missing a very important point. Next, it says something very interesting:

> Then Manoah knew that he was an angel of the Lord.

Opps! *"The angel of the Lord"* has suddenly become *"an angel of the Lord."* And it is the same in all translations. *An* angel means just any ole angel, not THE super special angel. It cannot be both; if we are to take the special meaning that theologians have given to "the." But there's more! The next verse says:

> Manoah said to his wife, "We are certainly going to die, for we have seen God." (13:22)

Now, does this actually mean that they saw God or any member of the Godhead? No. Did they die? No, and since they did not die, then we know that they did not actually see God. Perhaps Manoah was aware of what God told Moses, that no one can see God and live.

But the most important point in the above passage is that it refers to the angel as merely *"an angel."* This shows us that this angel was, in point-of-fact, an ordinary angel who was acting on God's behalf. Since the passage also uses the same references as in other passages that cause people to wrongly believe that it refers to a member of the Godhead, then we can also assume that those other appearances were also made by an ordinary angel.

A passage in Judges 2 says:

> The angel of the Lord went up from Gilgal to Bokim and said, "I brought you up from Egypt and brought you into the land that I promised your fathers. I said . . .

4 When the angel of the Lord spoke these words . . .

Now, consider this, the oldest texts from the Bible that we have in Hebrew were found among the Dead Sea Scrolls, which were written shortly before the time of Christ, but most are not completely intact. The oldest complete Hebrew texts we have are from the Middle Ages. However, the Septuagint is the Greek translation of the Hebrew, and it was made even before some of the Dead Sea Scrolls. Here is how it words it:

> And an angel of the Lord went up from Galgal to the place of weeping, and to Baethel, and to the house of Israel, and said to them, Thus says the Lord, I . . .

4 And it came to pass when the angel of the Lord spoke these words . . .

We see clearly that the Septuagint says *"an angel"* and begins his words with *"Thus says the Lord,"* while the Masonite text leaves out, *"Thus says the Lord."* Now, why would anyone add those words? They might take them out to shorten the text or for some other reason, but I doubt that they would be added.

And in verse 4, where it says, *"when the angel of the Lord spoke these words,"* it is not a confusion; it is not calling the angel THE Angel of the Lord; it is merely using correct grammar. You would never say, *"when an angel of the Lord spoke."* When you are referring to a specific angel who spoke specific words, you would say "the" not "an."

And digging even deeper, why did it say that the angel (that is, *messenger*) *"went up from Gilgal"* to Bethel? Did he first deliver a message to the people of Gilgal, then go to Bethel to deliver another message? That wording seems strange for an angelic visitation. Therefore, I suspect, since humans can be messengers as well, that the passage refers to a human messenger, not a spirit-being messenger, so it would have been better to call him a prophet.

Finally, in Psalms, David wrote:

> The angel of the Lord camps around those who fear Him, and delivers them. (34:7)

Well, now, isn't that special? We don't have just any ole guardian angel; we have Messiah himself guarding each of us! LOL. If theologians are right about their view of *"THE angel of the Lord,"* then this passage <u>absolutely requires</u> that Messiah guards each one of us as our own personal guardian angel! (There is such a shortage of angels in heaven, you know!)

This idea that The Angel of the Lord is Messiah was also believed by many among the Early Church Fathers, which led them to wrongly believe that Jesus was not only God and Man, <u>but also a literal angel</u>! Justin Martyr said:

> Now the Word of God is His Son, as we have before said. And He is called Angel and Apostle. (Apology to Caesar)

Melito was a disciple of John the Apostle and the Bishop of Sardis, after the one who was there when John sent the letters to the seven churches. He wrote:

> [Jesus was] among the angels, Archangel . . . the captain of the angels. (*The Ante-Nicene Fathers*, Vol. 8, page 757.)

And even the immanent Irenaeus called Jesus, *"Angel among angels"* (*The Ante-Nicene Fathers*, Vol. 1, page 577). But they were all wrong. In calling Messiah an angel, they were calling him a created being. You cannot be a created being and God at the same time, which is likely one of the reasons that this belief was <u>declared anathema</u> in 553 A.D. by the *Fifth Ecumenical Council*, which ended centuries of dispute about the matter. It states:

7. If anyone shall say that Christ . . . had different bodies and different names, became all to all, an Angel among angels . . . let him be anathema.

(This council also declared anathema the belief in the pre-existence of the human spirit, because those who believed in pre-existence also believed in reincarnation. But I happen to believe in pre-existence.)

As I have shown, the state of theology, when it comes to angels, is in a bad place; messed up by much faulty reasoning and analysis on the part of people who are not using God-given wisdom. I believe I have provided powerful evidence to support the thesis of this chapter, that *the Angel of the Lord* does *not* refer to Messiah, but to angels with authority to speak and act for God. That is their job here on Earth, to be emissaries of God.

Chapter 4

Historical Opinions About Angels

"I could not have made it this far had there not been angels along the way." – Della Reese

The previous chapters provide powerful evidence that God still uses angels to do his work among nations and individuals. God is using angels today, even when they are not seen. Most ministers throughout Christian history, both Catholic and Protestant, have believed in the continuing ministry of angels. I like to read what others have written about angels, as it shows the continued belief in them. Here are some choice quotes:

When God determine to make man he assembled together all the angels, that each one might contribute something towards the work; therefore he said to them: "Let us make man." But certain angels refused, saying: "What is man that thou regardest him!" (Talmud) (Fowler, *Our Angel Friends*, page 18)

***

Angels are spirits, but it is not because they are spirits that they are angels. They become angels when they are sent. For the name angel refers to their office, not their nature. You ask the name of this nature, it is spirit; you ask its office, it is that of an Angel, which is a messenger. (Saint Augustine)

***

Angels are intelligent reflections of light, that original light which has no beginning. They can illuminate. They do not need tongues or ears, for they can communicate without speech, in thought. (John of Damascus)

***

An angel can illumine the thought and mind of man by strengthening the power of vision and by bringing within his reach some truth which the angel himself contemplates. (Thomas Aquinas)

***

The Angels are the dispensers and administrators of the Divine beneficence toward us. They regard our safety, undertake our defense, direct our ways, and exercise a constant solicitude that no evil befall us. (John Calvin)

***

I can reach no other conclusion than that [angels] are especially interested in believers, and are constantly seeking their good. They influence, help, guide, watch over, defend and minister unto them. You say this is the work of the Holy Spirit. It is wholly distinct from that He works chiefly from within; they altogether from without. He attends primarily to the spiritual; they to the temporal. . . . We have proof of this in Christ's life. The spirit led, taught and filled Christ (Luke 6:1), but the angels defended, strengthened and ministered unto (i.e. fed) Him, Matt., 6:6. (Rev. John Balcom Shaw, D.D.) (Fowler, *Our Angel Friends*, page 92)

***

The Jewish Rabbis are of Opinion that the Prophets were acted by Angels. The divine influx (they say) came by their Ministry, who ordered and disposed the word in the mouth of the prophet according to the mind of God. It is a celebrated saying among them, that every prophet received his prophecy by the Ministry of an Angel, Moses only excepted. . . . They suppose the reason of that expression in Judg. 5.23 to be because Deborah being a prophetess spake according to Angelical Inspiration. They say that the difference between a divine and a deceitful dream, is, that the former is by the hand of an Angel, the latter by the hand of an evil spirit. So do they reconcile, Numb. 12.6. with Zach. 10.2. (*A Disquisition Concerning Angelical APPARITIONS*. By Increase Mather, President of Harvard College. BOSTON. 1696, page 3)

***

As to the nature of angels, we are told that they are spirits, but whether pure spirits, divested of all matter, or united to some thin bodies or corporeal vehicles, has been a controversy of long standing. The more general opinion is, that they are substances entirely spiritual, though they can at any time assume bodies, and appear in human shape. (Charles Buck) (Fowler, *Our Angel Friends*, Page 63)

***

In Scripture we frequently read of missions and appearances of angels, sent to declare the will of God, to correct, teach, reprove, or comfort. God gave the law to Moses, and appeared to the Patriarchs, by the mediation of angels, who represented Him, and who spoke in His name. Origen, Bede, and others think that angels were created at the same time as the heavens, and that Moses included them under the expression: "In the beginning God created the heavens;" others suppose that they are intended under the term "light," which God created on the first day . . . (Edward Robinson, D.D.) (Fowler, *Our Angel Friends*, page 155)

***

A writer of wonderful research (Huet) proves that belief in the existence of angels is found among all peoples and in all lands; that the Greeks received this belief from the Egyptians and Phoenicians; and that all antiquity has recognized the existence of spiritual beings inferior to God, and created to preside over the order of nature -- stars, the elements, the generation of animals. The world, according to Thales and Pythagoras, is full of these spiritual beings. They believed that the angels floated in the sky and in the air. Plato, according to Plutarch, speaks of a prince of an evil nature, who is over the spirits that were chased by the gods and fell from heaven. The belief in angel-guardians, or good spirits, destined to protect and watch over man from his cradle to his grave, was no less ancient and widespread. (Dr. Parker) (Fowler, *Our Angel Friends*, page 93)

***

Socrates had an angel; and he said that if any evil came to him at any time, he would be informed of it by his guardian angel. On that memorable day on which he was condemned to drink the fatal hemlock, he says: "My angel did not give me notice this morning of any evil that was to befall me today, therefore I cannot think it an evil, my being condemned to die." This is certainly a memorable statement. Who but an angel of God could have been the "knowing one" that revealed secrets to the mind of that great sage? (From "A Peep Within the Gates.") (Fowler, *Our Angel Friends*, page 110)

***

There has been a great deal of curious speculation concerning the relation of angels to worldly affairs. Some think that the angels dwell in the immediate presence of God, and sing his praise; and that during the intervals of song they fly from star to star to refresh and regale their minds with the glories of the sky. Others think that the angels bear a distinct relation to man, that they influence all his affairs, and that every one has his guardian angel who watches over him and to a certain extent protects him. The truth respecting angels probably lies in the golden mean half way between these two opinions. Then angels are doubtless charged with ministering to man, and they are interested in all of his affairs. They, like man, are the offspring of God, and, therefore, they have a fellow-feeling for men, and wish to inquire into their affairs. (Bishop Cyrus Foss, D.D.) (Fowler, *Our Angel Friends*, page 94)

***

You will always find that, in proportion to the earnestness of our own faith, its tendency to accept a spiritual personality increases; and that the most vital and beautiful Christian temper rests joyfully in its conviction of the multitudinous ministry of living angels, infinitely varied in rank and power. (John Ruskin) (Fowler, *Our Angel Friends*, page 100)

***

St. Bernard of Clairvaux (1090-1153) wrote; "*Angels are spiritual creatures, created by God without a body, for the service of Christendom and the church.*"

***

How merciful art thou, O Lord, that thou thinkest us not safe enough in our weak and slender walls, but thou sendest thine angels to be our keepers and guardians. (Ambrose, *Ministration and Communion of Angels*) (Clayton, *Angelology*, page 192-193)

***

Luther in his Commentary on Gen. 37. and Gen. 40. declares, that he was very much moved and offended at the infinite multitude of Satanical Illusions, with which the World was horribly deceived for a long time under the Papacy; and that for his own part he did constantly pray to God, that he would not reveal anything to him by Dreams or Visions, but by his Written Word; and that He would not send Angels to appear to him, knowing that when he was meditating on the Scriptures, God and His Holy Angels were near to him, who could instill irradiations on his mind without any visible Apparitions. Yet, he does acknowledge that some may have that which he never did nor desired to experience. ((*A Disquisition Concerning Angelical APPARITIONS*. By Increase Mather, President of Harvard College. BOSTON. 1696, page 7)

***

"If a man is saved from drowning, or escapes a falling stone, that is not chance, but the will of the dear angels." (Martin Luther) (Fowler, *Our Angel Friends*, page 119)

***

Thus God's strange and wonderful works of Providence are performed by angels; nor see I any reason to believe that God does ordinarily do anything himself immediately, (understanding by immediately, without any Second Cause) which he hath made some creature able and fit to do, but he works ordinarily by such means and instruments as he has fitted for his work. (*A Discourse of Angels, Their Nature and Office, or Ministry*, by Thomas Parkhurst, London, 1701, page 98)

***

In most of the battle that were fought by the Israelites in the conquest of Canaan, there was nothing visible but their own arms; but God had told them that he would, and accordingly he did, send his angel before them to expel those heathen nations, that were the then possessors. And why would we question God's doing the like nowadays, giving victory by the aids and conduct of those unseen champions?

It is the opinion of many Fathers and great Divines, both ancient and modern, that God does <u>make use of angels in governing and ordering of this world</u>, and the affairs of it, not only now and then extraordinarily, <u>but in his ordinary way of working</u>; . . . (Ibid., page 102)

***

It is acknowledged that malignant Spirits or Devils are permitted to blind, delude, and pervert men. The Scripture attributes this power to them; and it appears that this power of theirs is exercised not only on wicked men . . . Now, <u>that God should permit devils to go on with their work, and forbid good angels to exercise their power and skill, is not to be imagined</u>. (Ibid., page 143)

Again, Increase Mather wrote in 1696:

Angels both good and bad have a greater influence on this world than men are generally aware of. We ought to admire the grace of God toward us sinful creatures in that He hath appointed His holy angels to guard us against mischiefs of wicked spirits who are always intending our hurt both to our bodies and our souls. (*Angelographia*)

***

Emanuel Swedenborg (1688-1772) claimed to have frequently communed with angels. Although he said some believable things about them, he also said many things that were not. He taught that all angels were originally humans; therefore, all angels have a human appearance, and none are just beings of light. And that all people have two angels and two demons with them at all times! The angels try to lead people toward good actions, but the demons lead them toward bad actions. He called for a new form of Christianity called *The New Church*, also called *Swedenborgianism,* but it did not begin during his lifetime. However, it did begin in England about 15 years after his death.

***

Angels have manifested themselves to men and women through vision, hearing and feeling. Why then should we consider them purely immortal substance having no connection with the visible universe? Our knowledge of Angels leads us to believe they are connected with the world of matter. (Thomas Titupson; *Angel of Gody*, 1845)

***

The ministry of Angels may be divided into two parts, that of praising God, and the execution of His behests. (Alfred Edersheim; *Life and Times of Jesus the Messiah*, 1890)

***

While we struggle in His name against sin, and relying on His help to overcome, we are surrounded by invisible forms who watch with interest, and who are near in times of peril, weakness and doubt, to shield us from change and to strengthen and support. They may call to mind some passage from God's Word, thus lightening the inner man or woman by refreshing and invigorating the very spring of hidden life. (Charles Bell, *Angel Beings*, 1878)

***

A belief in the existence of [angels] is not, therefore, an essential article of religion, any more than a belief that there are other worlds besides our own; but such a belief serves to enlarge our ideas of the works of God, and to illustrate the greatness of his power and wisdom. (Kitto) (Fowler, *Our Angel Friends*, page 53)

***

And every disclosure of heavenly existence that is made to us shows us life without one trace of selfishness earnestly devoted to the service of others. Angels' life is very pure, holy and blessed, and yet these celestial beings, the angels, find their employments in serving. It is their joy to minister, not to be ministered unto. If we would be as the angels, we must have the same spirit. (Dr. J. R. Miller) (Fowler, *Our Angel Friends*, page 122)

***

Whatever assistance God gives to man by men, the same, and frequently in a higher degree, He gives to them by angels. (John Wesley) (Fowler, *Our Angel Friends*, page 208)

***

That there lives in the presence of God a vast assembly, myriads upon myriads of spiritual beings, higher than we, but infinitely removed from God, mighty in strength, doers of His Word, who ceaselessly bless and praise God; wise, also, to whom He gives charge to guard His own in all their ways, ascending and descending to and from heaven and earth, and who variously minister to men, most often invisibly. All these angels are interested in us and in our well being. They are present with God, witnessing the trials of our race. (Pussey) (Fowler, *Our Angel Friends*, page 217)

***

It cannot be said: God does not need angels, therefore angels do not exist; for God does not need man, yet man exists. (Edward Robinson, D. D.) (Fowler, *Our Angel Friends*, p. 223)

***

See! they eat, they speak, they sing, their voices are heard by human ears, their touch is felt upon human hands, as when they led Lot and his family forth from Sodom. In short, they command material forces and achieve material results. When they appear their bodies resemble a human form, nor is there any indication in Scripture that those bodies are not real, and only assumed for the time and then laid aside. For myself, I believe that they are material, though of a form of matter of which we as yet can form no true conception, but which, some day perhaps, in the progress of a sanctified science, we shall be able to understand, if not discern. At all events, their life-history, as far as the Bible gives it, shows them united in sympathetic and harmonious service of God, with man and with all creation. (H. C. McCook, D.D.) (Fowler, *Our Angel Friends*, page 233)

***

When we consider the words of angels, how short they are, how adapted to human comprehension in their simplicity, and yet always with a deeper meaning concealed beneath the primary one. Alas! commentators for the most part have passed over these words very lightly, noticing them merely as angelic words, not pausing to weigh their inherent value. Again, all the accounts given of the appearance of angels, are characterized by the same directness and simplicity. When angels are introduced to the normal waking consciousness of men, we do not find that they are seen flying down from heaven, or that there is anything marvelous in their deportment. It is not with shapes projected by the inherent force of the human intellect, that we have to deal; it is the words and deeds of angels themselves; of separate and independent beings, in a marvelous manner no doubt, but yet in very deed and truth manifesting themselves as objective realities to man. In the collective historical books of the Old Testament, we only find the appearance of speaking angels recorded thrice, while in the gospel narrative we read of at least eight distinct angelic addresses, and in the Acts of the Apostles of five. (Rudolph Stier, D. D.) (Fowler, *Our Angel Friends*, page 236)

***

Sometimes [angels] bring to light the hidden things of darkness, and show us the traps laid for our feet. (John Wesley) (Fowler, *Our Angel Friends*, page 248)

***

We ought all to have an experience like Jacob. . . . Life will never be the same if we have seen the angels. (G. H. Morrison, *Return of the Angels*, 1909)

***

The denial of the existence of Angels springs from the materialistic and unbelieving spirit, which in its most terrible form denies the existence of God. (Merril Unger, Bible Dictionary; 1957)

***

I am convinced that these heavenly beings exist and that they provide unseen aid on our behalf. I also believe in Angels because I have sensed their presence in my life on special occasions. . . . When the Christians die, an Angel will be there to comfort us* to give us peace and joy at that most critical hour and usher us into the presence of God whom we shall dwell with, the Lord forever. (Billy Graham, *Angels*, 1975)

***

The Angel is one of those Articles of Faith as unshaken as our belief in the existence of God. (Malcolm Goodwin, *Angels* , 1990)

***

Of course, some people will say Angels don't exist, never having seen one. And other people will ask why they appear only to certain humans. Others will say that Angels come to everyone. The question is who will recognize them when they come? (Sophy Burnham, *A Book of Angels* , 1992)

***

Angels are creations of God, and under the direction of the Holy Spirit they help us carry out our assignments as believers. (Terry Law, *The Truth about Angels*, 1994)

***

Angels, then, are real. Angels are spiritual beings, godlike but not God. Nor are they human— though they may appear in human form — they are immortal. (Larry Kinnaman, (*Angels Light and Dark*, 1994)

Chapter 5

Angels in Christian History

"It is highly probable, independent of Revelation, that there are many orders of beings superior to man. To suppose our own species to be the highest production of Divine power would indicate irrational and puerile presumption." (Robert Hall, in Clayton, *Angelology*, page 84)

We have many reports of Angels appearing after the time of the Early Church, a few were written down. It is reported by Eusebius that the venerable Polycarp (A.D. 69- 155) had a dream that he should be burned alive for the Gospel. He was captured, tried, and taken to the arena, at which time the Christians who were near, heard a voice from heaven that said, *"Polycarp be of good courage, and play the man now."* Today, we would translate this as saying, "Be strong Polycarp, and be a man!" Most people attribute the voice to an angel, and I agree. It is sad how many Christians refuse to believe this simple miracle.

In A.D. 208, a preacher by the name of Andeolus, who later became Saint Andeol, was holding a revival meeting in Bergoiata, a town in Gaul. It just so happened that Severus, the emperor of Rome, was passing through the city at the same time, saw the great crowd of people, and asked what the crowd was for. He was informed that they were waiting to hear Andeolus preach about Jesus. So, Severus sent for Andeolus and attempted to persuade him to renounce his faith. All efforts having failed, Severus ordered him tortured.

Andeolus was thrown to the ground and had his hands and feet tied with ropes attached to pulleys. He was stretched to the maximum and then scourged with rods that tore his flesh. Next, they tore his flesh with red-hot hooks, and was bound on a wheel that turned above a fire.

Andeolus showed no sign of pain, but said, as the wheel turned slowly around,

> *"Blessed be the name of God, and my Saviour Jesus, who have thought me worthy to suffer thus. Leave me not, O my Savior, nor suffer me for any pains of death to fall from you."*

Severus was present for all the torture and ordered Andeolus thrown into prison to await other tortures the next day.

> At the suggestion of a tribune named Cericius, Andeolus was thrown into the crypt of the temple of Mars, on the bank of the Rhone. At midnight, the guards were greatly alarmed by seeing this subterranean vault brilliantly illuminated, and hearing thousands of voices singing celestial music with Andeolus. They heard these words among others, *"Courage, dear brother; tomorrow you will be with us in paradise."* They then applied healing balm to his wounds; and when he was brought the next day to the tribunal, the emperor was amazed to find him in perfect health and joyous spirits. *"Off with his head,"* roared Severus in a fury, *"or the magician will corrupt the whole city!"* Then a soldier with a very hard wood sword stabbed him in the head. (Bollandists, Acta Sanctorum, vol. 1. pp. 38, 39, May 1.) (Brewer, *A Dictionary of Miracles*, page 10)

Theodorus, St. Euphemia, and many others of the period also suffered torture and were ministered to by angels before they died, such as St. George of Diospolis, St. Julian, St. Lawrence, and others. The important thing to notice is that the angels did not intervene to prevent the torture and death of the martyrs, but merely ministered to them in their suffering or gave them direct miracles of healing, but it did not stop their eventual deaths.

St. Anthony the Great of Egypt (circa A.D. 251-356) cultivated a garden and made mats to earn a little money. But all of his manual work left him little time for spiritual contemplation, and he became very low-spirited. But then an angel appeared and showed him how to make mats from palm leaves. After a few more visits, before leaving, the angel said, *"Do this, and you shall be saved."* St. Anthony followed the angel's instructions and was able to make mats more efficiently, which gave him time for prayer and contemplation.

(*Les Petits Bollandistes* (1880), vol. 1. p. 429.) (Brewer, *A Dictionary of Miracles*, page 5-6)

This story is believable because, in the Book of Enoch, the fallen angels were said to have taught humanity how to make weapons, and given them other knowledge. So why couldn't angels teach a saintly person how to make a better mat? It was not to make him rich, but to supply him with more money, which allowed him time for his spiritual pursuits.

In A.D. 370, a group of Arians became angry with Marcellinus, bishop of Embrun, because he so greatly opposed them. One day, a group of these heretics seized him and took him to the top of a steep rock, then pushed him down, but angels caught him and delivered him safely to the bottom. (Mons. Depe'ry, Hagiographie de Gap) (Brewer, *A Dictionary of Miracles*, p. 9) At first, one might believe that this miracle was invented by the Catholic Church, but other modern miracles done by angels suggest that it was, in fact, genuine.

St. Euphrasia was a nun in Constantinople who, about 412 A.D., was pushed by an evil spirit into a pond, but an angel held her head above water until she could be pulled from the water. (Surius, *Lives of the Saints*, vol. 2) (Brewer, *A Dictionary of Miracles*, page 8)

St. Cuthbert (634-687 A.D.) of Britain often saw and conversed with angels, and was even fed by them. Before he entered the priory of Mailros, he was healed by an angel of an abscess in the knee, and even cured by an angel of the plague. (*Bede, Church History, bk. iv. chap. 27-32.* From *A Dict. of Miracles*, page 8)

In the Middle Ages, a German preacher named Grynaeus, traveled from Heidelberg to Spire to hear another preacher who spoke in agreement with some Roman Catholic doctrines. Grynaeus went to him and explained his error to him. The preacher seemed to accept the correction and acted as though he desired more communication on the issue. Grynaeus proceeded to his lodging for the night. While eating the evening meal, *"a grave old man of goodly countenance, seemly and richly attired, who, in a friendly and grave manner"* informed Grynaeus that within an hour, officers would arrive to arrest him and *"carry him to prison,"* and urged him to leave at once. No sooner had Grynaeus gotten on a boat and left, when the officers arrived looking for him. *"No doubt this was an angel which God had sent to deliver this goodly minister from persecution"* (Clayton, *Angelology*, p. 199).

Another minister, also seeking to escape capture and avoid persecution, crawled into *"a dark whole in the house,"* and *"as soon as he was got in, a spider drew a web over the mouth of the hole."* When the house was searched, the men did not look in the hole, believing that he could not be in there because of the spider's web. Thus, he escaped from his would-be captors. (Ibid.)

Even though others were not delivered from persecution or death, there are times when God will send an angel to save someone because they have yet more to do for God. When God decides that it is your time to go, you will not get a guardian angel to protect your life, but angels will still be there helping you to the end. All but one of the 12 Apostles were martyred.

A fellow named James Bingham was burned at the stake for opposing the Roman Catholic Church; while he was burning in the flames, he yelled out:

> "O ye papists! Ye look for miracles; here now ye may see a miracle; for in this fire I feel no more pain than if I were on a bed of roses!" (Clayton, *Angelology*, p. 200)

As Vincent Ferrier was about to die (A.D. 1419) the windows of his chamber flew open of their own accord, and a crowd of winged creatures, no bigger than butterflies, very beautiful and purely white, filled the room. When he breathed his last breath, these winged creatures suddenly disappeared, leaving behind them an exquisite scent in the air. Everyone was convinced they were angels, who had come to carry in triumph the soul of the saint to the paradise of God. (*Les Petits Bollandistes*, vol. 4. p. 240) (Brewer, *A Dictionary of Miracles*, page 8)

Martin Luther tells the story of a poor woman who lived in a time of famine. She ran out of food and money, so she got herself and her children dressed up in their good clothes and proceeded to walk to a nearby fountain. As she was going, she met a man who asked where she and her children were going. She replied that her provisions were gone and she was going with her children to the fountain, because God, who provides for the ravens, can not only provide water but food for her and her children. The man urged her to return home, where she would find food. She did as he requested, and upon her return, found a large amount of flour. She did not know where the flour came from, nor did she know the identity of the man. (Isaac Ambrose, *War With Devils: Ministration of, and Communion with Angels*, Glasgow, 1769, page 285)

It is clear from the story that she had faith in God to provide for her needs, and so it is probable that she prayed and expected an answer, and God sent an angel to supply her needs. Rarely does an angel knock on the door and hand you the groceries, but it has happened.

Here is another story from the same book, which is interesting because it was at a time when people did not readily believe much in the miraculous; Luther himself said he would prefer not to have miracles because of the chance of being deceived, so he preferred the written Word of God:

> One, about the time of the reformation of religion, desired much of God the guidance and assistance of an angel; and from the thirty-seventh year of his age he had sensible manifestations of a spirit that assisted him, and followed him till his death. In his dreams or visions he was sometimes admonished of this or that vice, and sometimes [warned] of this or that danger, and sometimes resolved of this or that doubt, or sometimes persuaded to this or that duty. "Once I heard a voice from heaven, saying, I will save thy soul." Usually in the morning, about the fourth hour, the angel would beat at his door to have awaked him, and if he had done any good or evil, he would have manifested the approval or disproval of it by some sign. If in company he had spoken any unwary words, he was sure to [have it pointed out] and reproved for it by a dream in the night following. If he had read any book that was not good, the angel would have struck upon the book, to have caused him to leave it and lay it aside. Often would the angel have provoked him to prayer, and alms deeds, and other duties. Bodinus asking him, whether ever he had seen the form of this angel, he answered, that he never saw anything, but only a bright and shining light, in a round orb; and once after prayer upon his bed, that he saw a sweet boy in white apparel, of admirable beauty. (Ambrose, *War With Devils*, page 287-288)

This is certainly an unusual case, but not impossible. Notice that the angel first appeared as an orb of light, then later as a boy, I will discuss this later in the book. If the angel had actually appeared all those times to him, I would doubt this story, but since he merely did those things without appearing, it could have happened.

Even though Luther was not into seeing angels, he did believe in their work. Many of the Protestants who came after him believed more in angels than many Protestants do today. Increase Mather reported in 1659, that Robert Samuel, a teacher during the time of Bloody Queen Mary (ruled 1553-1558), was put into chains and given only a few morsels of bread and three spoonfuls of water each day. Then he dreamed that a man stood *"before him clad in a white Garment, saying to him, 'Be of good cheer, for after this day thou shalt hunger and thirst no more."* The next day, he was burned at the stake. He must have told another prisoner, or guard, about his dream for us to have it today. (*A Disquisition Concerning Angelical Apparitions.* Increase Mather, President of Harvard College, Boston, 1696, page 9)

This brings to mind the story of Joan of Arc, who had many miracles, but when she was in prison, an angel told her she would be delivered the next day. She must have told people about it, because the next day, she was burned at the stake. Many people would not call that being delivered, but when you consider that she would likely have spent many decades in a horrible prison filled with vermin and disease, with little food; she was taken to heaven, so it was deliverance from a literal hell.

In April 1659, Samuel Wallas of Stamford in Lincolnshire, had been sick for thirteen years, and given up by the physicians. On April 7, the Lord's Day, being sickly, he was not able to attend the public church services. While reading a book, he heard someone knock at the door. Since he was the only one at home, he took a staff and, leaning against the walls, made his way to the door. A wise old man with *"fresh complexion"* and white curled hair walked in, walked around the room, and said, *"Friend, I perceive you are not well."* Wallis then told him how he had been long ill and could not afford the expensive treatments offered by the doctors. But had *"committed himself and life into the hands of God, to dispose of as he pleased."* The wise old man then replied:

> "Thou sayest very well; be sure to fear God, and serve him, and remember to observe what now I say to thee: tomorrow morning go into the garden, and there take two leaves of red sage, and one of blood-wort, and put those three leaves into a cup of small beer, and drink thereof as oft as need requires; the fourth morning cast away those leaves, and put in fresh ones; thus do for twelve

dayes together; and thou shalt find e're these twelve dayes be expired, through the help of God, thy disease will be cured, and the frame of thy body altered." (*Remarkable Provinces*, Increase Mather, page 145)

The old man gave a few more instructions, then Wallas asked if he would like something to eat, to which the man replied; "*No friend, the Lord Christ is sufficient for me. Seldom do I drink any thing but what cometh from the rock.*" He wished "*the Lord of heaven to be with him*" and departed. Wallas watched the man walk away, but no other people in the street saw him depart. And though it had been raining all day, when he came into the house, he was completely dry.

Wallas followed the man's directions and was restored to health. How he was cured became well-known and was discussed by several ministers at Stamford, who concluded that it was indeed brought by a "*good angel.*" Increase Mather concludes the story with this warning:

> . . . it is not impossible but that holy angels may appear, and visibly converse with some. Yet for any to desire such a thing is unwarrantable, and exceeding dangerous; for thereby <u>some have been imposed upon by wicked daemons</u>, who know how to transform themselves into angels of light. (Ibid., p. 147)

The last few quotes above were from books by Increase Mather, the son of well-known minister Cotton Mather of early New England. Increase was also a minister who became president of Harvard College. Like his father, he wrote many books. In *Angelographia*, he recounts how angels have intervened in the affairs of men for our good. He said that it is well known that demons can put thoughts into people's minds and bring about many temptations and evils, so it is also <u>true that angels do the opposite</u>:

> Impression must needs be from a good Angel. And an other like passage is related in the life of that holy man, Mr. Dod: One evening (though he had other work to attend) he could not [resist the urge that] he must go to such a neighbours house: when he came to him, he told him, he knew not what he was come for; but he could not rest in his spirit, until he had visited him. The poor man was astonished, for he had in the violence of a temptation, put a rope into his pocket, with an intent to have destroyed him-

self, had not Mr. Dod's thus coming prevented it. Surely an Angel of the Lord was in this providence.

Bishop Hall speaks of one whom he knew, that having been for sixteen years a cripple, had these monitions in his sleep, that he should go and wash in St. Matherus Well in Cornwell, which he did, and was suddenly recovered. This he thinks was from angelical suggestion. Marcus Aurelius Antoninus did in a dream, receive the prescript of a remedy for his disease, which the physitians could not cure. A physitian of Uratislavium followed the counsil he had given him in a dream, concerning the cure of a disease which was to him incurable, and he recovered his patient. It added to the wonder, that a few years after, he met with that [prescription] in a book then newly printed. Histories report that the like to this happened to Philip, and to Galen. If angels may suggest things beneficial unto the minds of men who are strangers to God, much more unto them that fear him!

Mather believed that angels have stopped appearing to people, but that their work has not stopped. But we know today, that angels still appear. He goes on to tell of another instance where the Chancellor of *Navar* heard a voice in the night that called him by name, he awoke but then went back to sleep. A second time he awoke to the voice calling his name, and finally a third time, and told him to leave town, *"because within a few dayes a terrible plague would be there, and make the town desolate: He took the warning, and so escaped the danger"* (Ibid., page 70). Within a few days, the plague began in that town, and many people died. The voice was certainly that of an angel. You might be wondering why none of the other people received such help, were they all sinners? Surely there were more good people in the village, but perhaps God wanted the man to remain alive because God still had work for him to do.

In another book, Mather told the story of Mr. Patrick Simpson, a minister in Sterling, Scotland, whose wife showed signs of the early stages of demonic possession, and Satan told her that she would *"be given over into his hand."* This caused much fear and anguish for them both. Mr. Simpson then went into his garden and fasted and prayed all day. While Mr. Simpson was lying face down on the ground, an angel spoke in an audible voice and told him that his wife would become completely well within 10 hours, and it was so. Mr. Simpson said, *"O what am I, being dust and ashes, that the holy*

Ministering spirits should be sent by the Lord to deliver a message to me." (Mather, *An Historical Discourse Concerning the Prevalency of Prayer*, 1734, page 16-17)

In another account, Mather was unsure about the truth of a 15th-century woman named Christina Peniatovia, who claimed to have many revelations and visions. Her father was a minister, and from a noble family in Prussia. When her father learned that she claimed to have these revelations and visions, he greatly opposed her; but eventually became a believer himself, as did other prominent ministers of the day, including Commenius, her tutor and spiritual father.

An Angel appeared to her, and told her she should speedily die of an apoplexy: She was that night smitten with that disease. She made her will, and took her leave of all her friends: was for some time thought to be really dead: there was no breath perceived in her, but she was grown quite cold her hands & feet were become stiff like a dead persons; all persons went out of the room, leaving only two nurses to lay her out. But on a sudden she rose up in her bed, and called for her clothes, and was in such perfect health as before she had not been in, her lame hand & foot being made whole & perfect, to the astonishment of all about her.

The account which she her self giveth of this matter, is, that on the day before, there was a knocking or striking on the table, first one stroke, and after that five, whence she concluded, that the next day she should dye at five a Clock in the afternoon: That she heard a voice saying, Come, come, come. When that evening came, her sight & speech failed, and (says she) I felt my self go forth with my spirit, and be carried into heaven, where surrounded with a great shining, I saw an huge company clothed in white. And the Lord stepping forth took me in his embrace. She added, that the Lord told her, she should return again, and behold his goodness in the land of the living, that her disease should leave her. She then desired to know how many the dayes of her life should be. But that the Lord told her, that should be hid from her, commanding her to live righteously, & that He would no more visit her as formerly. Whereupon she worshiped him, and was restored to life, & to full vigor, health, and strength in that very moment.

This surely is a strange relation; yet reported as credible, by as grave & learned a man as Commenius, who was an eye and ear witness of these things. Now I must confess, I am not easy to believe, that Christina's death or her ascension into Heaven was real, but that they were both phantastical [strange, weird]. (Mather, *A Disquisition Concerning Angelical Apparitions*, p. 32 -38.)

Mather did not believe this account, but I do believe it, because I have read many different accounts and find nothing strange in it. She died and saw heaven, Jesus said she would be restored to health but not have the many dreams and visions as she had before. Many other people have also died and were told to return. Some were totally healed upon coming back to life, others had to recover slowly. (Examples, later.)

Mather was clearly a believer in angelic visitation, but he was also very skeptical of most such claims, and rightly so, believing that many were actually fallen angels, and he gave several such examples:

> No infallible Judgment can be made by the words which they speak, or the counsel which they give, whether the appearing spirits are good or evil Angels. Jacobus Vitriacus speaks of one who was frequently visited in his sleep by a daemon, that did reprehend him for some of his faults, and also excite him to acts of piety & devotion: but the daemon used this fraud with a design to instill some poisonous notions into his mind. (*A Disquisition Concerning Angelical Apparitions*, Mather, p. 38)

Mather rightly understood that this was a fallen angel, even though it urged him toward acts of piety and devotion; the reason being that it also condemned his faults and gave him false doctrines. Mather also stated that no good angel ever told a lie; *"that Spirit which shall be once found in a Lye, comes not from Heaven"* (Ibid., p. 14).

There were a couple of people, perhaps ministers, whom he called *"Dr. Dee and Killet,"* who had some sort of visitation from what they thought were *"good angels."* These angels gave them good religious advice for some time until the angels advised them to do wicked sexual acts: *"for although those Spirits did for a long time pretend to great sanctity, they did at last advise to filthy Nicolaitism"* (Ibid.). Mather rightly said:

> Carthusianus does greatly mistake, when he supposeth, that those Revelations must needs be Divine, which incite men to devotion

and spirituality. The Devil has often taken that course, that so he might the more effectually deceive. (Ibid., 39)

Mather gives another really good example of being deceived by fallen angels who were pretending to be good angels. A young man named Jacob Oluffso, lived on an island governed by Denmark. In the year 1667, Jacob was,

> afflicted with a disease that made him keep within doors a fort-night: on January 20th, being Lords day there appeared to him one in shining garments, and made the room where he was, full of splendor. He gave a kind salutation to the young man, asking him about his pain, and then stroking him with his hand, the young man was presently healed. This shining spirit used those words to him, *Be thou whole and sin no more.* He exhorted him to pray three times every day, and that he should admonish the people where he lived, that they should pray also, and that they should leave off their cursing & swearing, & desist from all other sins, that so the anger of God may be appeased: So did the spirit depart from him. But five dayes after he appeared again, and did then sing the 23rd Psalm.
>
> The young man had a strong impulse on his spirit to go abroad, where he saw in the southwest the heavens opened, & one coming down thence, who at length came & stood by him, habited [dressed] like a minister, & told him he should not at all doubt, but that he came from God. The next Lords-day, being January 27, the glittering spirit appeared to him the third time, asking whether he had performed, what he was commanded. He said, Yes, he had. But this Spirit replied, *You have not done it so earnestly as ought to have been.*
>
> He appeared several times after this. But at his third appearing, he told the young man that they must change the day of their keeping the Sabbath, from the first day to the last day of the week, withal adding, that whereas there had been on Saturday two Suns seen in the Heavens, that was sent as a sign that Saturday should be kept as an Holy Day.
>
> The news of these apparitions became publick all the country over, and many ignorant people (notwithstanding they were Protestants) put great faith in them, especially as to that of the new holy-day. But the ministers charging their people to adhere to the infallible Word of God, and not to regard visions, in a

while all vanished, and every one was satisfied, that this Shining Spirit was no other than a White Devil. The account of this matter was published by Lucas Jacobson Provost of the Churches in those Islands. (*A Disquisition Concerning Angelical Apparitions,* p. 40-41)

Even Mather, it appears, would have believed that this was a good angel except for the change in the Sabbath Day. That, it seems, was the trouble spot for him. But if you will notice, the angel told him to pray three times a day and live without sinning, "*so the anger of God may be appeased.*" This was a clear indication that it was a fallen angel. If you have accepted Christ's forgiveness for your sins, then you do not need to appease the anger of God. He knows that Christians will not and cannot live perfectly sinless lives, which is why he told us to ask forgiveness when we sin, and God will forgive them (1 John 1:9, 2:1; Matt. 6:5-15).

Notice also that the angel chastised him for not performing the legalistic religious acts earnestly enough. This angel was trying to get the people to depart from the true Gospel of Salvation to a very legalistic gospel of religious works, such as praying three times daily and never sinning. Now, it is good to not sin and it is good to pray, and if you want to pray three times a day, that is awesome, but if you are doing it "*so the anger of God may be appeased,*" then it is nothing but outward works of dead religion. Because we are not saved by these acts, we are saved by asking Jesus to forgive our sins and accepting that forgiveness; this is why it is called salvation by faith and grace, not works.

Also, no true angel of God will ever condemn someone for not living a perfect enough life! The angel that appeared to Isaiah did not condemn him for using swear words, but put a coal on his tongue and cured him of the problem (Isa. 6:5-6). And no true angel of God will give us new religious doctrines! It is not their job as messengers to give us correct doctrine or tell us how to live, God expects us humans to come up with doctrine, with the help of the Bible and the Holy Spirit.

The Apostle Paul was likely speaking prophetically when he said, even if an angel comes down from heaven and teaches any other gospel, do not believe it (Gal. 1:8). He knew that this would happen, and it has indeed happened several times; most notably the angel who claimed to be Gabriel and gave Muhammad his new religion that spread war, famine, and death throughout the world (the 4th horse of the Apocalypse in Rev. 6). And later an angel gave Joseph Smith the Mormon religion (if both men even saw an angel, they may have just made up their stories). And one or more Jews who practiced the mystical Kabbalah in medieval Germany came up with the book of Raziel, supposedly given by an angel.

Today, many people accept any supernatural experience as though it were from God, as though evil does not exist; as though Satan were not trying to deceive people. Demons and fallen angels speak through people frequently, and the people have large followings by relating the so-called wisdom of these spirits, who are channeled through these deceived persons.

Mather tells another story of a senator's son in Geneva who was given strange visions and revelations by a supposed good angel who, like the previous story, fooled many people to a certain point. When ministers became suspicious of the spirit, it said:

> They will not believe that I am a good Angel sent of God, but I will prove it by a miracle, and snatching some way or other a knife, thrust it into his breast, and drew it out again without hurt, crying "behold a miracle!" (*A Disquisition*, page 44)

It is not clear whether the angel stabbed himself or the young man (likely himself), but that was the final straw that caused them to realize that he was not a good angel. There have been a surprising number of bad angels pretending to be good:

> St. Francisca claimed to read her midnight prayers by the light that glowed from her guardian angel. (Gaebelein, *What the Bible Says About Angels*, page 66)

However, even though there is more than one saint named "Francis," I suspect that the above is likely the same one mentioned here:

> St. Frances had always her good angel near her, that he was visible to her, and suggested to her the good she should do, and diverted her from evil; he sometimes <u>even chastised and struck her before company, who heard plainly the blows he gave her</u>, but never saw the angel. (Page 37) (*Dissertations Upon The Apparitions of Angels, Daemons, and Ghosts*, by Reverend Father Dom Augustin Calmet, Translated from the French, London, 1759.)

In the above account, it appears that the Roman Catholic Church believes that the above was a good angel! Even though it "chastised" her and "struck" her! NO, it was not a good angel! In modern versions of the story, the abuse the angel inflicted is left out. <u>Beware of visiting angels; even if they do good, if they ever do evil they are not good angels</u>!

Many angel encounters have doubtless been lost, but we still have many in the historical record. *A Book of Angels*, (edited by L. P.) published in 1906, is mostly a theological discussion of angels, but there are a few angel stories:

> Many modern stories are told of angelic intervention in temporal danger, and some of these at any rate are well authenticated. A little child in America ran out into the street, but was run over by a passing tram-car. She was picked up and taken home as one dead. For a long time she lay in a kind of trance, though apparently unhurt. When she came to herself they asked her what she remembered of the accident.

> She told them clearly of a bright being in white who had lifted up the cruel wheels one after another so that they could not hurt her. The only traces of the accident upon her were two red marks across her body made by the wheels. This story comes from one who had seen the marks, and is told on unimpeachable authority . . . (page 246-247)

Why were there even red marks, you may ask? I suspect that the angel lifted up the trolley car just enough so that the child was not injured in an attempt to make the angelic intervention undetected. The book continues with the story of a prosperous Cornish farmer in England who took regular trips to the market to sell his produce, returning home on his wagon alone after dark:

> The vicar of his parish asked him once if he was not afraid, under the circumstances, to drive back in the dark by himself; he replied that he preferred to be alone, for he always meditated on the way home, and frequently felt the close companionship of the angels.

> One night two [coal miners] had plotted to waylay and kill him, and waited for his trap to return along the dark and lonely road. As the gig drew near, one of them cried, 'Good God! there are two of them.' . . . The men fled in terror; and one of them, being taken ill shortly afterwards, made a clean breast of the evil plot,

in the presence of a priest.

The farmer, on being asked for a solution of the mystery, simply replied that no one had accompanied him on that particular night, but that (as often before) he had felt the angels very near him. The truth of this story also rests on the strongest evidence, and it has often been re-told. . . . The facts of the story are simply so much additional evidence of what every faithful Christian confidently knows to be true, viz. that our God keeps His promises, and the inspiring, comforting words of Psalm 91 are no exaggeration. (pages 246-248)

I find it interesting that many Christians of the 19th century believed in angels and miracles, yet today, many do not. And back then, there were no Pentecostals or Charismatics.

A preacher of the late 19th and early 20th centuries who was fairly well-known at the time, but not as much today, was A. C. Gaebelein. He has his own angel story:

The great men of God in the past in every century record miraculous escapes from threatening dangers which they could not explain in any other way but by the ministry of the angels. . . .

A number of years ago, while travelling northward [by train], we committed ourselves especially into His loving hands. There was a feeling of danger in the heart. The Lord gave a night of peaceful rest. But in the morning we heard the story of what had happened during the night. The train was hours late and the crew told us that near to midnight the train had been flagged by a farmer and had been brought to a stop less than five yards from a deep abyss. A storm further north sent its flood-waters down the creek and washed the wooden bridge away. A farmer was asleep. He said a voice awoke him to arise. He heard the rushing water and hastily dressed himself and lit a lantern, when he heard the oncoming train, which he stopped in time. We have always believed that an angel of God acted then. (*What the Bible Says About Angels*, Gaebelein, page 98-99)

The biography of the Indian Christian mystic, Sadhu Sundar Singh (3 September 1889 - 1929), includes some angel stories. This is a great one about his trip to Tibet:

With a deep determination to make the name of Christ known in this hostile country the Sadhu continued his work, knowing that sooner or later bitter persecution would be his lot. At a town called Rasar he was arrested and arraigned before the head Lama on the charge of entering the country and preaching the Gospel of Christ. He was found guilty, and amidst a crowd of evil-disposed persons he was led away to the place of execution. The two favorite forms of capital punishment are being sewn up in a wet yak skin and put out in the sun until death ends the torment, or being cast into the depths of a dry well, the top being firmly fastened over the head of the culprit. The latter was chosen for the Sadhu.

Arrived at the place he was stripped of his clothes, and cast into the dark depths of this ghastly charnel-house with such violence that his right arm was injured. Many others had gone down this same well before him never to return, and he alighted on a mass of human bones and rotting flesh. Any death seemed preferable to this. Wherever he laid his hands they met putrid flesh, while the odor almost poisoned him. In the words of his Savior he cried, "Why hast Thou forsaken me?"

Day passed into night, making no change in the darkness of this awful place and bringing no relief by sleep. Without food or even water the hours grew into days, and Sundar felt he could not last much longer. On the third night, <u>just when he had been crying to God in prayer</u> he heard a grating sound overhead. Someone was opening the locked lid of his dismal prison. He heard the key turned and the rattle of the iron covering as it was drawn away. Then a voice reached him from the top of the well, telling him to take hold of the rope that was being let down for his rescue. As the rope reached him he grasped it with all his remaining strength, and was strongly but gently pulled up from the evil place into the fresh air above.

Arrived at the top of the well the lid was drawn over again and locked. When he looked round his deliverer was nowhere to be seen, but the pain in his arm was gone, and the clean air filled him with new life. All that the Sadhu felt able to do was to praise God for his wonderful deliverance, and when morning came he struggled back to the town, where he rested in the serai until he was able to start preaching again. His return to the city and his old work was cause for a great commotion. The news was quickly taken to the Lama that the man they all thought dead was well and preaching again.

The Sadhu was again arrested and brought to the judgment seat of the Lama, and being questioned as to what had happened he told the story of his marvelous escape. The Lama was greatly angered, declaring that someone must have secured the key and gone to his rescue, but when search was made for the key and it was found on his own girdle, he was speechless with amazement and fear. He then ordered Sundar to leave the city and get away as far as possible, lest his powerful God should bring some untold disaster upon himself and his people. Thus was Sundar delivered from a fearful death, and praised God for interposing on his behalf. (Parker, *Sadhu Sundar Singh: Called of God*, page 61-62)

Notice that the angel did not immediately rescue Sadhu, but let him suffer for several days. I suspect that he decided on his own to go there without being directly guided by Holy Spirit. After his release, Sadhu goes right back and endangers himself again. He managed to escape death that second time, but later he took another trip into Tibet and was never seen again. If God directs us to go somewhere dangerous, then we will likely get angelic protection, but we should not intentionally put ourselves in positions where we require angelic protection; we may not get it. It is almost like jumping off a cliff and expecting the angels to catch you!

Frank Laubach was a missionary on the island of Mindanao, Philippines, in the early 1900s:

Lonely and frustrated in his savage surroundings, [he] often climbed Signal Hill for prayer under the stars, unaware that he was followed by spear-bearing, head-hunting Moro tribesmen.

The Moros met with strange frustrations. Every time they crept out of the trees to follow the foreigner in the night, they found a big man had preceded them and was walking beside the missionary. There was something strangely terrifying about that tall companion. The Moros dared not attack.

"We would have killed you," the shamefaced group of Moros told Frank Laubach later, "but you were never alone. That big fellow always walked beside you."

Laubach had walked up the jungle path alone, and had prayed on the hilltop alone, except for the feeling that the living Christ was by his side. (Adapted from Courage in Both Hands, by Alan A.

Hunder, Ballantine Books) (Carter, *Hand on the Helm*, page 203)

***

Metropolitan Cyril (Smirnov) of Kazan and Sviyaz was sent to exile. One night he was thrown out of the train carriage at full speed. It was a snowy winter. Metropolitan Cyril fell into a huge snowdrift, as if into a feather bed, and was not hurt. He struggled out of it and looked around: woods, snow — no sign of a dwelling. He walked a long way in the snow and, growing tired, sat on a tree-stump. The frost was chilling him to the bone through the worn-out vestment. Feeling that he was beginning to freeze, the Metropolitan began to read to himself the prayer for the dying. Suddenly something big and dark approached him, he looked carefully — it was a bear.

"He will eat me!" — the thought flashed through his mind, but he had no strength to run, and where to? But the bear approached him, sniffed at him and calmly lay down at his feet. The beast was in good temper, it emitted warmth. He moved, and turning his belly towards His Eminence, stretched out and began to snore. The Bishop hesitated for a long time, looking at the sleeping bear, but then could no longer bear the paralyzing cold and lay down next to the bear, cuddling up to the warm belly. He lay, turning one or the other side to the beast to get warm, while the bear was breathing deeply in its sleep and enveloping him in his hot breath. When it grew light, the Metropolitan heard roosters crowing in the distance. 'Habitation is near,'- flashed the happy thought in his mind, and he carefully, without waking the bear up, rose to his feet. But the beast got up, shook himself and waddled to the forest. His Eminence soon reached a little village.

After knocking at the first door, he explained who he was, and asked for asylum. He was allowed in, and lived for more than half a year in that village. He wrote to his sister, she visited him, and then they came for the Metropolitan and took him away. (*Contemporary Cases of Miraculous Help*. Translated from Russian by Tatiana Pavlova / Natalia Semyanko. www.father alexander. org/booklets/english/chudesa_e.htm)

***

A Canadian woman who spent many years as a missionary in China, tells of many miracles that took place during those years. But here is one great story that she told about her grandfather in England:

> The most precious recollections of early childhood are associated with stories told us by our mother, many of which illustrated the power of prayer.
>
> One that made a specially deep impression upon me was about our grandfather, who as a little boy went to visit cousins in the south of England, their home being situated close to a dense forest. One day the children, lured by the beautiful wild flowers, became hopelessly lost in the woods. After trying in vain to find a way out, the eldest, a young girl, called the frightened, crying little ones around her and said: "When mother died she told us to always tell Jesus if we were in any trouble. Let us kneel down, and ask him to take us home."
>
> They knelt, and as she prayed one of the little ones opened his eyes, to find a bird so close to his hand that he reached out for it.
>
> The bird hopped away, but kept so close to the child as to lead him on. Soon all were joining in the chase after the bird, which flew or hopped in front or just above, and sometimes on the ground almost within reach. Then suddenly it flew into the air and away. The children looked up to find themselves on the edge of the woods and in sight of home. (Goforth, Rosalind. *How I Know God Answers Prayer*, page 6-7.)

Was this a real bird or an angel? Since it is the job of angels to do stuff like this, I believe it was an angel, not the Holy Spirit controlling a bird.

***

In 1926, a serious book was published by Sir William Barrett, in London, about the many accounts of people who appeared to see into the spirit world just before they died, called, *Death-Bed Visions*. Here are a few stories from that book.

Rev. J. A. Macdonald received this account from Miss Ogle, the sister of the dying person:

> "My brother, John Ogle, died at Leeds, July 17th, 1879. About an hour before he expired he saw his brother -- who had died about sixteen years before -- and John, look up with fixed interest, said, 'Joe! Joe! and immediately after exclaimed with ardent surprise,

'George Hanley!'

"My mother, who had come from Melbourne, a distance of about forty miles, where George Hanley resided, was astonished at this, and said, 'How strange he should see George Hanley; he died only ten days ago.' Then turning to my sister-in-law she asked if anybody had told John of George Hanley's death; she said 'No one.' My mother was the only person present who was aware of the fact. I was present and witnessed this: Harriet H. Ogle. (Barrett, *Death-Bed Visions*, page 20-21)

She further stated that John was not delirious and that George Hanley was not a family friend but a personal friend of John. The book contained several other similar stories:

"The mother of one of the foremost thinkers and theologians of our time was lying on her death-bed in the April of 1854. She had been for some days in a state of almost complete unconsciousness. A short time before her death, the words came from her lips, 'There they are, all of them -- William and Elizabeth, and Emma and Anne'; then, after a pause, 'an Priscilla too.' William was a son who had died in infancy, and whose name had never for years passed the mother's lips. Priscilla had died two days before, but her death, though known to the family, had not been reported to her." (Ibid., page 26)

The author of the book stated:

It is needless to quote a great number of cases, as doubtless many of my readers will be familiar with instances. Such cases are not confined to one country or one nation, but they appear to be more or less common all over the world. (Ibid., p. 27-28)

Yet he does include many other accounts. The next account he took from a book titled, *The Ministry of Angels*, by Mrs. Joy Snell, who had worked as a nurse for many years, and was blessed with the ability to see the souls of departed loved ones who come to the bedside of the dying. It should be noticed in this account that the souls of the dead are referred to as angels, as though it were an accepted belief at that time:

"It was about six months after I began work in the hospital that it was revealed to me that the dying often really do see those who have come from the realms of spirit life to welcome them on their entrance into another state of existence.

"The first time that I received this ocular proof was at the death of Laura Stirman, a sweet girl of seventeen, who was a personal friend of mine. She was a victim of consumption. She suffered no pain, but the weariness that comes from extreme weakness and debility was heavy upon her and she yearned for rest.

"A short time before she expired I became aware that two spirit forms were standing by the bedside, one on either side of it. I did not see them enter the room ; they were standing by the bedside when they first became visible to me, but I could see them as distinctly as I could any of the human occupants of the room. I recognized their faces as those of two girls who had been the closest friends of the girl who was dying. They had passed away a year before and were then about her own age.

"Just before they appeared the dying girl exclaimed, 'It has grown suddenly dark; I cannot see anything!' But she recognized them immediately. A smile, beautiful to see, lit up her face. She stretched forth her hands and in joyous tones exclaimed, 'Oh, you have come to take me away! I am glad, for I am very tired.'

"As she stretched forth her hands the two angels extended each a hand, one grasping the dying girl's right hand, the other her left hand. Their faces were illumined by a smile more radiantly beautiful even than that of the face of the girl who was so soon to find the rest for which she longed. She did not speak again, but for nearly a minute her hands remained outstretched, grasped by the hands of the angels, and she continued to gaze at them with the glad light in her eyes and the smile on her face.

"Her father, mother, and brother, who had been summoned that they might be present when the end came, began to weep bitterly, for they knew that she was leaving them. From my heart there went up a prayer that they might see what I saw, but they could not.

"The angels seemed to relax their grasp of the girl's hands, which then fell back on the bed. A sigh came from her lips, such as one might give who resigns himself gladly to a much-needed sleep, and in another moment she was what the world calls dead. But that sweet smile with which she had first recognized the angels was still stamped on her features.

"The two angels remained by the bedside during the brief space that elapsed before the spirit form took shape above the body in which physical life had ceased. Then they rose and stood for a few moments one on each side of her, who was now like unto themselves; and three angels went from the room where a short time before there had been only two.

"About a month after the death of Laura Stirman, which I have just related, another friend of mine died in the hospital, a Mr. Campbell, a man of 45. It was pneumonia that carried him off. He was a good and devout man and for him death held no terrors, for he was sure that it was but the transition to a happier, more exalted life than can be lived here. His only regret at dying was that he would leave behind him a dearly-loved wife; but that regret was softened by the assurance that their parting would be only for a time, and that she would join him some day in that other world whither he was going.

"She was sitting by his bed, and, believing as he believed, was awaiting the end with resignation. About an hour before he died he called her by name, and pointing upwards, said, 'Look, L--, there is B! He is waiting for me. And now he smiles and holds out his hands to me. Can't you see him?' 'No, dear, I cannot see him,' she replied, 'but I know that he is there because you see him.' B- was their only child who had been taken from them about a year before, when between five and six years of age. I could plainly see the little angel with curly flaxen hair and blue eyes, and garbed in what I call the spirit robe. The face was just that of a winsome child, but etherealized and radiant as no earthly faces ever are.

"The father had been greatly weakened by the ravages of his disease, and the joyful emotion occasioned by seeing his angel child seemed to exhaust what little vitality he had left. He closed his eyes and sank into a placid sleep. He remained in that state for about an hour, the angel child meanwhile staying poised above the bed with an expression of glad expectancy on his radiant face. Occasionally he looked lovingly at his mother.

"The breathing of the dying man grew fainter and fainter until it ceased altogether. Then again I witnessed what had now become a familiar spectacle to me -- the formation of the spirit body above the discarded earthly body. When it was complete the angel child grasped the hand of the now angel father, each gazed into the eyes of the other with an expression of the tenderest affection, and with faces aglow with joy and happiness they vanished.

"Later on in the day, the widow (Mrs. Campbell) said to me 'I am very glad my dear husband saw B-- before he died; it was natural that B-- should come for him to take him to the angels, for they loved each other dearly. I shall now be able to think of them as always together and happy. And when I receive my summons I know that they will both come for me.' (Barrett, *Death-Bed Visions*, page 109-113)

(Michael defeats Satan, 1630-1635 A.D.)

Mrs. Snell continued with another bedside story:

"After I had left the hospital and had taken up private nursing I was engaged to nurse an old lady (Mrs. Barton, aged 60), who was suffering from a painful internal disease. She was a widow and her only daughter lived with her. . . . The time came when the end was very near. The mother had been for some time unconscious, and the daughter was kneeling by the bedside, weeping, her face buried in her hands. Suddenly two angels became visible to me, standing on either side of the bed. The face of one was that of a man who, when he departed from this life, was apparently about 60 years of age. His beard and hair were iron-grey ; but there was stamped on his features that indescribable something indicative of exuberant vitality and vigour, which shines forth from all angel faces I have seen, whether in other respects they present the semblance of youth or old. age. The face of the other angel was that of a woman, apparently some ten or fifteen years younger.

"The dying woman opened her eyes, and into them there came that look of glad recognition I have so often observed in those whose spirits are about to be released for ever from their earthly tenements. She stretched forth her two hands. One angel grasped one hand and the other angel the other hand, while their radiant faces were aglow with the joy of welcoming to the better world, her whose earthly pilgrimage was finished." (Ibid., 113)

Chapter 6

Angels and War

"I remember the moment I came to Jesus Christ as Savior and Lord. The angels rejoiced! Since then I have been in thousands of battles with Satan and his demons. . . . As I prayed and believed, I am convinced that God 'put a hedge about me,' a hedge of angels to protect me." (Billy Graham)

It may come as a surprise to many people, but angels actually engage in human-like warfare. I am not speaking of war in the heavenly realm, though there is evidence of that, I am speaking of war here on earth. Angels will kill human soldiers during warfare, in order to make sure that the side they want to win actually wins. Throughout history, there have been eyewitness reports that support the belief that angels engage in literal warfare.

When Moses led the Hebrews out of Egypt, Pharaoh changed his mind and chased after them with chariots and horses. Jewish legend believes that angels *"hurled arrows, great hailstones, and fire and brimstone at Pharaoh's forces"* (Gaebelein, *What the Bible Says About Angels*, page 45).

The angel Gabriel appeared several times to Pastor Roland Buck in Boise, Idaho, in the late 1970s (*Angels on Assignment*), and one of the things that Gabriel told Roland was that when the Egyptians were racing toward the Hebrews, many angels were attacking them by pulling off the wheels from the chariots and throwing lightning bolts at them.

(When I first read his book in the mid-1980s, I actually did not believe it. Forty years later, when I started re-reading it as part of the research for this book, I expected to be speaking against the book, but I am older and wiser, and I now believe it.)

In 2 Kings 6, Elisha prayed that God would open the eyes of his servant so he could see what Elisha could see, and he saw thousands of horses and chariots, and angels waiting to engage in battle. We already learned that just one angel killed 185,000 Assyrian soldiers in one night (2 Kings 19:35). Many are the speculations about how they were killed, whether by a plague or something else.

In 2 Maccabees 3, we learned how Heliodorus was attempting to confiscate the gold and silver of the Temple, when a mighty warrior wearing gold armor on a horse *"adorned with beautiful trappings,"* suddenly appeared, rushed at him, and struck him. Then two other warriors, *"scourged him unceasingly, inflicting on him many sore stripes"* (3:26). Heliodorus was picked up off the ground by his men, put in a litter, and carried away near death. Clearly, these were angels who came in answer to the prayers of the people.

Later, an angel killed King Herod because he did not give glory to God, but took it for himself:

> Immediately an angel of the Lord struck him, because he did not give God the glory. And he was eaten by worms and died." (Acts 12:23)

In this case, it is clear that he was stricken with an illness that killed him, likely within days, but it was caused by an angel.

Below are many different stories from early to recent times that tell of angelic intervention in wars, mostly to save soldiers.

A Battle for The Roman Empire

In 394 A.D., Thodosius was fighting against powerful pagan invaders in the Italian Alps, led by Arbogast. The fate of Rome was at stake; would the mighty Roman Empire, which had not long become a Christian empire, remain so? Or would it be defeated and become pagan once again?

The Christian army was surrounded by rocky cliffs and boulders; to escape, they needed to penetrate the invading army. The night before the battle, the pagans believed they were assured of victory and celebrated with drunken revelry. Arbogast vowed that he would soon stable his horses in the Church of Ambrose. The prospect of Christian churches being pillaged and Christians being tortured or persecuted was a real possibility.

> He had lost great numbers of men; those who remained were deeply discouraged, and he doubted whether they could be per-

suaded to meet the enemy again. . . . Theodosius wandered away alone into the hills and remained all night in fervent prayer that God would help the right and vindicate His own cause. As the dawn came up behind the eastern hills the Emperor fell asleep and had a wonderful dream. In his dream he saw two radiant knights, clothed in white and mounted on white horses, come towards him. They told him that they were John and Philip, the Apostles of the Lord, and that he should be of good courage, for God had heard his prayers. Theodosius awoke, but only to begin praying again; nor did he cease until, just as the sun leapt up behind the Nanosberg, an officer came running to tell him of a wonderful dream that one of his soldiers had had — and described the same vision that had visited and comforted the Emperor.

Then indeed Theodosius knew that he should prevail, but he neglected no smallest point that could aid him to victory. When all was ready he made the sign of the Cross, the preconcerted signal of attack, and hurled his men on the foe, who was somewhat dazed and disorganised after the night's excesses. Still Arbogast's men fought so fiercely that the issue seemed once more wavering in the balance, and then the great Emperor, like another David, rising in his saddle, shouted, "Where is the Lord God of Theodosius?" and dashed into the thickest of the fray. Like those other valiant ones, who carried no weapons, his soldiers said, "Let us perish with him!" and flew to follow; and <u>then the Lord God of Theodosius let loose His servant, the terrible "Bora,"</u> the wind that science cannot account for, that blows once in a century or once in a decade, as the case may be, and always carries death on its wings. From behind the spurs of the Alps it roared down that day, as if placed under the Emperor's orders, and in its fury the very darts of Arbogast's men were turned back and buried in the bowmen's flesh. (Fraser, Mrs. Hugh. Italian Yesterdays, Vol. 1. Dodd, Mead and Company: New York, 1913, page 202-203)

The powerful winds added distance and force to the arrows of Theodosius's army, while actually turning back the arrows of Arbogast. The wind was so powerful that the pagan archers could barely stand up against it. And so God provided a mighty wind to bring victory instead of defeat. (Other sources include: Hodges, George. *Saints and Heroes to the End of the Middle Ages*. Henry Holt & Co.:

New York, 1913. And: *The Horizon Book of Ancient Rome*, 1966. And, Carter, *Hand on the Helm*, page 147-150)

A Goth Invasion

In A.D. 433, the Germanic Goths invaded Gaul (France). St. Albin was then archbishop of the city of Embrun. He prayed to St. Marcellinus for protection. The Goths laid siege to the city and eventually reached the immediate fortifications. But the Goths were defeated by the intervention of a legion of angels who fought them, turning their weapons back upon them, and throwing them from the walls of the city. This was seen by the Gauls and the Goths. (https:// catholic southernfront. wordpress.com/chapter-957-saint-michael-the-archangel-and-the-apparitions-and-prodigies-of-other-saints-during-wartime/)

Saved From Attila the Hun

In 451, Attila the Hun approached Rome to attack it. Thereupon, Pope Leo went to Attila to plead that he leave them and not attack. To everyone's astonishment, Attila withdrew his army. When asked why he withdrew, he replied,

> *"While pope Leo was speaking, I distinctly saw two shining beings of venerable aspect [large size], and manifestly not of this earth, standing by his side. They had flaming swords in their hands, and menaced me with death if I refused to withdraw my army."* (Damasus, *Lives of the Popes of the Middle Ages*)

Many people do not believe this story, but why would it not be true? I believe it totally. One reason is that a similar thing is recorded in the Bible as happening to Balaam. An angel stood in the path and blocked his way, with a sword in his hand:

> Then Yahweh opened the eyes of Balaam, and he saw Yahweh's angel standing in the way, with his sword drawn in his hand. (Numbers 22:31) (WEB)

The other reason I believe it is true is because it is part of recorded history. Attila the Hun did not attack Rome, which should have happened since Rome was no longer a military force in 451 A.D.

Joan of Arc

In 1429, France was in a state of despair; there was a famine, a breakdown in law and order with roaming bands of robbers, and

Charles was likely to abandon his claim to the throne. To make matters worse, it was during the one-hundred-year war with England; the military was in such a state of hopelessness that 1600 English troops defeated 4,000 French soldiers. In response to the crisis, clergy traveled throughout the county and urged the people to pray for God's help.

Little did they know that God had already prepared a peasant girl to save the nation. Joan of Arc (c. 1412 – 30 May 1431) said she received visions of the Archangel Michael, Saint Margaret, and Saint Catherine of Alexandria from the age of 13, who told her to wage war along with the armies of Charles VII (who had not yet officially become king), against the English. At the age of 16, she went to a nearby town and asked the army commander to take her to the French Royal Court at Chinon. She was turned away but returned the next January and insisted on joining the king, saying that she was their only help.

> "Although I would rather have remained spinning [wool] at my mother's side . . . yet must I go and must I do this thing, for my Lord wills that I do so." (Pernoud, Régine. *Joan of Arc By Herself and Her Witnesses*, p. 35.)

She was 17 when she first met with Charles VII in 1429. To make a long story short:

> When the Dauphin Charles granted Joan's urgent request to be equipped for war and placed at the head of his army, his decision must have been based in large part on the knowledge that every orthodox, every rational option had been tried and had failed. Only a regime in the final straits of desperation would pay any heed to an illiterate farm girl who said that the voice of God was instructing her to take charge of her country's army and lead it to victory. (Richey, Stephen W. *Joan of Arc: A Military Appreciation*.)

Yet, once Charles VII became king, rather than listen to Joan and wage war, he negotiated with the English and disbanded his army, while the English still held much of France. So, Joan gathered a group of fighting men under her command and waged war directly with the English with, *"sudden, repeated, and decisive victories"* (Ibid.). She was captured by the English in May of 1430, and burned at the stake as a heretic one year later.

Because of her trial and retrial after her death, there was much eyewitness testimony by people who knew her while she was growing up, or fought with her in battle. These documents still exist. These firsthand testimonies show that Joan had a dynamic personality and confidence, which allowed her to whip-up the morale of the French to a high level so they could engage in battle and win; whereas they had previously been beaten down with despair. At the same time, her presence on the battlefield caused doubt and fear among the English. Even though she was captured, the French were able to keep fighting and became victorious. Which means that she accomplished her mission.

Joan is reported to have said of angels,

> "I saw them with my bodily eyes as clearly as I see you. And when they departed, I used to weep and wish that they would take me with them." (Gaebelein, *What the Bible Says About Angels*, page 22)

Why would God want the French to win a war against the English? The book of Daniel says:

> . . . the Most High rules over the kingdom of men and gives it to whomever He wills. (4:32)

So this tells me that God did not want England to rule France but wanted the French to be a separate nation. It did not necessarily mean that he approved of the French rulers more than the English, or somehow was with the French people over the English. Not at all. This also means God did not necessarily approve of the French church over the English church, as both were ruled by the Roman Catholic Church during that period. God merely wanted France to be France, and not under the thumb of the English, the way Ireland and Wales have been.

Angel Saved Christian Town

In the mid-16th century, the Asian tribe of Badagars were a warlike people and were intent on killing a local missionary, Francis Xavier, and wiping out all Christians in the towns of Trauancor and Comorinum. Xavier went alone to confront them. The advancing army came to a stop, "spellbound" by what they saw. The leaders of the army claimed that a giant figure stood beside Xavier with lightning in his eyes. So the army retreated. (Lewis, *Angels A to Z*, page

68) (*A Dictionary of Miracles, Imitative, Realistic, and Dogmatic: with Illustrations*, Ebenezer Cobham Brewer, 1894, page 391)

Saved By Warrior Angels

In 1900, menacing groups of rebels were gathering outside the walls of Peking. They were called "Boxers," a close translation of their own Chinese title, meaning "Righteous, Harmonious, First." Encouraged by dowager Empress Tz'u Tsi, they were revolting against the government of China because they believed it was adversely influenced by foreigners. *"Death to the foreigners"* was their bloodthirsty battle cry.

Christian missionaries were exempt from this fate in recognition of their unselfish service. But such special consideration was not always to be depended upon. So, many missionaries, including the family of Reverend Chauncey Goodrich (Congregational missionary to China, 1865-1925), had fled to the Methodist Missionary Compound in Peking. The men took turns watching the compound.

Chinese servants of the Goodrich family who went into the compound with them said that Boxer revolutionists were afraid to attack the mission compounds because of a prevalent belief among them that "shen" (spirits, genii, gods) were on the side of the missionaries and would appear and protect them.

Tensions grew until June 20th, when the missionaries and their families left the compound and marched into the British Legation for greater protection. Chinese employers of the British Embassy also said that the Boxers certainly would not attack the missionaries. But local authorities insisted that every precaution be taken, so from June 20 to August 14, only government soldiers and marines were allowed on the Peking wall to keep a lookout for enemy movements.

But once the missionaries were no longer seen on the walls, the number of Boxer attacks increased. It was during an attack by a superior force that the defenders noticed strangely illogical behavior among the attacking insurrectionists. With more than adequate forces, they had fought their way to within seconds of their objective when they abruptly halted and began to point upward. The whole attacking force, seemingly filled with consternation, suddenly turned and fled. Some were captured, and when asked why they were running, they replied in obvious terror:

We saw the walls suddenly swarming with angels in white. Everyone began shouting that the 'shen' (the gods) had come down to fight for the foreigners and our cause was lost.

(Adapted from *Knights Masterbook of New Illustrations* by Walter B, Knight (Wm. B. Eerdmans Publishing Co., 1956). With additions from letters of a missionary's family. (Carter, *Hand on the Helm*, page 157-158)

Saved by Female Angel

Arch Whitehouse says in his book, *Heroes and Legends of World War I*, that after the battle of Mons, during the retreat, some Coldstream Guards got lost in the area of the Mormal Forest and dug-in to survive as best they could. Then a tall, slim female angel wearing a white flowing gown approached the men and led the Guardsmen across an open field to a hidden, sunken road, which they followed and allowed them to escape.

There were likely many praying Christians among those men, with praying relatives back home, so an angel was sent to save the whole group! But can angels be female? Gaebelein said that a servant girl of John Wesley said she had seen a female angel:

> . . . clothed in white, "glistening like silver" and "unspeakably musical," who foretold to her certain events which came to pass. Upon questioning her about her experience, Wesley said that he was "soon convinced that she was not only sincere, but deep in grace; and therefore incapable of deceit." Wesley was troubled, though, that the girl identified the angel as female, but excused her by saying that "from the face, the voice, and the apparel, she might easily mistake him for a female . . ." (*What the Bible Says About Angels*, page 70)

Some people won't believe anything not clearly stated in the Bible, as though the Bible could contain everything. They say that there are no female angels mentioned in the Bible; therefore, they do not exist. It is true that the Bible does not say that female angels exist, but it also DOES NOT say that they do not exist. To make the claim that they cannot exist because they are not stated to exist in the Bible is not good reasoning, that sadly does exist. Because there have been many honest reports of female angels, it was no mistake.

Saved From Bullets

During World War I, a man regularly prayed for his son, Jimmie, who was fighting in France:

He prayed for an hour and his wife set down the time of prayer. Jimmie was in a dugout and buried alive with nine others. All lost their lives but Jimmie. One was cut in two, right through the center of his body. The faithful, Holy Spirit put prayer on the father away off in Scotland that his boy's life might be saved.

At another time as the father sat down to his breakfast, he could not eat. As he took the food into his mouth, he sickened, and said to his wife, "We must go to prayer." He travailed in soul for hours and they noted the date. Later they found that at that time Jimmie and another boy were returning from a village. His own army thought he was from the enemy's side dressed in English clothes, and turned the machine gun on them.

They showered the artillery on these two boys; the bullets flew so thickly the dust came up into their faces, but they were unharmed. Suddenly, the Captain saw that these boys were from the British Army and ordered the machine gun stopped. All Jimmie got was a little scratch back of the ear. (*The Later Rain Evangel*, Sept., 1923)

This is an example of the Holy Spirit causing someone to pray in intercession for someone who is in danger. It usually happens with someone related to the person in danger, but sometimes a person is called upon to pray for a total stranger. They have no idea who they are praying for or what kind of danger they are in.

Prayer For Supplies

During WW2, the average age of the men in the 511th Parachute Infantry Regiment, 11th Airborne Division, was 21. And since war tends to cause many to start praying, the Colonel of the regiment, Orin D. "Hard Rock" Haugen, required all the men to attend Sunday service.

This group of men were known as "The Angels," and prepared their very heavy packs for the trek into the jungles and mountains of Leyte and Luzon. The Bibles were heavy, so most of the men had to set them aside. PFC Everette M. Hagemeyer had to set his Bible on the ground, "Goodbye, Good Book!" But the men knew that God was going with them, even though their Bibles were not.

The men soon encountered Japan's 16th and 26th Infantry Divisions. They had many miracles during their battles, some are verifiable, such as the miracle which the men received through Chaplain Lee Walker.

Up in the mountains, it was rainy and overcast, and the men were suffering from a lack of food, but there could not be a food drop because of the bad weather. But this did not stop Chaplain Lee Walker, who was determined to visit the men. He made a jump from a small Piper Cub airplane and promptly held a service.

> "With helmets and rifles in hand, the battle-tested paratroopers all meekly knelt in the same mud they had slept, fought, bled, and buried friends in as Chappie prayed on their behalf. His words of faith and humble pleadings warmed their hearts and renewed their spirits."

Chappie Walker packed his things to leave when the sky began to clear, and men began cheering when a C-47 transport flew over and dropped badly needed supplies. The men were certain that God had heard the chaplain's prayer, and it became known as "Chappie Walker's Miracle." (https://511pir.com/unit/unit-history/los-banos-raid/89-miscellaneous/287-god-and-the-angels-on-leyte-1944?)

An Angel-Battle

Another angel-battle occurred in July 1918, near Bethune, France. The Germans saw what appeared to be cavalry approaching from a distance, so they began shelling in that direction and let loose much machine gun fire, but no rider fell, and they kept coming. As they got closer, the Germans charged toward them, then suddenly retreated in panic. German prisoners of war later told the story that the cavalry that charged them was dressed all in white, and the leader had golden hair and was carrying a sword. This story was corroborated by many witnesses on both sides of the conflict. (Lewis, *Angels A to Z*, page 69)

Christian Crew Saved Many Times

"Alley Oop" might have been the name of this bomber. But Captain Paul Helander had a multitude of good reasons for calling his shining new B-24 Liberator "The Good Shepherd."

At first the fellows couldn't understand why Paul didn't choose a more glamorous name for his plane, which led his squadron in flights from England over enemy territory. But when "The Good Shepherd" continued to fly unscathed over targets like Berlin, Cologne, and Hamburg, the boys began to think his place led a charmed life.

For twenty missions "The Good Shepherd" came and went, flying serenely through flack-studded skies and enemy fighters.

"Then came our toughest assignment," said Helander. "We were up at 3 a.m. Our target was Berlin . . . in daylight. High over Berlin our 'Good Shepherd' received a direct hit."

Captain Helander, who was awarded the Distinguished Flying Cross and other medals, then related how he was seriously wounded, how the co-pilot brought the plane home, and how he awoke in a British hospital the next day. None of the other crew members was hurt.

Weeks later both Helander and "The Good Shepherd" had been patched up. But a new crew had been assigned to the plane. As Helander and his men watched their faithful ship take off, little did they realize they would never see it again. Over Munich that day "The Good Shepherd" had its last flight. It was shot down, and no information concerning the crew's safety was ever received.

The secret of "The Good Shepherd's" charmed life while Helander was at the controls was simple. One night, Paul Helander at the age of ten gave his life over to the Lord Jesus Christ, the Good Shepherd. Paul had learned with the Psalmist that "the Lord is my Shepherd . . . He leadth me." In all of life's sunshine and sorrow Paul had in his Saviour a real Friend, a Counsellor, a Guide.

Each time before the big bomber left for a mission Paul would huddle with the crew of "The Good Shepherd" and they would pray for help and guidance. A prayer of thanksgiving was offered as the plane reached its base.

"On the last flight of "The Good Shepherd", said Paul thoughtfully, "I watched the fellows climb into the plane. They did not know the Lord, and they left on that mission without prayer. That is why I believe they never returned." (Dennis, *These Live On*, page 18-19. The stories from this book originally appeared in numerous other publications shortly after WW II.)

If they made numerous missions and were never shot down, and it was in answer to prayer, how exactly did that happen? I believe that several angels went with them on every flight and deflected anti -aircraft fire and bullets from hitting them.

Angels Supply Gas

For weeks Chaplain Johnson had been planning this mission. Serving his men on an island in the South Pacific, he was anxious to observe the exact dangers faced by his men during combat.

Now that the CO had granted permission. Johnson began to prepare in the early hours of the morning to take part in a bombing raid over a group of Jap occupied islands several hundred miles away.

The mission was a complete success with only little enemy opposition. The full squadron of planes directed their course homeward. After covering a short distance, the plane in which Johnson was flying began to lose altitude. The engines seemed to fade out.

The God of heaven, however, was navigating and piloting this plane and had provided an island below on which to land. A safe landing was made near the beachhead on one side of the island. The fliers learned later that the Japs were just one-half mile in each direction, yet their landing had not been discovered.

After a thorough examination of the engines, the staff sergeant very slowly came to Johnson and said, "Chaplain, for many months now you have been preaching to us fellows about the great needs of praying and believing God to answer in times of great distress and trouble. You have told us that God answers prayer and that He does it right away. Well, sir, now is your chance to prove what you have been preaching. We're out of gas . . . home base several hundred miles away . . . and almost surrounded by Japs."

What would you have done?

Chaplain Johnson knew Christ as a Friend and Companion and had seen God answer prayer when offered in the Name of His Son. He knew how to talk direct to heaven.

Johnson began to pray. As he prayed, he began to lay hold of the promises of the Scriptures, and he began to believe that God would work a miracle in their behalf.

All afternoon Johnson was on his knees. As the sun was setting, a ship was sighted on the horizon. It seemed to be heading in toward the island, but it passed and gradually faded away. Night came, and the crew improvised bunks on the ground. Johnson continue to pray.

About 2 a.m. the staff sergeant was strangely roused. Walking to the water's edge, he there discovered a metal flat which had drifted upon the beach — a barge on which were fifty barrels of high octane gasoline.

Within a few hours the crew reached their home base safely. A careful investigation revealed the skipper of a U.S. tanker, finding his ship in sub-infested waters, had removed his gasoline cargo to remove the danger of a torpedo hit. Barrels of this gasoline were placed on barges and put adrift some 600 miles from where Johnson and the plane crew had been forced down. God had navigated one of these barges through wind and current and beached it only fifty steps from the stranded men. God does perform miracles. He does answer prayer. (Dennis, *These Live On*, page 48-49)

I can just see an angel flying slowly above the water as he pushes the small barge of gasoline through the water toward its desired destination. But the angel most assuredly had a smile on his face and did not consider it drudgery or a menial job.

Angel Saved Overboard Sailor

Each surging wave pounded over the deck of the small ship, stretching and straining every timber. Sailors struggled from place to place by clinging tenaciously to the slightest handhold.

Suddenly, a mountainous wave engulfed the small vessel, throwing the ship into a dangerous lurch. A cry for help, a violent stream of blasphemous oaths, and a gurgle which faded into the roar of the next wave. "Man overboard!" But rescue was impossible, hopelessly so, in such a heavy sea.

Far away, in Philadelphia, lived the sailor's mother, a Christian mother. In the dark of the night she awoke thinking of her son, who had shipped months before on a small cargo ship. She was impressed that he was in danger. Even though she did not understand her awakening, after praying for perhaps two or three hours, she felt in her heart that God had answered.

For days afterward she wondered why she had been awakened in the dead of night. Somehow she could no longer feel the need to pray for her boy; rather, she daily praised God for something that she knew He had done for her son.

One day, several weeks later, her front door burst open. "Mother, I'm saved!" Soon he was telling her his story.

He told how a few weeks before his ship had been tossed and beaten in mid-Atlantic by a terrific storm, and he had been carried overboard. Even though a powerful swimmer, he only went deeper. As he was sinking, the awful thought came to his mind, "I'm lost forever." Suddenly he remembered a hymn that he had often heard in his boyhood days:

> *There is life in a look at the Crucified One,*
> *There is life at this moment for thee,*
> *Then look, sinner, look unto Him and be saved,*
> *Unto Him who was nailed to the tree.*

He cried in the agony of his heart, "O God, I look, I look to Jesus." Then he was carried to the top of the waves and lost consciousness.

Hours later, when the storm had ceased and the battered ship was again out of danger, the sailors came forward to clear the deck. There they found him lying unconscious, crowded up against a bulwark. One wave had carried him over, and another had brought him aboard the ship again. His first words when he finally regained consciousness were, "Thank God, I'm saved."

When he had finished his story, his mother, with moist eyes, told how God had awakened her in the darkness of that very night, to pray for him. Together they rejoiced in God's answer in saving his life and his soul. (Dennis, *These Live On*, page 52-53)

There are many old books that are no longer in print, such as this one, that are full of miracle stories, yet some used copies are still available at various websites.

9 P.M Prayer Miracle

It was the morning of Sept. 1st, 1940, in the underground operations of the 11th Group Fighter Command of the Royal Air Force. British Prime Minister Winston Churchill and his military advisors discussed their next move after the previous retreat to Dunkirk. Intelligence reports indicated an invasion of England by Hitler's forces was being prepared.

The British had already lost hundreds of planes in the war, and few were readily available. Then suddenly the alert came; 40 planes were reported approaching England from one direction, 60 more from another direction, and more than 80 from another direction. The Royal Air Force sent up 25 squadrons of planes from the 11th Fighter Command, and tensions rose in the underground command center. Reinforcements were requested from the north, but only three squadrons were available.

"What other resources have we?" Churchill asked.

"None, Sir," was the reply. The room was silent.

"The odds were great; our margin small; the stakes infinite," Churchill wrote later. [1]

Then, inexplicably, the war pieces on the wall map were moved eastward. The entire Nazi air flotilla had turned back. Having lost 185 of their aircraft, they retreated. Miraculously, against all probability, the Royal Air Force had won the battle!

Exactly how the Royal Air Force had won against unbelievable odds may never be fully explained, but British Intelligence officers received information from three different members of Hitler's forces. One was a pilot captured after his crippled plane was drowned in England.

"Why did your formation retreat when only two planes were attacking you?" the intelligence officers asked the prisoner.

"Two!" exclaimed the pilot. "There were hundreds!" [2]

The prisoner was dismissed, and the British intelligence officers exchanged puzzled glances. Then a Luftwaffe officer, captured later, asked them, *"Where did you get all the planes you threw into the battle over Britain?"* The British interrogators masked their surprise. [2] There had not been a sky full of Royal Air Force planes! The answer came when a captured Nazi Intelligence officer exclaimed:

"With the striking of your Big Ben clock each evening at nine," the Nazi told the British Intelligence officer, "you used a secret weapon which we did not understand. It was very powerful and we could find no countermeasure against it." [3]

Every evening at 9 p.m., the entire British Commonwealth

stopped for a "Silent Moment of Prayer." This prayer movement was started by industrialist W. Tudor Pole, who had fought in WW I.

Just imagine being an angel and flying a fighter plane in WW II while shooting down enemy planes! As exciting as it would have been for a human, I am sure it was even more exciting for the angels because the angels experienced no fear of death or injury, only thrills!

1] Albert La Fay, "Be Ye Men Of Valor," National Geographic, 08/1965.

2] Sharing Magazine, 02/1961, San Diego, California.

3] Round The World At Nine O'clock (London: Big Ben Council).

Hand on the Helm, Katherine Pollard Carter, Whitaker House, 1977, page 3-6.

Angels Turn Back Planes

A former missionary to China and Tibet, H. A. Baker, relates the account of an American who spent many years in China, and could speak both Japanese and Chinese. Some Japanese men from their air force told him how they were sent to attack a certain town in China during WW II. They were in the lead plane, and as they neared the town, a white cloud covered it. *"As his plane neared the cloud he saw a group of angels."* His plane was hit by turbulence and became difficult to control. He repeatedly tried to steer the plane toward the town, but the turbulence made it impossible, so he went around the town, and the other planes followed. But that was one side of the story.

This same American was able to learn that the town was occupied by many Christians who had been praying hard because <u>they had been made aware of an impending attack</u>. The Christians did not see the angels, but they did see the planes approach and go around. (*Heaven and The Angels*, page 132-133) The Christians in the town were not tipped off about the planned attack by a spy; they were told by the Holy Spirit or an angel, which caused them to pray against it.

Angel Turns Torpedo

A letter appeared in *Christian Home*, a weekly newspaper in Council Bluffs, Iowa, and was later reprinted in *Weekly Unity*, of Kansas City, MO, March 10, 1946. A woman wrote and recounted the miracle her son had during WW II:

> My son who is a real Christian boy, is now somewhere in the Pacific war zone. Many months before he left our shores he and I

memorized and repeated over and over again that wonderful 91st Psalm. We agreed together that the promises it contained applied to us. We stood upon them in faith, believing and made a covenant with God.

We agreed that, no matter where "Son" might be, at prayer time we would repeat again those verses. It was a sort of tie, binding our hearts and minds no matter how many thousands of miles might lie between us. A few days ago I received a letter from my boy which to me is evidence beyond all possible doubt that God's promises are real and operative. An excerpt from the letter reads as follows:

"Our convoy was under heavy attack from both air and submarines. Antiaircraft guns chattered incessantly and the crash of heavy guns was deafening.

"Every battle station was manned and operating. One submarine was sighted off our starboard and within firing range. Momentarily we expected to see the wake of a torpedo headed our way, and it was not long in coming. It was a tense moment and I knew that many of the fellows on deck with me were praying.

Suddenly I remembered our covenant with God and the 01st Psalm. I began to say it over again. I know you too must have been praying, for before our very eyes God wrought a miracle. When the torpedo was a short distance from our vessel it seemed as though something went wrong with its mechanism, for it swerved sharply in its course and passed to our stern and disappeared.

Shortly after that a second torpedo was fired by the sub and again its wake showed that it was aimed directly at us. I kept on reciting those verses. Somehow I was not afraid for I knew that god was able. This time, at about the same distance from our vessel, the torpedo seemed to go crazy. It spun in the water, took a sharp angle to its right and passed by the bow of the ship. That's the last we heard from the submarine. As for the attack by air, we suffered not a hit nor a scratch." (*Weekly Unity*, page 6)

Miracle Causes Russian to Believe in God

This next story is from a Russian fighting the Germans who invaded Russia in WW II:

In 1941, when I was 22, I was sent to the front. I was a signal-man. I took part in the Leningrad defense. The Nazis were trying to take the city, which was surrounded. Trying to take the city at any cost, they sent an avalanche of fire on us. My battle friends were dying one after another. And then, during one of the bombings, when the barrage swooped on the city and, it seemed, that the end of the world had come, a real miracle happened. The night sky was suddenly illuminated with pink light, and the image of the Savior appeared on the rosy sky. All the soldiers in the dugout, without any mutual agreement, fell on their knees from the suddenness of it, and started to pray… The image of the Savior disappeared. The sky became normal, but the hell on earth stopped. And we could not regain our senses for a long time… I started to believe in God from that moment. With this faith, I survived the entire war and, after the Victory, returned home without a wound. The image of Christ remained in my memory forever. (*Contemporary Cases of Miraculous Help*. Translated from Russian by Tatiana Pavlova and Natalia Semyanko.)

Angel Saved Sailor

One seaman, fighting against the Nazis at the Baltic Sea, found himself in the ice-cold water. He swam, tiring out. The cold waves were submerging him. His clothes were wet. His arms and legs grew numb, became uncontrollable. Where could he swim? Where was north? South? The fog was like an impenetrable wall. His heart beat at top speed.

He had exploded the enemy's ships, now they exploded his launch. Nobody survived. He would die, too. He had to face the truth: those were the last moments of his life. Even if any ship passed by, he wouldn't be noticed: there was impenetrable fog. He was far from shore. The cold was piercing. It was getting harder and harder to breathe. There was nothing to hope for, except a miracle. But all his life he thought, — and he was so taught at the Moscow University, by very intelligent professors, — that miracles did not exist, that there was no God, that all that was a lie and the invention of illiterate fools or swindlers.

In those moments he remembered his dearly beloved grandmother, who had said just the opposite when he was a child: 'Just say — Our Father. Call God your Father… And can the Father leave His child in trouble?'

And the seaman, hardly recollecting the words of the prayer, gathered his last strength, whispered: 'Our Father Who art in the Heavens! Hallowed be Thy name…'

Before the seaman even finished the prayer, the dense fog suddenly dissipated, revealing a Soviet ship which was in that region accidentally. They noticed the seaman and took him aboard. This rescue from inevitable death, particularly after he had read the prayer, appeared to the seaman to be so miraculous, that he believed in God. (Ibid..)

Mother's Prayers Saved Son

I did not believe in God. When it came time to join the army, my mother, frequently going to church and praying for me, gave me a piece of paper, with a prayer written on it, and said: 'My son, let it always be with you.' Later, I found out that the 90th Psalm was written on the piece of paper. I was assigned to the para-troopers. One is not allowed to have superfluous things in their pockets in the army, so I sewed the prayer into the lining of my uniform jacket, near the left shoulder.

I was making my first parachute jump. I shall never forget that moment when, having fallen down to the air abyss, I pulled the ring and... the parachute did not open.

I pulled the ring of the spare parachute — it did not open either. The ground was approaching fast.

In those few seconds I could not, naturally, take out my mother's prayer and read it. Therefore I only slapped the place where it was, and cried: 'Lord, rescue me!'

In reply, I heard the flapping of the opening parachute.

Everything would come later: the inquiries of officers and friends, my mother's joy and tears, but even before I reached the ground, I promised myself that I would enter the seminary.

Later, upon graduating from the seminary, I joined a monastery, now I am a hieromonk. (Ibid..)

Angel of Stalingrad Battle

This next story would have been widely published had it oc-curred in Europe or anywhere in the West, but it happened in Com-munist USSR during WW II. But the account was written down and discovered years later in the archives:

In world history there are events, which remain forever in the memory of mankind, they make up the golden fund of the history of nations and kingdoms. The brilliant victory of our nation in the Stalingrad battle belongs to their number. It surpassed all previous armed battles in its scope, force and consequences. The Stalingrad battle became the turning point of the entire Second World War.

Researchers analyzed mainly the correlation of techniques, human reserves, combat training and level of morale of both the Soviet and Hitler armies. However, behind the frames of scientific monographs there was something beyond the limits of human knowledge, therefore carefully hidden in confidential folders of special repositories in the state archives.

While I was working in the State Archive of the Russian Federation I found a document, unique in its way: it was the report of the representative of the Council on the Affairs of the Russian Orthodox Church Comrade Hodchenko to the then-chairman of the Council G.G. Karpov. In it, a regular atheist, an opponent of religion, informed the higher bosses about things which contradicted his own ideas and beliefs. The representative reported no more no less a Miracle, which a whole military unit that had come to the Ukraine from the Stalingrad front had witnessed...

After the shattering defeat near Moscow, the German command was counting on delivering the main blow to a southern region, in order to break through Rostov to Stalingrad and the Northern Caucasus, and from there to the Caspian Sea and north along the Volga River. Therefore the defense of Stalingrad appeared to be the major strategic task to the Soviet leadership. In the middle of July, 1942, the army of general Chujkov was sent to the Stalingrad region, which took on the major brunt of the struggle against the enemy, whose force was made up of 26 divisions.

In September of 1942, the fascists prepared for the last, "decisive" storming of the fortress on the Volga. By that time, the greater part of the city was already in their hands. There were heavy street battles for every district, house, for each meter of the Volga grounds throughout the month. On November 11 the Nazis made their next attempt to storm the city. Our armies found themselves divided into three parts. But during the most critical moment of the battle, the soldiers of one part of the celebrated army saw something that made them shudder: a Sign appeared in the autumn night sky of Stalingrad, indicating the rescue of the city, the army and the swift victory of the Soviet armies.

Unfortunately, in the report of the representative, it does not say what exactly the soldiers saw in the Stalingrad sky. It can only be assumed, that the Stalingrad sign and the appearance of the Kazan icon of the Mother of God in Stalingrad (the miraculous icon was among our armies on the right bank of Volga, and moliebens and panikhidas were constantly served in front of it) are somehow connected. In any case, the Stalingrad sign clearly showed, that God's help does not abandon the Russian people in the most critical moments of its history. The further succession of events — the encirclement of the enemy and counterattack of the Soviet army — served as the best proof of that.

After all that happened, the legendary commander, subsequently the celebrated marshal, Chujkov, could be seen in Orthodox churches. The hero of the Stalingrad battle stood in church; put candles before the icons . . . Certainly, he remembered the night before the battle and the marvelous Face of the Mother of God, which had appeared in the clarified autumn sky! (*Contemporary Cases of Miraculous Help*. Translated from Russian by Tatiana Pavlova and Natalia Semyanko.)

These stories show that miracles and angelic intervention happen to all genuine Christians, not just Protestants or Catholics, and even to those who are going to become Christians. And the fact that some miracles included the icons of Mary has no bearing on it, as it does not mean that God endorses icon worship or Mary worship. It merely means that the Russian Orthodox Church was the dominant Christian church in that region, and using a sign of Mary in the sky was the best way to show the people a Christian sign. This sign meant only that God was with the Christians and was going to give victory because of their prayers, and it was also proof of the reality of Christianity. It was not an endorsement of Russian Orthodoxy over Protestantism, or any other branch of Christianity.

You can be sure that there was a legion of angels fighting to make sure that the Russians won the battle, because God did not want the Germans to win. It does not mean he was with the Communist government of the USSR, but merely against the Germans.

Prayers Save 146 Church Members

Posted by Robert Lenk in Norman OK USA on Oct 17 2015:

During part of WW II, my dad Fred Lenk was pastor of a Presbyterian Church in Kenmore, New York, USA. The church had 146 members in the different military branches. The church prayed every day by name for each member in the war for safety, and all came home with no war injuries. One night, my dad woke up at 2:00 AM, and he knew that he needed to pray for one man in the Navy. Dad prayed for that man from 2:00 AM until 4:00 AM when dad felt like it was then OK, and he wrote down the date and time. Months later, that man was home on furlough, and dad talked with him. Allowing for time zone differences, the man said that at that exact time, he was on board of an American submarine sitting on the ocean floor at a depth of 150 feet in the Pacific Ocean. During that exact period of time, a Japanese destroyer was making many passes to drop depth charges in an attempt to destroy the submarine. By the end of the two hours, there had been explosions that were close but not close enough to break the hull of the submarine. (www.crossrhythms.co.uk/articles/life/)

Angels were not seen in the above account, but if prayer was needed to prevent the submarine from being hit by depth charges, which are bombs, then angels must have been there to push away the bombs, or perhaps shield the sub from the effects of the blast.

Angel Causes Engine to Not Work

It was a hot and humid morning when the crew of a U.S. gunboat got ready for their mission during the U.S. Vietnam War. Stephen F. was manning the machine-gun on the lead boat of the convoy, but when it came time to leave, the boat's engine would not start. It would not even try to start; there was no sound at all, it was dead. So the lieutenant in charge went to another boat, and the convoy headed out. Just as the last boat left, Stephen's boat started, and they headed out as the last boat.

But somewhere along the river, the Vietcong opened fire upon them from both sides of the river, and the lead boat sustained heavy damage. All of the sailors on that boat were killed except the lieutenant, who was hit in the neck and paralyzed. But the last boat did not receive any significant fire. This is one of the ways in which Stephen's life was saved due to his mother's many prayers for his safety during the war.

Even though there was no angel seen, and the miracle did not seem overtly huge, an angel was no doubt there to stop the engine. The Holy Spirit is not busy all around the world doing stuff like that; it is God's workers, the angels. (A personal testimony given to me.)

Angels Save Children

Towards the end of World War II, while the Russian army was advancing against the Germans at Danzig, in present-day Poland, the children were sent to live in a building that also served as their temporary schoolhouse. This building survived the bombardment and was known as *"the island of peace."*

They had prayer each evening at the school. During one prayer service, a boy who did not have any religious background said to one of the nurses, *"It came up to here on them,"* while he tapped his breastbone. The nurse asked the boy to explain; he had seen very tall men glowing with light standing around inside the building. And *"they were so tall the gutters on the roof came up to their chests."* (Lewis, *Angels A to Z*, 69)

Why are angels almost always much taller than humans if they merely take on the shape of humans? I find that very strange; perhaps they have a particular size and shape, based on their job function.

Angels Saved Children in Congo

During the Jeunesse Rebellion in the Congo (1963-65), a rebel army advanced on a school where approximately 200 children of missionaries lived. The Christians knew their lives were in great peril, and were praying hard. The school only had a fence and a few soldiers for protection, but there were hundreds of rebel soldiers. The rebel soldiers attempted to attack, but then retreated. This occurred numerous times for three days. One of the wounded rebels, who was later captured and questioned, said that the reason they could not conquer the compound was because it was defended by hundreds of soldiers dressed in white. (Lewis, *Angels A to Z*, p. 69-70) (*The Catholic Southern Front*, chapter 9/57, *Saint Michael the Archangel and the apparitions and prodigies of other Saints during wartime* https://catholicsouthernfront.wordpress.com/)

These soldiers who were defending the compound were not merely deflecting bullets; the inference was that the rebels were being shot at by angels! Why are angels virtually always wearing white? This is not a coincidence. Jesus said several times in the letters to the seven churches of Revelation that we, too, will be wearing white in heaven. <u>The rebel did not say they were white soldiers</u>; he merely said they were dressed in white, and since this was Africa, they were most likely black angel-soldiers, because angels do take on normal human appearance.

Angel Saved Future Pastor

Robert Bogrean was orphaned at age 4, then raised by his grandmother and *"shuttled between relatives."* His life was difficult, and he had to delay college plans when he was drafted into the US Army in 1970:

> I remember going to church on a regular basis when I lived with my grandmother, but once that was over, church became a rarity reserved for Christmas and Easter. . . . So with my orders in hand, I stepped off the plane. There I was, a radio technician ready to serve my country.

> Somehow I knew, from the beginning, that I was not going to like Vietnam because it was too loud and much too hot. I shared a small tent with three other men and between my duty, their snoring and the sound of the distant bombing, it was very hard to concentrate and nearly impossible to sleep. Since I was the newest man on the radio team, I was assigned the night watch with a promise of a rotation when another new person arrived. I really did not mind the night watch, for it gave me time to sort out my thoughts and even gave me some time for prayer, especially when the gunfire got too close. All remained fairly routine, until April, 1971.

> I remember that the rain started early in April and it continued for several days. I did not mind the rain as the others did, because it seemed that the rain washed away the despair and death of the war. I recall leaving my tent that night and sloshing past several rows of tents that seemed to sag in the darkness. I was just passing the last row of tents, when a flash of light seemed to surround me. At first I thought it was lightning, but it was not like that harsh glare that lightning produces, it was much softer and seemed to be just around me. I tried to run, but it felt like my boots were stuck in the mud. The light changed and that is when I saw the angel.

As the glow started to diminish, a figure of a man stood in front of me. He appeared to be about my age and was wearing a long robe, that was dry. The man started to speak to me, but at first his lips did not move then slowly they became more pronounced. He told me that I would be safe while I was in the war, but that I was to tell the others about God's angels. I wanted to interrupt and tell him that I knew nothing about angels, but that thought was blocked. Instead my heart and my mind were filled with a series of Biblical references about angels. Then the angel said, "Do God's work, and the angels will do theirs." That night, I found a Bible and began to study the references that I had been given.

From those passages, I began to see how angels were a reality of my life and the lives of those around me to this day. Today I am married, have a family and have pursued the career of a minister. Each day, come rain or shine, I thank God for sending His angel to a rain-soaked hillside in Vietnam, to open the heart of a soldier to the warmth and beauty of angels. (Robert Bogrean, *Angel Watch*, Nov/Dec 1998, page 10)

Six-Day War Miracles

Many miracles were recorded during Israel's Six-Day War as the surrounding Arab nations attempted to invade Israel in a surprise attack. From the miracles recorded, there is no doubt that many angels were involved. For example, an Israeli tank force was unknowingly approaching a mine-covered road when a sudden dust storm blew up so strong that none of the drivers could see anything at all, so they stopped. It shortly ended, but the wind had uncovered the mines that were easily seen on the road ahead of them. (Carter, *Hand on the Helm*, page 37)

One army unit was traveling from Bethlehem toward Hebron when they saw an old man standing near the tomb of Abraham. He was dressed all in white, had a flowing white beard, and was *"standing with hands raised heavenward."* An officer attempted to speak to him and said:

> "There's a war on. If you stay here you are quite likely to get killed" . . . When the old man showed no sign of having heard him, the officer sent a soldier to repeat it at close hand. But as the soldier reached out to grasp the aged arm and get his attention, the old man disappeared. (Ibid.)

When the surprise attack first began, it took some time for the Israeli soldiers to reach their defensive positions, but the enemy troops would have overrun the borders, except--

> - thousands of soldiers dressed for battle appeared both in the north and the south. These "angelic soldiers" remained there defending their positions until the "real" Israeli troops and equipment arrived, and then they disappeared. (MacNutt, *Angels are for Real*, page 114)

Judith MacNutt said of the Israeli army today:

> One of my longtime friends was a major in the Israeli army. He and the soldiers under his command told me numerous stories of angelic intervention that occurred regularly on their maneuvers. (Ibid., page 114)

God is not defending Israel because Judaism is the true faith; it is because God has decided that Israel will exist as a nation, and so it will not be defeated until the final war when the Antichrist invades, shortly before the return of Christ, as recorded in Bible prophecy.

In the book *Heaven is For Real*, Colton Burpo went to heaven when he was a child during a hospital operation (but didn't die). Later, his parents gradually found out what he saw in heaven. Colton said he saw a future war here on earth in which Jesus and angels will fight with good people against Satan, monsters (demons), and bad people. Colton said his dad (Todd) will be fighting in this war with Jesus with a sword, or a bow and arrow; he did not remember which. Since swords are what angels use in the spirit world to fight the demons, I suspect it is a sword, which means that his dad will likely have gone in the Rapture. It means that Raptured saints will be fighting with angels here on Earth.

Todd Burpo is the pastor of a Wesleyan church in Colorado, not among the Charismatics who are apt to promote spiritual experiences or trips to heaven. Angel visits and trips to heaven are not limited to one group, though they are less likely to happen to people without the capacity to believe in them. I guess God does not want to shake their earthly-acquired beliefs too much.

Chapter 7

Angels of the Modern Era

The early fathers regarded the ministry of angels as a consoling and beautiful doctrine, and so much at that time was it held in veneration that the founders of Christianity cautioned their early converts against permitting their reverence to degenerate into adoration. We now go to the opposite extreme, and seldom think of their existence. (Dr. George Townsend) (Fowler, Our Angel Friends, page 71)

In spite of our advancing knowledge of science, people have continued to believe in God and angels in the 20th and 21st centuries. In the 1980s, there was a TV series that starred Michael Landon called *Highway to Heaven* that lasted 5 years. Then, in 1994, the TV series called *Touched by An Angel* began, that stared Roma Downey and lasted nine years, plus many years of reruns for both shows.

There have also been many books written that are filled with nothing but first-person testimonies of angelic encounters, as well as magazines such as *Angels on Earth*. A few stories from them are included below, along with many others I have pulled from a wide range of books, magazines, news reports, and videos.

A Lonely Life

A dear saint whom God had wonderfully blessed was compelled because of the Lord's dealings with her to lead a rather lonely life, so far as human companionship was concerned. Spiritually inclined she reached out after the things of God, and the man or woman who walks with God is often much alone. Spiritual food and Christian fellowship are often found outside our own home and family life, and in her search after God she frequently had to go alone to religious services, sometimes becoming quite fearful about being out late at night. So she cried to the Lord about it and He comforted her with this verse, "The angel of the Lord encampeth round about them that fear Him and delivereth them," which promise We often proved to her.

Several years ago we were having a special series of Lectures at The Stone Church on the Book of Revelation, and this sister was greatly interested. One night the meeting was held unusually late and as the speaker pronounced the benediction he said as he had kept the people quite late and many had long distances to go he felt led to ask the Lord's special protection upon them and prayed that the angels might have charge over them and keep them. As he did that, the Spirit spoke to this sister and said that was for her. She said, "Yes, Lord, I do believe You will give Your angels charge over me," and started out. It was a dark night and there was not a person on the street as she walked along the Avenue, but her mind was on the teaching of the evening and she had blessed communion with the Lord. As she neared the corner where she was to turn she saw a man going across .the street and disappear up 41st Street. She commenced to pray and asked the Lord to protect her. Just as she came to the corner she saw him standing with his back against a house, evidently watching which way she would turn. As she started up 41st Street he walked ahead of her three or four steps, keeping quite near as they both walked along.

At once the thought came to her that she was in danger, and the Spirit told her he was a "hold- up" man. She began to pray for guidance, whether she should turn back and take an Indiana Avenue car or go on, but the Spirit seemed to press her forward. Then the enemy said to her, "Now you will have to go under the Elevated Road and he will catch hold of you in that dark place, you had better turn back and run," but she felt that prayer that was offered at the close of the meeting would be answered. While there was not another person on the street, all at once a man appeared in front of her and walked right between her and the "hold-up" man. She felt perfectly at rest and had the greatest confidence in this man.

She thought, "How strange it is that I feel so safe in this man's company, and that he has come to protect me!" They walked on, the three of them together; the man directly in front of her walked very deliberately, and the "hold-up" man hastened his steps. As they went on he turned down the first alley he came to, but the "guardian angel," for it was none other, continued walking ahead of her until she was within two or three doors of her home; then he disappeared down a stairway that led into a store. When she reached the house and thought it over the Lord gave her the verse, "The angel of His presence saved them." (*The Later Rain Evangel*, Feb., 1915)

The Unbelieving Farmer

A farmer whose wife attended the meetings of the Pentecostal folks, became filled with hatred because she insisted on going to the meetings of that despised company. He said, "I will not have my farmer friends make fun of me because you go to those meetings." She answered, "I will obey you in everything but this, and in this I will obey my Lord, and worship as He leads me."

He became beside himself with rage, and one day he entered the house with a large knife in his hand and said he would kill her if she would not promise to give up her religion. She knelt down on the floor, thinking her time had come, and he stood over her with his knife. Suddenly he found himself on the other side of the room, and said to her in a frightened tone, "Who was that?" An angel had come down to protect the woman and fear fell upon the sinful man. He slunk out of the room and never again interfered with her belief after that. (*The Later Rain Evangel*, Sept., 1923)

Saved From Assault

At a street meeting [by a Pentecostal preacher] a man who was a Catholic stepped up to the speaker as he closed the meeting and asked, "Who protected you?" "Well, God always protects me," he replied. "Somebody protected you tonight," said the Catholic. "I came here with the determination to knock you down, but some one grabbed my arm and held it." He was angry because of the exaltation of Jesus above the Virgin Mary. (Ibid.)

If the person holding the arm down could be seen with human eyes, the man would not have asked, *"Who protected you?"* So I believe an unseen angel was holding the arm down.

Saved From a Gangster

As a young woman, I lived and worked as a maid in the home of a Detroit doctor. On my evenings off I went dancing downtown at Arcadia Hall. The Charleston was the craze, and in 1927 I knew all the steps.

One night I danced almost exclusively with a handsome blond who was attentive and polite. When the orchestra played Good Night, Sweetheart, he asked if he might see me home in a taxi. Despite my employer's warnings about strangers, I felt safe accepting this offer.

Inside the cab, I gave my escort the doctor's address. He ignored me. "Just cruise around," he ordered the driver. He looked at me sideways. "I'm Silk Shirt Bobby," he said. "From Chicago." I panicked. A gangster! I pressed myself against the door. He moved closer, and I saw the gun in his jacket.

I gripped the door handle. Please, Lord, protect me. With that prayer on my lips, I threw myself out of the moving cab. I braced for the fall onto the cobblestones, but a man caught me by the elbows and lifted me gently upward, as if partnering me in a waltz.

Still frightened, I didn't say much on the way, but the man accompanied me home and led me up the steps. I felt his kind eyes on me as I put my finger to the bell. Before I pressed it, the doctor threw open the door.

"Thank goodness you're back!" he said. "I worry about you coming home alone at this late hour."

I looked beside me. I was alone. My partner had slipped away as gracefully as he had arrived. (Betty Shier, Englewood, Florida, *Angels on Earth* magazine, Jan/Feb 1999, page 43).)

A Modern Prodigal

In 1939, Charles A. Galloway, Jr., was a rebellious teen who had been raised in a Christian home in Jackson, Mississippi. But he grew restless and bored with school, desired to get more out of life, and dreamed of being a prizefighter; so he ran away from home at the age of 16.

"I just need to be a man," he told one of his friends before he left. "Gotta set out on my own."

Charles was smart, tall, and strong, but he had little money, so he watched the railway cars to determine where they were going and which ones he might be able to hop onto. Some were protected by *"railroad bulls,"* men who were paid by the railroad to assault men who jumped onto the trains. The bulls would literally throw people off.

> They were not worried about people stowing aboard while the train was moving, since to do so would have been foolishly dangerous. For that reason, it was rarely attempted. . . .

> Charles could imagine the dangers associated with jumping onto a moving train, but he was not afraid. He determined he would wait until the train was moving and take his chances. If his timing was right, he believed he could run alongside a slow-moving train and jump aboard one of the cargo cars without incident.

If he failed to make the jump, he could fall under the moving wheels, but the train was moving slowly, and he easily made the jump. He used this method several times until he reached a small town in Missouri, where he found work with a traveling carnival/circus as a "roustabout." He wrote a letter to his parents:

> "I can't tell you where I am, but I'm safe," he wrote in that first letter. "I may even get to do some prizefighting."

He traveled with the Red Top Circus for eight months and was allowed to fight, which made him more money than being a roustabout, and he never lost.

> "I think you'd be proud of me," he would write. "Sure, I'm not in school. But I'm living out my dreams. Please don't worry about me."

His parents were concerned and kept praying for him daily.

> "Lord, please protect our son," they would pray aloud. "Keep him safe and bring him home."

Because of the cold weather in February, the circus closed. When his money got low, he headed south, and two weeks later he was in Hayti, Missouri.

> He really wanted to find another circus, somewhere he could resume fighting. That afternoon Charles scouted the area only to discover that the nearest traveling circus was about twenty miles

south. He knew just the train to take him south, and he hid himself near the railroad station's warehouse, under the loading dock. There he waited for the perfect moment. As he crouched in the shadows, he noticed that the train, which was still being loaded, would be pulled by two locomotives. That meant the train would pick up a great deal of speed much more quickly than usual. It might even be traveling close to full speed as it left the station. But he had jumped on fast-moving trains before and was not afraid.

When the time was right, he ran toward the boxcar and jogged alongside it. Suddenly, the ground beneath him narrowed and he was running alongside a steep ravine. A few feet ahead he could see that there was no land at all alongside the tracks--only a steep drop-off. Charles knew he had just one chance. Jumping before he had picked up the proper speed, he thrust himself upward and landed partially in the open boxcar. But with nothing to hold onto, his body began sliding out. As Charles struggled to pull himself inside the car, he could feel the train gaining full speed. Terrified at his predicament, he looked over his shoulder. The train was winding along the top of a very steep and narrow canyon ridge. If he slipped out he would either fall beneath the train's wheels or plummet down the steep canyon to his death. He closed his eyes and tried to will himself into the boxcar. Instead, he could feel himself slipping.

"Please, God!" he cried out, his eyes squeezed shut. "Don't let me die here." But Charles knew there was no way to survive the situation; he was seconds from certain death.

At that instant he opened his eyes. In front of him stood a fantastic-looking muscular black man in his thirties. The man was staring at him intently but said nothing; he only reached down and pulled the boy by his arms into the speeding boxcar. Charles lay face-down on the floor of the car for several seconds trying to catch his breath and regain his strength. When he looked up to thank the man, he had vanished. The boxcar was completely empty. One of the two side doors was closed, as it had been since the train began moving. He glanced outside and shuddered. There was no way the man could have jumped from the train and survived. He had simply disappeared from sight. Charles sat down slowly in a corner of the car and began shivering.

Suddenly he knew with great certainty that he needed to get home. He stayed on the train until it reached Jackson and immediately returned to his parents' home. He told them about the man on the boxcar.

"An angel, son," his father said, as his mother took them both in her arms. "God was watching out for you," she said. "See, he brought you home to us."

Charles nodded. "Things are going to be different now. You watch."

Charles returned to school, was baptized in a local river, then graduated from high school and became a prizefighter. He was drafted and served with the 339th Bomb Squadron in the 96th Bomb Group of the Eighth Air Force during WW II. He flew 28 missions over Germany and returned home. Decades later, he still tells people about how God sent an angel to save him:

"My entire life would be different if it weren't for that single afternoon," says Charles, whose faith and love for God is always evident these days. "God used that angel not only to save my life but to change it into something that could glorify him forever." (*There's An Angel on Your Shoulder: Angel Encounters in Everyday Life*, Vol. 1, Kelsey Tyler, page 23-28)

Landing a Jet

The following incident occurred in 1958 when I was a navy jet-fighter pilot. Our aircraft carrier was steaming in a northerly direction in the Pacific Ocean, east of the Sea of Japan, one late fall day. Farther to the east a typhoon was moving north as well. The seas were heavy but not too rough to prevent air operations. Our flight, the last one for the day, launched around three P.M. and lasted for an uneventful hour and a half.

When we returned, however, we found the ship pitching up and down and rolling in such heavy seas that our planes had great difficulty landing, either because of the uneven deck or because the plane ahead was fouled up in the arresting gear, blocking the landing area. Six times I tried to land and six times was waved off. I became anxious. Each landing approach consumed 150 to 200 pounds of fuel . . . . I was down to 450 pounds of fuel.

On my eighth attempt I was again waved off.

"What is your fuel state?" the Air Boss asked by radio.

"One hundred fifty pounds." The Air Boss asked for my intentions. I could either climb to parachute altitude and eject before I ran out of fuel or make one more attempt to land, with no chance of parachute escape, but if I failed, the plane would go into the sea. It was by now early evening and the ship was laboring in seas so rough that the rescue helicopter had landed. My plane was the last one in the air. I decided that my chances for survival after parachuting into a cold, mountainous sea with night approaching were nonexistent. Even in calm conditions a water landing was not advised, as the aircraft was known to blow apart on water entry. I told the Air Boss that I would make one last attempt.

As I flew downwind and prepared to turn onto the base leg of my approach, I prayed out loud into my oxygen mask but not over the radio: "Lord Jesus Christ, I need your help now or I will die. This is beyond my ability to control." My wife of six months was expecting our first child. I prayed, "I want a family. I want to see my children. But if it is your will that I should die now, then I accept your will. I will fly this plane to the best of my abilities until the end." I turned onto my approach heading. Suddenly a feeling of great warmth, love, and indescribable joy overcame me. My anxiety was gone. Although my hands were on the controls, a far better pilot than me was flying the plane. I knew instantly my prayer was being answered and that I had nothing to fear.

As the plane let down to the carrier from a distance of about two miles and an altitude of about 1,000 feet, I looked at the ship in utter amazement. It appeared to be floating on top of a huge upwelling of water. The waves were not penetrating the upwelling and the ship was floating level as in a calm sea. This lasted for some twenty to twenty-five seconds. Just as the tail hook engaged the arresting wire, the divine assistance ceased and the ship heeled sharply to starboard. But I was safely aboard. The aircraft line chief told me later that my aircraft was bone dry of jet fuel when checked before refueling. . . .

This contact with the Supreme Being affected my life. It made human goals of wealth and control and position seem of little consequence. It's made me very uneasy in the presence of unprincipled men and women, even to the point of feeling chills.

Since then I have turned my life over to Christ. I have had a wonderful marriage of thirty-three years, children and grandchildren, and been able to retire from business at the age of fifty-eight after the usual ups and downs.

Odd that people will trust their savings in the hands of a banker or investment broker but not think to put their happiness in the hands of God. (Name withheld by request, Burnham, *Angel Letters*, page 3-5.)

Unbeliever Saved From Drowning

A fellow in Russia who did not believe in God, relates how he became a believer after being saved from drowning:

'God does exist,' the old man, tall, bent, with grayish hair and expressive features often used to say. His name was Theodore Mikhailovich Makhov. At that time, all the schools and universities taught that God did not exist, and considered believers backward or insane. Theodore Makhov started to believe in the existence of God after he was saved from the waters.

Once, he was going home on the ice across the river Pekhorka, which is in Podmoskovye (a region close to Moscow). It was late evening —it grew dark early in the winter. He could not see the road. Somewhere in the middle of the river he fell into an ice-hole. The river was so deep in that place that, even in summer, not every diver could reach the bottom.

When he found himself under the water, he started to drown. If it had been dark on the ice, there was complete murkiness under it. He began to thrash, in order to swim out. In a few seconds he came up, but did not find the ice-hole, he hit his head on the ice. Then he really began to drown, because he had no idea which way to go to swim out. Sinking to the bottom, he appealed to the Lord with all his might:

If You exist, save me, help me! He begged not with words (he had no air), but with his mind — his entire essence cried aloft. At that very moment, the water under the ice lit up.

I saw no one, only it was like daylight, he was explaining afterwards. The light approached me. And some force took me by the hair, it seemed, and started to pull me up. I don't know how, but I was pushed out onto the edge of the hole. Someone helped me to get out. Most likely God or His Angel saved me from under the ice… First I crawled, and then I got up on my feet and began to walk. My coat was heavy with water, and ice-cold. I got home before I had time to freeze...

Yes, whatever they might say, God does exist! Otherwise, I wouldn't be alive. (*Contemporary Cases of Miraculous Help.* Translated from Russian by Tatiana Pavlova and Natalia Semyanko.)

My First Car

Victor Cooper, of Bokeelia, FL, wrote:

For my seventeenth birthday in 1971, my parents bought me my first car — a powder blue 1963 Oldsmobile F-85. I sure was proud. I washed and waxed it every Saturday morning.

One summer afternoon I drove away from home in the Cincinnati suburb of Norwood. I'd just gotten a green light and was turning left off Worth Avenue onto Rhode Island Street, when I noticed a car coming from my left. I assumed he would stop for the red. He didn't. [He was running a light that had just turned red.]

Maybe he was changing radio stations. I really don't know. Regardless, he was speeding through the light on a no-miss, T-bone collision course. It was not only a possibility but a certainty that the front of his car would slam into my driver's-side door.

My experiences over the years have taught me that people tend to use the word *miracle* too loosely. But I was there, and *miracle* is the only word fit to use. Only the hand of God could have prevented that sure catastrophe.

The other car *literally* passed through mine like Casper the friendly ghost passes through walls. As it did, the other driver, ostensibly a boy about my age, turned, and our eyes met. His face was no more than eighteen inches from mine, and I'll never forget his look of complete shock. I must have appeared the same way to him.

In this instant, time seemed to slow considerably. Immediately afterward both of us stopped, got out, and stood, just staring at each other. If I knew who he was and where to find him — I don't know whatever became of him — he would tell you the same.

After a few moments I got back into my car and drove two blocks to a Sohio gas station. I pulled in and parked, sitting in stunned silence, trying to grasp what had happened. I'd been raised in church, and I realized I'd just experienced divine intervention.

As I got out and examined my car, I knew what had occurred, yet many years went by before I ever told anyone. I was truly amazed by the magnitude of the event, but I figured people would think I was being sensationalistic.

In time I became a Southern Baptist clergyman, and I've shared this from the pulpit with two different congregations. Some have nodded in polite disbelief; there were others who hoped it was true but simply could not accept it. Humanly speaking they're correct, yet, as Jesus said, "with God all things are possible" (Mark 10:27). Several people from both churches came up to me afterward, said they believed it, and then proceeded to share miracle stories of their own. I believed every one of them because I know what happened to me one day in Cincinnati long ago. (Garlow, *Real Life Real Miracles*, page 235-236)

Angel on the Loud Speaker

Next is a great rescue story that was submitted by William N. Lindemann of Tahoma, California. It is a different kind of angelic intervention, which is why I have chosen to include it here.

William Landemann was raised in the outdoors. He was in the Boy Scouts for 10 years and often wandered the woods alone. He could hunt and fish, canoe, and backpack. So it was perfectly normal for William to head out on a walk one February morning around a frozen lake near the University of Wisconsin at Madison in 1975. Though he was dressed for the sub-zero weather, he was completely unaware of the approaching blizzard.

William had been raised Catholic but was no longer attending services, as he preferred to commune with God while on his nature walks. He left that day without telling his roommates where he was headed. Arriving at the lake, William decided to walk across it rather than around it, as it was about 25 miles around, 9 miles long, and 5 miles wide.

He estimated it would take about 4 hours to complete his walk on the frozen lake. Since it had been frozen for about 2 months, the ice was very thick. He passed many people skiing and ice fishing. He brought nothing to drink, so he ate snow when thirsty.

He reached the middle of the lake, then turned around and headed back, when the sky began to grow dark. Storm clouds began to drop large snowflakes, the wind began to grow strong, and the temperature dropped. He could no longer see other people on the ice or even his hand in front of his face. He leaned into the wind and kept walking.

William became so cold that he pulled his arms from the sleeves of his coat, into the chest area. He lost track of how long he had been walking and began to stumble and fall in the snow, barely able to stand again, so he began to crawl and call out for help.

He began to wonder if he had been going in circles, and depression began, with tears freezing on his cheeks. *"Please, dear God, help me find my way!"* he prayed.

Immediately, he heard a male voice over a loud speaker coming from the rescue station, which was only blocks from his house. *"Be careful,"* said a voice, *"the breakwater is open and deep."* William continued to crawl and began to hear the lapping of waves getting closer. So he knew he must have been close to an area with broken ice.

"Be careful, stay to the right, climb the concrete wall when you reach it." The instructions were very reassuring and gave him hope. He finally saw the light of the rescue station and crawled to the door. Then someone pulled him up and helped him into the warm building. The man had dark hair and a beard, and offered him a cup of hot coffee. *"You were lost out there,"* the man said.

William nodded. *"Yes, I didn't know where I was. Couldn't see anything."* The man stared at William with crystal-blue eyes like he had never seen before. *"Yes, I know. I knew you were lost so I sounded the foghorn. Then I sent some advice about the breakwater, in case you had lost your bearings."*

The weather cleared up while they were talking, and William headed back home. But before he walked out, he said, *"Why were you here, anyway?"* The rescue station is normally closed all winter. *"Doing research,"* the man said, smiling. William thanked the man and headed out.

When he arrived home, he realized that he had been gone for 7 hours and told his roommates the whole story. One roommate, Dana, said the station could not have been open. The next morning, William walked back to the rescue station to find it locked up. There had been no snow since the blizzard had stopped, yet there was snow piled up against the door, with no signs of it being disturbed. William dug into the snow to see the sign that said, "CLOSED FOR WINTER." It even included the exact dates from fall to spring.

William decided to call the sheriff's department. *"No one has had access to the rescue station since it was closed down in the fall,"* was the response. William then called the university that said, *"No, the county doesn't allow any research at the rescue station during the off-season."*

William then remembered his prayer for help. *"To this day I have no earthly explanation for my rescue, but this experience cemented my belief in a Higher Power and the guardians that watch over us."* (Based on two different published accounts: *Angel Stories*, page 37-42, and *There's An Angel on Your Shoulder: Angel Encounters in Everyday Life*, Vol. 1, Kelsey Tyler, page 71-77)

Beaten Up By Angels

Arthur Blessitt is well-known for carrying the cross around the world, often in very dangerous situations. He tells the story of when he was in Nicaragua in 1978, and after walking all day, he arrived at his truck and camper trailer. His driver and interpreter were with him, and they were told by the few nearby locals that they should not stay the night on that road but to go into the next village because *"They will kill you"* (Blessitt, *Arthur A Pilgrim*, chapter 13, online edition).

A civil war was going on in the nation at the time, which made things more dangerous than normal. But Arthur told the people that he never runs from danger. He was awakened by someone banging on the door and yelling. He opened the door to the sight of guns in his face, and was pushed back into the trailer as a few of the armed men followed. They looked around, then grabbed him by the arm and pulled him out of the trailer. They put him up against the truck, and the men lined up with guns pointed, forming a firing squad. Arthur said:

> Now, this is what flashed through my mind. If I'm going to die I
> don't want to die without a Bible. The guns were all aimed at

> me as I suddenly turned to the right, took about two quick steps
> and reached to put the key in the truck keyhole. I did it on the
> first try. I was thinking, even if they shoot me I think I can get
> the door open before I die and grab a box of Bibles. The men
> were screaming, "No, no!" (Ibid.)

He opened the door and reached in for a box of Bibles. He sat
the box on the ground, and as he was opening it, he could see the
feet of the men around him, but when he raised up again, they were
all on the ground and moaning with pain. They got up and ran to
their truck, and raced away. The two men with Arthur said:

> "Arthur, we could hear the blows of meat against meat. We
> thought they were killing you. Then we heard them yell 'O-o-o-
> oh' and they came falling back. One of the men fell into the
> doorway."

It is clear that angels beat the living daylights out of those gun-
men, literally. Later, Arthur learned that Paul and Jan Crouch of
TBN had gone to bed and were about to go to sleep when Jan saw the
ceiling light up with Arthur's face, and she knew that he was in great
danger. They both prayed for angelic protection, and God sent it.

Now, you may ask, why were the prayers even needed since
many prayers had already been prayed by Arthur and many others
before and during every trip that he took? But sometimes it takes a
lot of prayer for God to change the course of events about to happen. We can only speculate about how much prayer we need, and
under what circumstances we can expect to be saved when we are
about to die. Many Christians die for their faith every year; would
God have saved others who were martyred if they had more prayer?
Would God have allowed Arthur to die if Paul and Jan had not been
available to pray? Or maybe God just wanted the story told around
the world to build our faith and teach us to pray for angelic protection.

I suspect that the more important you are to the plans and pur-
poses of God in the world, the less prayer it takes for miraculous
intervention. The late minister, Terry Law, said that one --

> major factor that appears in biblical patterns of angelic assistance
> is that God has an overall plan for this planet and for His chil-
> dren. If human events directly affect His plan, you may be sure
> that angels will be involved. (*The Truth About Angels*, page 23)

Even though the Apostle Paul had divine intervention more than once, he was eventually martyred. Paul said his mission was accomplished before he was beheaded, *"I have fought a good fight, I have finished my course, and I have kept the faith"* (2 Tim. 4:7).

Angel of Flight 811

On Feb. 23, 1989, Shari Peterson, from Denver, boarded Flight 811 for Sydney from Honolulu, stopping first in Auckland, New Zealand. The Boeing 747 never made it there, and it was a miracle that over 300 passengers survived.

Shari had worked at several travel-related jobs, including hiring and training flight attendants. At this time, she was working for a travel agency and was going to Australia to escort a group of vacationers. She still has her boarding pass for the ill-fated flight. She was happy to get an upgrade from coach to business class and was given seat 9F, but when she went to the seat, she found a man already sitting there who refused to leave. *"I'm not moving,"* he said.

She settled into seat 13H and was planning to take a sleeping pill to help her get some sleep on the 8-hour flight. But the thought came to her that she better not do that because there might be some kind of emergency. She thought it was an odd thought but went with it. She pulled a book out to start reading, and a young male voice whispered in her right ear, which was on the aisle side, *"Tighten your seatbelt, you're in for the ride of your life."* She looked around, but there was no one standing there.

"The hairs on my neck stood up. I knew something way out of the ordinary had just happened and that I should listen." She tightened her seatbelt. People were relaxing with pillows and blankets and dimming the lights in preparation for sleep. Then she heard some grinding noises and a *"loud pop like a paper bag exploding,"* followed by a huge noise.

Another passenger on the plane, Attorney Bruce Lampert, said, *"in an instant, there was an incredible explosive decompression of the aircraft, not an explosion."* A latch on the front cargo door had failed and caused the decompression and structural failure of the fuselage, likely because of the aged plane. Nine people and seats, and the floor by the cargo door, were sucked out of the plane! This included 9F where she should have been sitting.

Shari said, *"The whole side of the plane ahead of me on my right just disappeared, in the blink of an eye."* She said, *"that's how fast it was. Just like that, blinking. They were there, they were gone, now there's a hole. . . I closed my eyes and thought, This can't be happening! When I opened them again, I could see the engines on fire outside."*

The lights had gone out, and the passengers were screaming in terror. The engine noise and the wind blowing into the cabin made it difficult to communicate with fellow passengers. The temperature in the cabin reached freezing in only a few seconds, with wires hanging down and papers and other debris flying around.

"I looked down through where part of the floor used to be and saw moonlit clouds miles below. A beautiful sight, but immediately I thought, This isn't going to end well," said Shari. The plane was fully loaded with fuel and flying on only two engines, so the pilot dumped fuel in case of a crash-landing and returned to Honolulu. The pilot later said that they had not yet become fully pressurized; if they had been, they would have just blown up in the air.

Shari believed she was going to die and surrendered to it. She saw her life flash before her and thought to herself, *"Did you do good? . . . Yea, in my life, I did okay. It was all about how did you treat people, and how did you affect people. . . . None of it was material, not one second of it; it was* Who did you love and who loved you back, and how did that go?"

She also prayed: *"And I started praying, desperately crying out for help. Then in my mind I saw a giant hand swoop down out of the sky under the plane, and I knew we were going to be okay."*

It took 20 minutes to fly back, but it seemed a lot longer. Any altitude that the plane lost could not be regained because it had only two engines, so the pilot kept as much altitude as possible and made a sharp turn to make the landing, which was surprisingly perfect. *"I've*

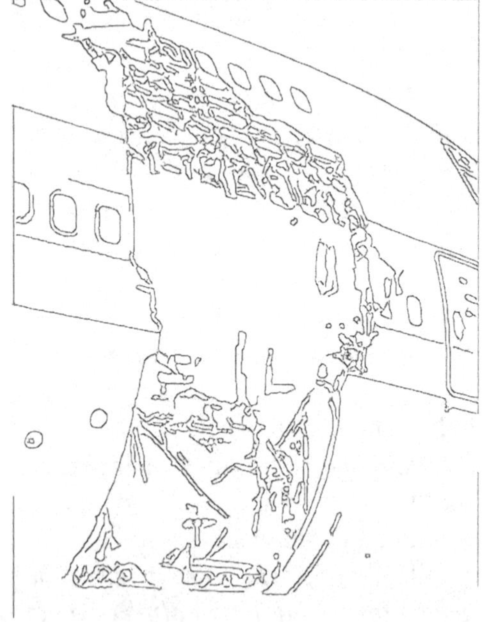

been on a million flights, still the most perfect landing ever. And he [the pilot] *said he did not land that airplane; it was divine intervention."*

Another passenger on the plane, Mike Rutherford, said that a couple of weeks later he spoke with the captain of the flight: *"In talking to him he informed me that the authorities had attempted to simulate the identical conditions in the simulator. They informed him that from this model they concluded that it was impossible for him to have brought the aircraft back in one piece!"*

After Shari finally exited the airplane, she was sitting on the tarmac in the rain with her head down, very stressed: *"I'm sitting there and all of a sudden felt this downy softness surround me. It felt like somebody had come up behind me and was holding me, but it was soft, and I thought, Angel wings? I don't care, it felt just really good. And I heard in my ear again, You're okay. You did alright. . . . It was an incredible moment."*

Shari said: "I am very humbled when I think about that night. I've asked myself many times why I was allowed to survive, why it wasn't me in 9F. I don't have an answer to that. I grew up in the Methodist Church and was always fascinated with God. But I wondered, why don't the stories we read about in the Bible ever seem to happen today? It bothered me.

"Now I know; Miracles do happen! They happen today just as they have throughout history, and sometimes just as dramatically as in the Bible stories. I've learned to be much more real in my approach to life, relationships, and faith — because you never know when you wake in the morning where you might end up. You've got to be fearless and not so concerned with what people think of you. Be a warrior for your own soul and know you are not alone. God intervenes in our lives — I am living proof." (Garlow, *Real Life Real Miracles*, page 15-21)

PASSENGERS IMMERSED IN DARKNESS, NOISE, FEAR, Desert News, Feb. 26, 1989 (Scripps Howard News Service) www.deseret.com

Eyewitness Report: United Flight 811, Mike Rutherford. www.airdisaster.com.

Aboard Flight 811: Passengers' Routine Dissolves Into Terror, Robert Reinhold, Special To the New York Times, Feb. 26, 1989.

Shari Peterson, Surviving Flight 811; Funky Brain Podcast, Dennis Berry. youtube.com

A Female Angel

Letter sent in to *Angel Letters*, newsletter:

In September 20, 1990, my three-year-old little girl went outdoors to play. As I watched through the sliding-glass patio doors, she opened the back door, turned to close it, and then squatted down almost immediately. I turned away, and a few moments later heard a crash. A huge limb had fallen from our largest elm tree, right near my little girl.

Later, I asked my daughter why she hadn't been playing in the yard, driving her little, red, battery-powered jeep. She said without any hesitation, "Mommy, a good god told me to sit down and not go under the tree, and I did just what she told me to do." This "good god" was a beautiful girl with long golden hair that flowed past her shoulders. She came from the sky and had wings. She had a light so bright about her, said my daughter, that it hurt her eyes, but, when she touched the light, she was surprised how cool it was. It did not burn. The angel had specific jewelry on, especially a necklace that was "so shiny." She wore, said my daughter, "all colors."

Certain changes have occurred in my daughter's behavior since the incident, most noticeably a serene calmness. She prays for her angel and also insists on saying a grace at every meal, a tradition that had not been in our family before. She has drawn numerous pictures of "Rebecca Rose" almost every day since the incident, and wants stories of the Bible read to her at night.

Now, several more months have passed. She says that she cannot see "Rebecca Rose" anymore — is not allowed to — and she longs to have her back; but she says that she has been told she will see her again in ten years. (Name withheld by request, Las Vegas, Nevada, Burnham, *Angel Letters*, page 55-56)

A Red Pickup

One snowy night, I was going home from my daughter's house after baby-sitting my two-year-old grandson. My friend had accompanied me and when we reached the intersection, we were stopped by a policeman.

"There's an accident up ahead," he told us. "You've got to turn back and take a different route."

[The] road back is very winding and steep. That night it was very icy and extremely treacherous. Both my friend and I prayed silently because we were slipping and sliding all over the road.

Suddenly, a little red pickup truck appeared in front of us. Slowly, we followed it all the way to the bottom of the hill. As we reached level ground the truck simply vanished.

Both my friend and I agreed that the red truck was driven by a guardian angel. (Barbara Shymanski, Scranton, Pennsylvania) (*Angel Voices*, page 33)

A Leg Cut Off

Carol Batey received a phone call in the middle of the night in December 1994. It was her husband's coworker, Ron, which immediately meant that something must have happened on the job. Her husband, Joe, worked for the railroad. Joe's left leg was cut off in an accident, but he would live. She found out the details from Joe in the hospital:

Upon realizing his leg was severed at the railway yard, Joe said a heavenly voice had spoken to him saying, "Joe, don't worry. Everything will be all right."

He said it was a misty morning but it was clear as daylight. Although feeling excruciating pain in his crushed right foot, a spirit of peace came over him to ease his fears and worries. The voice then commanded him to remove his severed left leg from the tracks and push his body back, or the moving train would hit him in the head.

With a damaged left leg and right foot, and his severed leg in his lap, he obeyed the voice. The voice told him to remove his radio belt and make a tourniquet for his left leg. Joe obeyed. Finally, the voice directed him to call on his radio for help. Ron was nearby and heard Joe's distress signal. He called 911, unaware that Joe was being protected and comforted by divine guidance. (*Angel Voices*, page 58)

Many times, difficulties work to our good; we just cannot know the future the way God does. Carol Batey relates how the accident affected them:

In the next two weeks, the outpouring of love from near and far was extraordinary. We received cards, gifts, food and checks

> from friends and strangers from all over America. Churches
> prayed for us and people we'd lost touch with were suddenly
> found.
>
> We spent Christmas in the hospital but our faith in God had been
> dramatically restored. And when I heard Joe tell the story, I
> understood why he had such a glow. . . .
>
> Despite the adjustments to our life, God's blessings continue to
> flow abundantly. His co-workers built a handicap ramp at our
> home, another painted our house. The [railroad] union brought us
> food for months and the railroad provided in-home care with a
> nurse's aid named Mrs. Ruth – a woman blessed with a gift for
> ministry. (Ibid., page 58-59)

You may be wondering, why didn't the angel do anything to prevent the accident? I can only surmise that God allowed it because God wants us to have challenges in this life that we need to overcome. The prevailing message of Jesus to the seven churches in Revelation is that God wants us to "overcome." The word occurs seven times in Rev. chapters 2 & 3:

> "To him who overcomes I will give permission to eat of the tree
> of life, which is in the midst of the Paradise of God." (Rev. 2:7)

This hardship actually resulted in great good. It is not merely that God can bring good from any situation, but that God allows hardships of all kinds to come upon us because it makes us better people. Notice that she said the end result was that their relationship with God was "restored."

Plus, suppose that if the accident had not happened, and suppose that they divorced 5 years later, it would have been traumatic for the children. So in the long-run, they were better as a family with the accident than without. But that is just one reason why God allowed it.

Saved From Car Wreck

Former Georgia state senator Mike Crotts relates how his wife and son were saved from a potentially bad car wreck:

> Phyllis and Caleb had to drive about 25 miles in the pouring rain
> that day. At one point on the expressway, the rain became so tor-
> rential that she could not see one car-length ahead of her. She
> noticed cars were stopping on the right shoulder to wait out the
> storm, but she was in the left lane and fearful about crossing two

lanes of traffic to pull over. With the median wall to her left, she continued carefully when she heard tires squealing with that sound of someone trying to slam on their brakes! To her right, a car was spinning out of control and heading directly toward her. She braced for the impact crying out, "JESUS! Help me!"

Determined to avoid the median, she concentrated on looking straight ahead when a beautiful 9 ft. tall man in a shimmering garment appeared, holding his outstretched hand toward her. She quickly glanced to her right again and saw a second very tall man in a shiny garment appear and stand with his hand outstretched toward the spinning car. Both men had shoulder length hair (one light and one dark) with beautiful countenances and she could only see their heads and hands, no wings. In that moment, surrounded with peace and wisdom, Phyllis knew to take her foot off the pedal and just coast as the spinning car next to her regained control. Less than a mile down the expressway, the rain stopped, and the sun came out. (Crotts, Mike. *Dead for 34 Minutes*, page 66-67)

Lost At Sea

In 1992, two fishermen in a small open boat became lost at sea. The engine died, and they were carried out by the currents. Martin Simon was one of those men. They drifted for several days while rescue planes and boats in the Caribbean looked for them without success. The other fisherman refused to listen to Martin's advice not to drink the ocean water and died along the way. Martian was desperate and did lots of praying to God to save him.

It was nine days before he was rescued, which was a true miracle. About the 4th day of drifting, strong winds blew a yacht off course and sent it in Martin's direction. John Beattie had left his teaching job in the UK to sail his 35-foot yacht named Warrior Queen alone, but was having lots of problems: engine trouble, sailing difficulties, freezing wind and water, so he decided to pick up another fellow at a stop to sail with him, Hamish.

John and Hamish were blown off course by fierce winds. The bad weather kept them awake for several days, then they both slept. John said,

"I knew that as long as you were well away from hazards and well away from shipping lanes, and hundreds of miles from land,

that it was fairly safe to sleep and let the boat sail herself through the night."

On the 9th day of drifting, Martin saw a yacht in the distance, and it was heading right toward him. It was early morning, and both John and Hamish were asleep as the Warrior Queen approached Martin. Martin saw the boat and yelled and waved his arms, but he did not see anyone on board. He said to himself, *"Lord, what is going to happen to me now, that's my only hope."* His yelling awakened Hamish, who at first thought it might be a bird, but he went to investigate.

Suddenly Martin saw Hamish for a brief moment, then he disappeared again to awaken John, who came on deck and saw that they had passed the boat, so he started the engine and turned around. *"I literally could not believe my own eyes,"* said John.

They threw a line to Martin, pulled him close, and got him onboard. They then gave him water and took him to the nearest harbor on the island of Antigua. *"I knew that this was a man very much on the edge of life. . . . had we not came across him, he would have died that day, for certain,"* John said.

"We had sailed within feet of each other in an area, literally bigger than the size of Texas." John said it was like there were only two people in the whole state of Texas, and one decided to walk across the state, and they came within feet of the other fellow.

Martin said, *"God made it happen that way, because I prayed a lot, and that prayer was answered."* Martin was taken to the hospital, where he spent six weeks before making a full recovery. While there, he met his future wife, Karen, so he got a double blessing.

Later, John wrote a book about his trip called, *The Breath of Angels.* Then a TV show called, *It's A Miracle,* hosted by Richard Thomas, did a segment on the miraculous rescue (available on Youtube).

Stuck in Snow

On the evening of Jan. 2, 1999, the worst blizzard in twenty years hit the area of Shirley, Illinois. The wind was 20-30 mph with over 14 inches of snow. The wind created snow-drifts that were 3-4 feet deep. The next morning, Jeff and Ruth Elliot and their two teenaged children, Jennifer and Eric, went out to shovel snow at their rural home. It took them about 4 hours to completely dig out the home and driveway from the snow.

While they were shoveling, Eric was clearly having difficulties; he had to stop and often rest, was out of breath, and just did not feel well. He had been having bad headaches for several weeks. Then suddenly, he became cross-eyed and collapsed in pain. They called the doctor, who told them to go straight to the hospital, about 10 minutes away.

Jeff and Eric headed out in the family pickup truck, but the truck got stuck in a snow drift on the country road. Jeff attempted to dig the truck out of the snow, but it would not budge. All the while, Eric was drifting in and out of consciousness. Jeff was very concerned about being able to make it to the hospital and called his wife on his cell phone.

At the thought of her son not being able to get the help that he needed, Ruth said, *"I just fell apart, I was a basket case."* They agreed to pray, then hung up the phone.

Ruth and Jennifer held hands and prayed. *"We just prayed with all of our heart,"* Ruth said. While they were praying, Ruth spontaneously saw in her mind a vision of three angels descend and begin pushing the truck. At the time, Jeff was again attempting to drive out of the snow, and suddenly,

> *"I stepped on the gas and it felt like we were being pushed by a Mac Truck. The power was incredible. And we continued on down the road just hitting drift after drift and not getting stuck. And I realized that something unusual had happened but I wasn't quite sure what, at that point. . . . When we were stuck in that snow drift, I've been stuck before and you just don't get out of something like that. I've never felt power like that, after being stuck like that."*

Eric was barely conscious when they arrived at the hospital. The doctors found a tumor in his brain the size of an orange, which required emergency surgery to save his life. Many people from their church prayed, and the surgery was successful. Eric had to relearn how to walk and talk again.

If that blizzard had not hit, they might not have noticed Eric's severe condition that day, and so it likely would have worsened until it was too late. The family is thankful for all the miracles they had that week, but *"Especially the vision of the angels, that is something I will never forget the rest of my life,"* Ruth said. A faith-based movie was made about the miracle called, *Hoovey,* Eric's nickname.

(*It's a Miracle*, TV show, episode "Snow Angel," hosted by Richard Thomas. And, *Family shares son's journey to recovery in film 'Hoovey'*, the Fayetteville Observer, Feb. 19, 2015.)

Angel Walks In

The next story is amazing in its claims, but I believe it is true because it was related by H. A. Baker (1881–1971) in his book, *Heaven and the Angels*. I consider him a highly credible source because he listed his sources, and was a missionary to Tibet and China from 1911 to 1950:

> When I was in Shanghai a friend asked me if I had ever heard about the angel who visited some little children in Ohio, and she offered to copy the account from a typewritten record she had. When she gave me the copy another missionary friend, Miss Longstreth, said: "Why, I know all about that angel's visit. The children's parents told my parents all about it before the account was ever published. From what publication the account is copied I do not know, but that is unimportant, as I have the story verified by one who knows it to be true. I later had a friend visit the home of this angel's visit and had photos taken of the place and of some of those who saw the angel. The story is as follows:

> "For the glory of God and the encouragement of His obedient children, I recall this bit of marvelous history, which occurred in the month of February, A. D., 1887, in the northern part of Dark county, Ohio.

> "About three miles from Roseville there lives a man and his wife, by the name of John and Hattie Hittle. They had six children whose names and ages were as follows: Ora, twelve; Henry, ten; Lizzie, eight; Ida, six; Nettie, four, and Pearl, two.

> "They were very religious people and enjoyed the blessing of sanctification. They were, and still are, members of the Massasinawa Class of Greenville Mission of the Indiana Conference of the Evangelical Association. Their home has for many years been the home of itinerant preachers.

> "There was a protracted meeting in the neighborhood to which the parents and Ora were going while the rest of the children were to stay at home alone. They had never stayed alone before, and there protested it on the plea that they were afraid; but the mother told them not to be afraid, for God and the angels would

take care of them.

"Finally, they consented, and after the parents were gone they lowered the blinds, locked the doors and gathered together on the sofa to have their family worship. Pearl had been put to sleep in the cradle in the bedroom. After they had all said their prayers they happened to get hold of the "Foster Child's Story of the Bible" which had been presented to Ora on his twelfth birthday. They began looking at the pictures, and presently came to the picture of an angel, whereupon Henry exclaimed:

"'Oh! I wish I could see an angel once!'

"And the rest said, 'I wish I could, too!'

"They had hardly said this when they heard a sound on the porch as of a rustling of silk garments; then a knock on the door. So they all jumped up and ran to the door to see who was coming. They raised the curtain and looked out, and behold! To their surprise, an angel came right in through the door, or glass of the door, the latter being locked, and stood among them. He asked them where their parents were and they told him they had gone to meeting. Then Lizzie, who happened to be standing by the rocking chair, said to him:

"'Take a chair and sit down.

"He answered, 'Oh, I can't stay long.' But he took the chair and drew it up toward the stove and sat down, saying as he did so:

"'You have a nice stove and a good, warm fire.'

"Then the children noticed that he was bare-footed. As the weather was cold and the ground covered with snow, they would naturally suppose he must have cold feet. Therefore, Henry said to him:

"'Put your feet on the railing of the stove and warm them.'

"The angel did so, and then called the children to him. They were still wondering in their minds why he should be bare-footed in such cold weather, and this made them take particular notice of his feet, which looked perfectly white and glistened like wax.

"He then reached out his hands and took Ida on one knee and Nettie on the other, and caressed them by putting his hands on their heads as if he were blessing them. At the same time he kept talking to them all, telling them to be good children and keep on praying to God, etc. His voice was clear and charming, his hair fine and wavy, and he wore a beautiful little crown on his head.

"After he had held them awhile, he put them down, and rising from the chair, began to walk around and look at the pictures on the wall. As he walked, they noticed that his garments were loosely thrown about him and extended a little below his knees. They could now have a better opportunity to see his wings, which were quite large and fairly glittered for whiteness.

"The children followed him wherever he went, and presently they came to the bedroom, where Pearl was sleeping. With the children close at his side he went to the cradle and took Pearl in his arms and kissed her, and then laid her down again, saying as he did so:

"'When Pearl gets older you must tell her to be a good girl and pray, too.' Then he said to them: 'Well, I must go now', and began to shake hands with each one of them and thus bid them good-bye.

'It is impossible to describe the loveliness of his hand as they took hold of it. It felt like snow, or some downy cushion and, like his feet. it was perfectly white and glistening. He wore a most heavenly smile upon his countenance. His voice was tender and sweet. His entire demeanor was marked with gentleness and kindness, and his whole appearance was that of grandeur and beauty. They felt perfectly at home and enraptured with his presence, and it made them feel sad when he told them he must go.

"After he had bidden them good-bye, he started for the door, while the children were still standing at the bed-room door. When he came to the door he paused a moment, and the children noticed that he had a long staff in his hands, and in an instant they saw him gliding out through the unopened door in the same manner that he had come.

"As soon as they saw he was gone they instantly made a rush for the door, literally tumbling over one another to get there first, and they saw him standing on the edge of the porch, and a bright cloud had gathered about him. They saw him glide out into the yard. His body was now in an inclined position with his feet extending backwards and his wings partially folded, while the lower part of his garment and the bright cloud seemed to roll and fold themselves together in a unique manner. He went on in this way until he came half way between the house and a pear tree which was standing in the yard, and then he ascended, his beautiful white feet being the last thing they saw of him. Then one of the children exclaimed:

"'Now he is gone!'

"Another said: 'I wonder why there was no bright cloud around him while he was with us in the room.'

"Still another said: 'I wonder how long it will take him to get to heaven.'

"The next thing in order was to wait until the return of the parents and Ora that they might tell it to them. They could scarcely wait until they came, they were so anxious to tell them. In the meantime they carefully examined the door from top to bottom, rubbing their hands over it to see if there was not a crack, or a break, of some kind where he had come in and gone out; but, to their astonishment, they could not find the least sign of a crack either on the door, the glass, or on the casing of the door.

"After awhile they heard their parents coming and they were all up and ready to meet them. The mother went to the house first, while the father and Ora put away the team. Who can imagine the bustle and excitement as the mother entered the house; Henry, Lizzie, Ida and Nettie, each trying to tell it first. They jumped, they laughed, they clapped their hands and were perfectly wild with joy. So great was the noise and holy racket that the father and Ora heard them at the barn and wondered what in the world vas the matter with the children.

"'Who do you suppose was here, mother, while you were gone?' they all exclaimed with one accord. 'An angel, yes; an angel! Oh! Mother, an angel was here.'

"When the mother had quieted them sufficiently, they went on to describe him, how he looked, what he had said and what he had done.

"Their shining faces, their exultant spirits, their positive declarations, and the unison of their assertions soon overwhelmingly convinced the mother of the truthfulness of her children's story and of the reality of the vision which they had seen. Besides, being a spiritual woman and having an insight into spiritual things, she could the more easily be persuaded of the facts in the case. She listened with suppressed emotion until her heart could no longer contain the joy which filled and thrilled her whole being. Then, going to the bedroom she threw herself upon her bed and gave vent to her feelings with loud shouts of "Glory to God." She felt that the very house was hallowed by the presence of the Lord, and that from henceforth, more than ever, her home should be like a little heaven on earth. After rising from the bed she seated herself in a chair near the stove and buried her face in her hands.

"Presently the father and Ora returned from the barn and as they entered the room where she was sitting, she exclaimed:

"'Oh, Father! You ought to hear the children tell of the wonderful visitor they had while we were gone', where upon the children began to tell the story to their father and older brother.

"'Ah!' said the father: 'you are only excited; it is simply your imagination. You did not see an angel.'

"'Yes, yes — father; sure, sure', came from every one of them.

"So positive were they, and so overwhelmingly happy that the father couldn't stand their simple arguments, but was compelled to believe what they were telling him was true, and he also began to praise the Lord and to participate in their joy.

"This simple story has been told to only a few of their most intimate friends. They deemed it too sacred to be told to everybody, lest they could not appreciate it. The writer became their pastor in the spring of 1896, and not until the evening of January 7, 1897, did they tell me about it; and the way it came about was this:

"Ida and Nettie had been to school during the day and the question came up whether, or not, the Lord revealed Himself to men now as He did in olden times through the ministry of angels. The teacher seemed to be skeptical, and said he did not believe such things were possible at the present time. He had never heard of this instance and therefore, knew nothing about it until Ida declared her belief in such things from the fact that they had seen an angel in their home when they were children. So when she came from school she was telling her mother what the teacher had said, and how she had convinced him contrary to his former belief. I overheard their conversation and began to wonder what they were talking about. Then they happened to think they had never told me the story and at once began to relate it. As the children were all at home they were soon seated around me and with shining faces were busily engaged in making known to me this remarkable incident, and it has made an impression upon me that shall never leave me. While they were telling me I felt that such a good thing should not be kept secret any longer. Therefore the day following I wrote out a minute account of it, just as the children had told me. Of course, they were no longer little children, for all, except Pearl, had grown up.

"The reader may imagine what a thrill of joy and gladness filled my soul, while by the help of God I undertook to write this story. Here I was in the very room where it occurred. To my left was the same sofa upon which these children had their family worship on the memorable night in February, ten years before. A little farther on to the left was the very door through which the angel had come and gone. To my right was the same rocking chair in which this heavenly messenger had been seated. In my lap lay the same book, opened at the very picture which had brought from them the wish that they might see an angel once, and upstairs is the stove which he said was nice.

"Nearly five years later (November 27, 1901), I visited them again. All the children, except Ora, are still at home, and in the evening while seated with them in the same room, and talking together about this same matter, I found that after the lapse of nearly fifteen years it has not in the least lost its freshness in their memories. For with shining faces and with hearts glowing with gratitude to God for His goodness to them, they still love to talk about the wonderful visitor whom He, in His kind providence, had seen fit to send them in the days of their childhood. Their whole lives have been influenced by it." (page 137-142)

Angel in China

A teenage boy of the Ka Do tribe was visiting a remote village, when he was asked by a sick woman, who had never heard of angels, to pray for her. As he prayed, the power of God powerfully came upon them both. The woman saw a bright angel with wings, and she was healed. Baker reported that there were many instances in which angels were seen when the sick were healed through prayer. (Baker, *Heaven and the Angels*, page 129)

Angel Hands

In another case related by Baker, a saintly Ka Do Christian woman had been very ill for a long time. Then one day, *"a light from above descended upon her, and two light-radiating hands and arms appeared."* One hand went under each shoulder and gently raised her into a sitting position. Her mother, sitting nearby, was surprised to see the sick woman suddenly sit up. And the woman had been healed. (Ibid., page 129)

Saved From a Bomb

A foreign-educated Chinese friend of H. A. Baker sent him a letter about how he and a friend were eating lunch in a hotel near the Palace Hotel in Shanghai at the beginning of WW II. Then a Chinese plane mistakenly dropped a bomb on the Palace Hotel and destroyed it, causing much damage to nearby structures. They heard an audible voice say, *"Get under the table."* As soon as they did, the ceiling collapsed, killing many people around them. The Chinese friend believes an angel warned them. (Ibid., page 130-131)

Angel Stops Car

Evangelist Charles S. Price relates an angel story in *Golden Grain* magazine of Nov. 20, 1940. He tells the story of an old Christian man in the early 1900s who was driving a Model T Ford, when a blizzard blew in. Because of the blinding snowstorm and roar of the wind, he could not see or hear an approaching train. As he approached the railroad tracks, the motor died. Then suddenly, a train *"thundered passed"* right in front of him. After the train fully passed, his motor started up with no issues, and he continued on his way. He knew that God had sent an angel to stop his car. (Baker, *Heaven and the Angels*, page 134)

Lost in Woods

In 1936, in Angelhom, Sweden, a little five-year-old boy named Rune followed a dog that ran into the trees and became lost in the dense forest. First, the mother and father searched, and then friends joined in the search. The next day, search parties went looking. After five days, they feared that the boy was dead from exposure and the cold nightly temperatures. On day six, 400 people were out searching for the boy. When they were about to give up the search and return home, the father heard his son's voice not far away. He found the child in good condition. And a doctor who examined the boy found nothing wrong. The child said, *"At night I looked up to the stars and prayed to God to help me get home again. One night I got cold, but the angel kept me from freezing."* (Ibid., page 136-137)

Saved From Electrocution

While doing laundry I noticed a pool of water forming on the floor. I had to step into the puddle to reach the iron spigot that put water into the overflow tub. As I turned the knob, a bolt of electricity from the washing machine shot through my arm, rooting me to the spot. My young daughter, Sharon, skipped in and pulled the frayed plug from the socket. She skipped away as if she hadn't a care in the world. I was fine.

Later I explained to Sharon about electricity and the danger she had put herself in. "What are you talking about, Mama?" she asked. "I haven't been in the laundry room all day!" (Betty Salter, Unadilla, GA, *Angels on Earth* magazine, July/Aug 1999: page 2.)

Angel Stops Car

Driving my son to school one day, I saw a red Mercedes screech to an impossibly short stop right in front of two children who had dashed into the street. Pressed against the front of the car was a transparent impression of an angel. Thin as a veil, it had been powerful enough to stop two tons of speeding metal dead in its tracks. (Donna Hephurn, *Angels on Earth* magazine, May/June 1999, page 2.)

Angel In the Elevator

A court reporter, I was on my way to a law office for a 7:00 A.M. deposition. I pulled into a parking garage across from the building. Nobody was around at that hour.

As I headed out of the garage I noticed a man in a brown uniform walking behind me. *A repairman,* I figured.

Inside the office building I hurried to the elevators. Getting on one, I reached into my purse for my comb. When I looked up I saw the man from the garage. He moved close to me — uncomfortably close — then pinned me to the wall. The elevator door started its slow slide.

God, send help! I prayed as my fate was being sealed by the closing door. It had only inches to go when someone slipped effortlessly through the crack. The assailant looked to see what had caused the change in my expression. He glared at the tall, imposing man in the pin-striped suit, then let me go and stepped away. The gentleman passenger gazed at me reassuringly, but our strange threesome rode in silence.

When we reached my floor, I got out and turned to wish the gentleman a good day. Instead I watched in amazement as the door closed on my would-be attacker — standing absolutely alone in the elevator. (Joyce Oglesby, Corydon, Indiana, *Angels on Earth*, Sept/Oct 1998, page 23)

Angel Dog

One day in 1977, [a big yellow dog] planted himself on the door-step of our house in the country, and there he stayed. The dog was quiet and gentle, and our three small children played with him all afternoon. We called him Sir because he was enormous. Soon after we went to bed, Sir began barking and growling. He sat on that step all night long, making a fuss. By morning we were ready to give him the boot. That is, until we heard that an escaped convict had stolen a taxi the previous night and prowled around our area, abandoning the taxi in a field about a quarter mile from us. Police traced footsteps to a hill overlooking our house, where the convict turned away, thanks to Sir, our angel dog. (Marcia Holton, Helix, OR, *Angels on Earth*, Sept/Oct 1996 page 2)

Yes, angels can take on the form of animals. I have read several such stories, and I believe they are true.

Angel Lifted Car

Barbara C. Porter, of Tempe, Arizona, had a dream several times for a few weeks. She dreamed of a car accident, screeching brakes, smashing glass, crunching steel, and even the smell of burning rubber; then red, flashing ambulance lights and the death of Laura, her only child, and two little granddaughters, crushed in their Isuzu Trooper SUV. She tried to convince herself that it was only a dream and the family was safe, but it still *"haunted her."* So she prayed many times for God to watch over their *"every step."*

Laura and her husband had several jobs in Ohio, while she also attended college. One of their jobs was singing in churches. One of the songs was, *"All night, all day, angels watchin' over me, my Lord."* They even named their first child, Mychael, after the archangel Michael.

All that day, the premonition of the accident would not go away but kept flashing through Barbara's mind, *"the crunching car, burning fuel, smashing steel, flashing ambulance lights."* She repeated to herself the words of the song, *"All night, all day, angels watchin' over me, my Lord,"* as a form of prayer. Even while at work, at the supermarket, and back home watching the evening news, she kept praying until the fear finally left.

Then Laura called and explained to her mother the accident she almost had:

"This afternoon I was driving home with the girls," she said. . . .

"We had to take a detour and ended up on a two-lane highway. Traffic was heavy going both ways. At one point, a big semi was rumbling toward me in the other lane, when from behind it a black Porsche darted out into my lane, trying to pass.

"I slammed on my brakes and could hear screeching behind me as other cars tried to avoid hitting me. I was afraid to look in the rearview mirror. I couldn't turn either way; one direction I would hit the semi, the other I would roll the car into a ditch. And anyway, there wasn't any time. The car was coming right at us."

Barbara took a deep breath and feared the worst.

"But, Mom," Laura said, "the most amazing thing happened. The black Porsche was lifted right up above us! It was as though it had been picked up like a toy and set down in the ditch to my right.

She got out of the van and did not find one scratch. The Porsche driver only had a bruised elbow.

I asked the other drivers, who all said the same thing: The Porsche had simply flown over our car. Even the police were at a loss to explain why the skid marks stopped abruptly — only inches from our van.". . .

"Mom, I really believe an angel lifted that car out of our way.

I'm sure I saw the faint form of an angel as it carried the Porsche away from us in a blinding light."

"I believe so too, darling," I said." (*Angels on Earth*, Sept/Oct 1996, page 36-37)

A Group of Dancing Angels

A seventeen-year-old girl agreed to wait under a lamppost for someone to pick her up for choir practice at Holy Trinity Church in Lowell, Massachusetts. As she waited, two men walked by her, then suddenly turned around and started walking back toward her:

> I was young and rather naive, but I just had the feeling that they meant me harm.

So she started praying to the Virgin Mary. That was all she knew to do. She did not believe she could run away from them, as the street beyond the lamppost was very dark and all the houses had their lights turned off:

> While I was standing there saying my prayers, seven little children, about the age of five or six years old, ran out of an alley and they were all carrying very large sticks. They walked over and formed a circle around me, all the while chanting, "Ah, ah, ah, . . ."

> I asked them what they were all doing out at such a late hour, after it was 9 p.m., but they did not answer or look at me. All the children just kept walking around me making the "ah" sound.

> As I watched the children, I realized that I had forgotten about the two men and having remembered them once again, I became even more frightened. I turned around to see where they were and discovered that they had walked away. There was no one around, the night had become very quiet and the children were also gone.

She looked for the children and saw the last one disappear back into the alley. She quickly ran to the alley and looked, but they were gone, and the alley was a dead end. She ran home and told her father what happened.

> He looked at me in awe and said, "My child, those little ones were angels." I laughed at his comment and said, "Oh, no dad." As the years went by and I grew older, I often thought about

what happened that night and yes, I now truly believe that those little ones were indeed angels. (*Angel Watch,* Sept/Oct 1998, Anonymous, page 12)

If you are a believer, whether Catholic or Protestant, God is not limited by doctrine. He is not going to deny angelic help because someone does not have 100% accurate doctrine; who would that be? Oh, the church you attend; point well taken.

Saved From Motorcycle Wreck

I want to share this story with you about an angel that saved my wife and changed our lives forever. Both my wife and I love to ride motorcycles, we mostly ride on weekends, but there are times we have taken longer trips. It was on one of these longer trips that we met our angel.

We were riding across the mountains, after spending several days in Virginia. The weather had been clear and beautiful, just perfect for traveling. My wife was in the lead, as we came around a sharp curve in the road. When she swerved outward to take the curve, she came face to face with an oncoming car. The man driving the car began to brake and also swerved. My wife hit the side of the car and was thrown from the motorcycle, landing underneath the car. I stopped my motorcycle and ran to help my wife, terrified as to what I might find.

To my surprise, my wife was sitting next to the car, with a little dirt on her face but not even a scratch! She began looking around and asked me where the man was that pulled her from under the car? By this time, I was joined by the driver of the car, who helped me get my wife to her feet. She continued to insist that when she hit the pavement, a man from the opposite side of the car gently pulled her free, and place her beside the road. All of us looked for this other person, but he was never found. We returned home knowing that we had come face to face with an angel.

I was never one to go to church, believing that prayer and worship were personal, but our experience with the angel changed all that. Now, I attend services of my choice, realizing the combined power of prayer. (Kenneth, South Carolina, *Angel Watch,* May/June 1998, page 14-15)

Sometimes, it takes being saved by an angel to change a person's life.

The Flying Car

When I resided in Colorado, I advertised that I would give private drawing lessons in exchange for transportation into the mountains to view the scenic vistas. I had a young rabbinical student who wanted to learn to draw and we spent quite a few afternoons driving around the front range, near Boulder. The air was always very fresh and invigorating. Huge outcroppings of old, rusty granite rock and deep green pine forests were our subjects.

One afternoon, after a fine day of drawing, we were driving down Sunshine Canyon Road, while on our way back to Boulder. The road was cut into the edge of a steep ravine which wound rather dangerously up from Boulder, to the top of the first peak in the range. There were no shoulders on the road, to speak of, and the wall of the mountain came down one side of the road and on the other side, a cliff dropped off for hundreds of feet. There were no railings, nor any other protection.

As we rounded a corner, I will never forget what we encountered. An enormous dump truck filled the inside lane, including whatever shoulder existed between it and the mountainside. In our lane, coming right for us, was a beige station wagon attempting to pass the dump truck. My friend and I gasped, for there was no time for any of the vehicles to stop. Everyone was traveling much too fast. My friend swerved to the right to avoid hitting the station wagon, and I felt as though we were going to go over the cliff. There was no shoulder there, and no room for two cars and a dump truck on that section of the road. We traveled right around the station wagon and back onto the road.

When it happened, I felt an incredible sense of suspension. When we passed the station wagon, we both gasped again and blurted out, "There is no room for us!" There was not any room for us to go around, how did that happen? Something held us aloft around the station wagon because we definitely were off the road and should have crashed.

Neither of us said the word "angels," but there was surely an intervention that saved both of our lives that afternoon. I am very grateful and wanted to share this experience with all of you. But, this was not the only time that I have been assisted by the "traffic guardians."

On another occasion, I was with a group of friends and we were dropping someone off at their house at the end of the day. I was in the back seat and had to get out of the car in order to let my friend out. When we pulled up to the driveway, I reached for the door handle and suddenly, I was unable to move! It was the most frightening experience that I have ever had. I was totally paralyzed. It felt as though there was a vice around my head, and not one muscle in my body could move. This lasted for only a few seconds, about as much time as it would have taken me to actually open the door and get out of the car.

When I was able to move once again, my hand touched the door handle, and immediately another car smashed into the side of our car, right where I would have been standing, had I been able to get out of the car. If it had not been for "someone" holding me back and stopping my movement, I would have been seriously injured or killed by the collision. (Patricia Preble, *Angel Watch* March/April 1998, page 4-5)

Saved From the Holocaust

In 1938, Poland was suffering through Hitler's invasion, and things became increasingly dangerous. People who had been friend-ly to the Jews were now throwing rocks and making threats.

It was also a time when men prayed for the silence of the con-stant bombing and for the help of the angels.

Levi and Fredia were forced to close their bakery because they feared for their lives. They heard reports of the murder of many Jews, so they made plans to flee the country.

Over the next several weeks, our Christian friends hid us in the back rooms and chambers of their homes. This was not only an inconvenience to them, but there was also a danger of them being arrested for the crime of trying to save our lives.

After a month of living with their friends, they heard about a man who could get them across the border the way he had helped many others. They made their plans, packed, and left.

It was planned that we would travel by night and rest in the forest during the daylight hours. . . . We were advised not to talk with anyone, or answer any questions. We were given a special password to share only with the man at the border.

They traveled through a forest so dense that the trees often blocked out the sun. After three days, they were told they were only three miles from the man who was to help them.

My heart raced, for I knew that if this escape failed, our lives would be lost.

Darkness soon came, but we had to wait far into the stillness of night before we headed towards the edge of the forest. As we stepped out into the clearing, we were greeted by a wide-open road and gently fallen snow. The children asked to walk as we proceeded down the road, but they soon became tired and asked that we again carry them.

Suddenly, out of the shadows two figures approached us, that of a man and a woman. As they came closer, I could see that they were dressed as poor peasants. We stopped as they continued towards us. They stopped and asked us who we were and where we were going. Levi said nothing, yet I was impelled to share our story with them and tell them of our hopes of making it across the border. It was then that the woman told us that the house of the man that we were seeking had been taken over and was no longer safe. She told us that the man we sought was now staying with his son and she provided us with the directions to the son's house.

We listened intently and immediately decided to proceed to the son's home. Then we turned back to thank the couple for their assistance and found that they had disappeared, leaving not even a footprint in the fallen snow.

Later that same night, we made contact with the man that we were seeking. He was amazed that we had been able to find him and he informed us of several arrests along that same stretch of road, that we had been traveling on. We shared our experience with him about the man and the woman that provided us with the detailed instructions to his son's house. Two days later we crossed the border to safety, eventually making our way to the United States. To this very day, I still miss my homeland but I will never forget our struggle for freedom and the angels that helped us to safety. (Fredia Heinzoff, *Angel Watch*, Nov/Dec 1998, page 5-6)

Saved on a Train

Lonnie Glosson was a legendary harmonica player from White County, Arkansas (died at 93 on March 2, 2001). He had no doubt he had been saved by a guardian angel more than once. He frequently told how he rode the rails back in the 1920s:

"I was in Little Rock and was catching #8, a fast mail train, out to go home to Kensett. #8 did not carry anybody, only mail, . . . it slowed down to about 15 miles an hour. I got back under a viaduct where it was dry to catch the train. I caught it – but where I caught there was no steps – only a straight rod running up the corner of the car – and as I was hanging on my hands started slipping down all the time I was swinging back and forth in between the cars. My knees almost to the ground. And as I swung out the last time there was a switchstand that was going to hit me square in the stomach. So I lost my memory and when I come to myself I was sitting up in the blinds on the other car. I was really scared and shaking like I had a hard chill. I do not know how I got up in that blind. After the train got to Kensett I got down and I tried to get up in the blind while the train was stopped. But there was no way to get up there.

"There just had to be a Higher Power just pick me up and set me up there. That is why I believe in guardian angels.

Another time he felt strongly that he should not get on a certain train, but he did anyway, and once on, he felt strongly that he should get off:

"It was going about 15 miles an hour when I jumped off and went back home. Believe it or not, that train only got 12 miles out – as far as Tuckerman – and it derailed and killed the engineer, fireman and two mail clerks. There was a boy who caught it the same time I did who stayed on and he was killed, too. I sure was lucky. That had to be my guardian angel helping me. . . .

"I have had a guardian angel over me all of my life. That is why I have lived to be 92 years old. These things actually happened – the honest truth and facts." ("Saved By An Angel," *White County Heritage*, 2001.)

Van Goes Through a Car

The following story may not be believable to some people, but I have read other accounts like it:

> As we were being driven from out hotel to the site of a meeting in Canada, we proceeded through a green light but the person driving a van coming from the other direction ran through their red light and obviously didn't see us.

> We were in an ordinary automobile, when the driver of the van proceeded through the red light — drive right toward the engine of our car and went right straight through it! I was sitting in the front seat and even though the motor extended way out in front of our car, the driver's face was no more than six or eight inches from the windshield of the car in which we were riding!

> The van proceeded down the street, but not for long! The people climbed out of the car with the most shocked looks on their faces we've ever seen. They were looking to see what had happened to their vehicle but there was nothing the matter! We all said the same thing, "Did you that angel?"

> An angel somehow supernaturally let that van run right through the motor of our car with no damage whatsoever! There was no accident . . . (*The Angel Book,* Charles and Frances Hunter, page 128)

Most Christians have heard by now about what are called "alien abductions," which is when aliens go into a person's house and literally float them through the walls of their house and into their UFO. This has been described by literally thousands of people. It seems that there are up to ten dimensions of the universe, and the aliens are able to activate one of those other dimensions, which allows for two solid objects to go through each other. So angels can do that also.

Saved From a Car Wreck

I have my own story that must have included one or more angels, when God saved me and an elderly couple from having a bad accident on the highway.

I was twenty years old and driving a delivery truck loaded with fruit and vegetables. It was December or January, and when I started out that morning about 5:30, a light rain started. I did not realize that it was freezing on the roads.

Shortly after the sun was up, I left a restaurant at the south end of Marlow, Oklahoma and headed south on what was then a two-lane highway. Because my truck was heavy, it was getting traction on the rough asphalt.

I had not yet gotten up to full highway speed when I topped a hill going about 40-45 miles per hour, and I saw that not far ahead of me was a car that was doing only about 20-25 miles per hour. I gently   touched the brake, and the truck immediately went into a slide.

It fish-tailed to the left and continued to turn until I was facing the opposite direction, north, and in the north-bound lane.

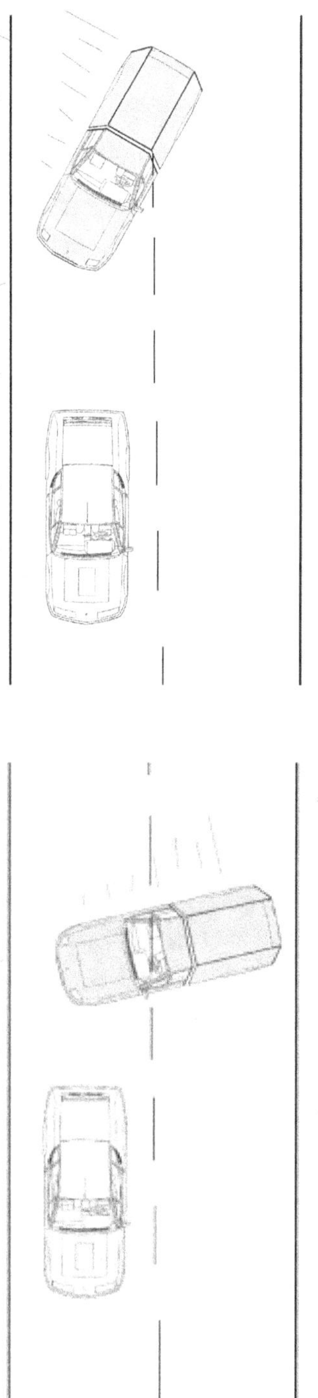

But the momentum of the truck was still carrying it south, straight down the highway in the northbound lane— backwards.

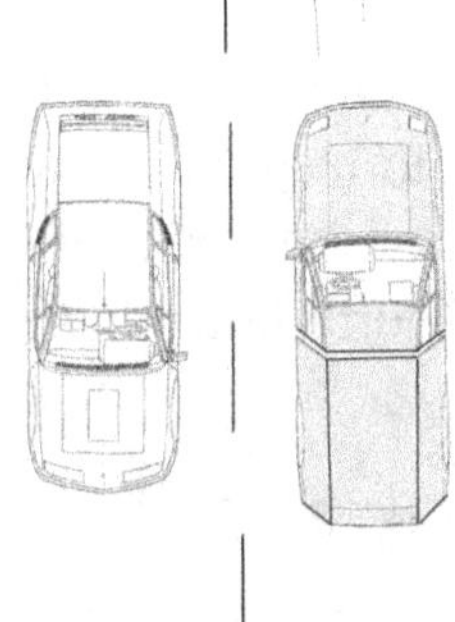

I then passed the car that had been ahead of me, while I was going backward. The driver of the car had a look of astonishment as he and I looked at each other as I passed.

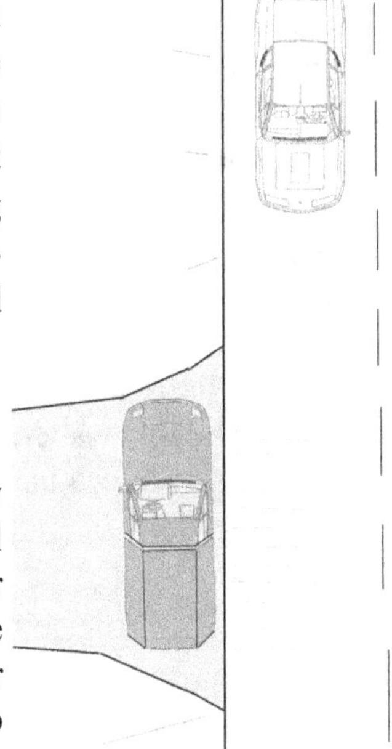

The truck stayed in that lane while moving backwards for several seconds, long enough to pass the slow-moving car and several more car lengths.

After I was far enough in front of the car, the truck suddenly shot across the road, going totally sideways to the opposite side and went off the road, still facing north, and went into the entrance of a farmer's field and came to a stop.

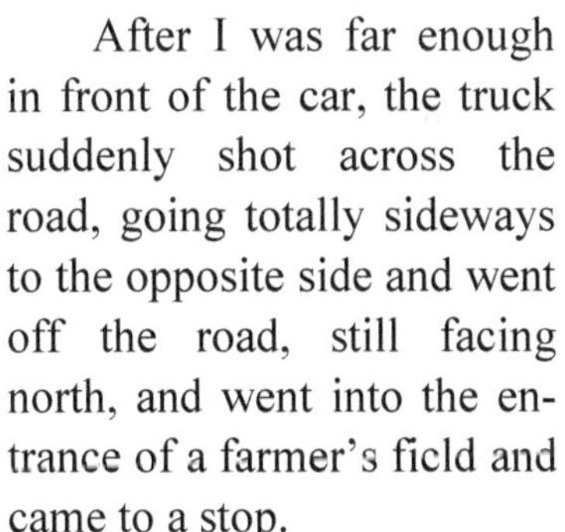

The car immediately passed me; its occupants still had amazed looks on their faces. If the truck had gone off the road at any other spot, it would have gone into a ditch, and I could have been injured or killed. As it was, the truck and I were undamaged. The truck engine died as it came to a stop, so I started it, made a U-turn and continued slowly south. I will never forget the shocked and confused expression on the face of the elderly male driver.

When I arrived home after work, my mother asked me what happened because she felt moved to pray for me that morning (she worked the evening shift). She knew I had been in danger. Though I did not see an angel, there is no doubt that there was one flying above my truck, moving it along like a child moves a toy truck.

Wallet Appears

I had another, less dramatic, occurrence of angelic help about a year before that. I had just cashed my paycheck and had all the money in my wallet. It felt good to have a wallet full of money. I dressed and prepared to go to work the next day, but I could not find my wallet anywhere. I looked everywhere in the house and the car. I was very upset because my entire paycheck and wallet were gone, including my driver's license. I was on my way out the door, prepared to drive to work (at a different job than the one above), and hoped I would not get pulled over by the police.

But before I reached the front door, a voice in my head calmly said, "Look again." I stopped in my tracks; "What? I looked. It's not there," I thought to myself. The voice calmly repeated, "Look again." I thought, "Okay, I will look again." I walked into my bedroom, and there it was, laying in plain sight on the dresser. I did not have a dresser cluttered with a lot of stuff back then. At that age, my dresser had only a few items on it, because I was rarely at home. The black wallet was very easy to see on the white dresser scarf. It could not have been missed. I am certain that an angel retrieved the wallet and spoke to me to look again.

My best friend and I discussed how it could have happened. The angel could have found the lost wallet, or he could have created another one to look just like the original, and even put other money into it that someone somewhere had lost; or perhaps money that had been burned up in a fire.

An Angel Dog

A young girl came home late one night using public transportation. She was terrified because she was being followed by a suspicious-looking man. So she prayed. When she got off the bus, there was a large white dog, a Great Pyrenees, sitting there waiting for her, which she had never seen before. The dog stood up and put its head under her hand, thus signaling that it was with her, and walked with her all the way home. The man also got off the bus but decided to go elsewhere. Once she arrived at her front door, the dog was gone. (Burnham, Sophy. *A Book of Angels*, p. 113-114)

Saved From Train Wreck

International minister, Terry Law (1943-2020), tells of when an angel saved him from injury. He was traveling in Eastern Europe and was in his bed in the train-car, lying about a foot from the wall, when he sensed a presence in the room:

> Suddenly, I felt I should change my position on the bed and put my back against the wall. About thirty seconds after I did that, we had a head-on collision with another train. After a tremendous, grinding crash, our train came to a halt. . . . The man in the next car had his nose smashed and blood was running down his face. People all around me were screaming and wailing. I found out later that six people were killed. (Law, *The Truth About Angels*, page 66)

Apparently, there was only one guardian angel on duty that night; the angels for everyone else must have been on vacation!

Another time he was in danger, he was traveling in a van on a mountain road in Canada, when an angel appeared to his father, who was a preacher. The angel told him that Terry was in *"grave danger"* and gave him a vision of the van going off a cliff and flying through the air. Terry's father knew what he had to do, and merely said, *"In the name of Jesus, take care of that situation!"* (Ibid., page 171). The angel disappeared, and a short while later he returned and said it was taken care of, and that they were safe.

Perhaps a deer was going to jump out in front of the van and cause it to swerve and fly off the road; or perhaps the brakes were going to fail. This, of course, is just an example of what might have been the case. And it is another example of the fact that you do not automatically have a guardian angel protecting you from danger. You need to pray for it, at least frequently; every day is not too often. If it were automatic, the angel would not have needed to warn his father, who then asked the angel to fix the problem.

Angel in the Hay Loft

A young Presbyterian preacher, still in college, preached the Sunday morning service at a country church. After the service, he was approached by a farmer named Lee, who asked him to come to his farm because he needed to talk to him. The preacher and Lee were standing in the barn below the hay-loft, and the farmer said,

> I heard a voice up in the hay-mow. Clear and plain the voice said, "Lee, God wants you to build a calf feeder. This will be the best calf feeder ever, and here's how I want you to build it." Then the voice gave me exact measurements. How high, how wide, how long, and how every piece should fit.

Lee showed the preacher-boy his calf feeder, and it was a wonder to behold. It allowed each calf to get plenty of food without being pushed aside by another calf, with many other features.

> "Whose voice was it? An angel? I've wondered about it a million times. Whoever it was, he told me several times he was speaking for God. What do you think?"

The preacher-boy believed it was an angel, because his own life had been saved twice by an angel; once when he was a teenager, and once when he was a college undergraduate working at a dangerous job. The farmer eventually patented his cafe feeder. (Shedd, *Brush of an Angel's Wing*, page 37)

Angel Pushes Truck

In 1982, Rodney and Ellie Hein were on a mission trip to Mozambique, Africa, when they needed an angel, and instantly received one:

> One of our vehicles was in trouble and we all got out to push. I became too tired to move, and collapsed on top of the hill while Rodney and the men tried to get through an exceptionally deep gully. In spite of every attempt, the truck wouldn't budge. The narrow track made turning back impossible.

> We needed a miracle. I lifted my eyes to the beautiful, clear, African skies and began to call on God to send an angel. Almost immediately, as I looked into the brightness of the sky, I saw a large figure step out of the heavens and stand behind the vehicle. His face and hands were like shining bronze. He put his hands on the truck, and the truck moved easily up the hill. As soon as the

truck reached the top, he disappeared. Astonished, I rubbed my eyes. . . .

At the top of the hill Rodney jumped out of the truck and, with an incredulous expression on his face, said, "It felt like someone was pushing the truck for us!"

"He was," I yelled back. "I saw him." (Hein, *Mozambique: The Cross and The Crown*, page 40-41)

Saved From Car Wreck

Linda M. told me about her experience with a supernatural intervention in the Spring of 2023 that could be attributed to her guardian angel (or at least to guidance from the Holy Spirit), which prevented her from being in an accident. On a Wednesday night en route to her church's midweek service, she was waiting at a traffic light when a thought came into her mind telling her she needed to stop to fill her van with gas on the way home after church. She glanced over to the QT station and argued that QT was always too expensive, then noticed the same price she had seen earlier that day at her regular gas store. So she argued that she did not actually need gas, and could wait until later the next day to fill up. She drove on to church and forgot about the experience.

After church, she was driving home in the dark and approached the same station at the posted speed of 60 miles per hour, with no thought to stop when she was again urged to stop for gas. This time she argued that she was going too fast to change lanes and turn in, but a glance in her mirrors revealed all the vehicles around her were no longer close. So Linda braked and pulled into the station. She tried to get the pump to accept her credit card, but it was not working. So she gave up, scolding herself for even stopping.

She started to leave, feeling silly for listening to that inner voice. She suddenly heard guidance to go to another pump. Frustrated and confused, she did and filled the van's gas tank. Just as she started to pull out, a lot of traffic came along the side road and delayed her from proceeding.

After getting on the interstate highway, she was passing Fort Hood, now called Fort Cavazos, when a Texas state highway patrolman passed her and looked at her, causing her to realize she was going only 60 mph versus the speed limit of 75. She was preoccupied due to the strange event regarding stopping for gas.

Moments later, the patrolman suddenly sped up, pulled across in front of her, and exited. She thought he had gotten a call. Little did she know that at the on-ramp past that exit on the right, a bad accident had occurred a few minutes earlier, and cars were in a deep ravine. One vehicle was smashed from the front and rear; a fire truck was just arriving with firemen running into the ravine, and people across the divided highway had stopped and were running down into the ravine to help accident victims. All lanes were blocked.

Linda suddenly began crying as she realized her delays had likely prevented her from being one of the accident victims. She prayed the rest of the way home, thanking God for His protection. We do not often receive such direct guidance, but it behooves us to listen to those angel voices that lead us for our good.

Daily Confession

Charles and Francis Hunter were a married ministry couple who daily prayed:

> Thank You, Father, that angels are in charge of me. I am surrounded by angels at all times who minister to me and protect me, even from accidents. I am accompanied by angels, defended by them and preserved by them because You have ordered them to do so. (Hunter, *The Angel Book,* page 47)

So it should not be a surprise that they have seen several angels and were saved from a car wreck by an angel. (below)

No Brakes

They were being driven on the freeway by their daughter, Joan:

> It was early morning and traffic was heavy . . . To her horror and ours, she discovered she had no brakes.

> We were about to plunge into a truck or other cars. A bad crash was inevitable. All three of us instantly screamed "Jesus!" We are not sure what happened, but a small hole opened, seemingly not large enough for our car to go through. We missed the truck and the brakeless car came to a halt at the red street light! We know at the spontaneous impulse of calling on Jesus, God surely used one or more of His angels to protect us. (Ibid., page 59-60)

Chapter 8

Angels that Heal, Comfort, or Direct

Let us hold fast to the other and kindred truth that God employs His angels as "ministering spirits" to the humblest and lowiest of His children. (Theodore L. Cuyler, D.D.) (*Fowler, Our Angel Friends*, page 39)

Sometimes an angel does not merely save a person from an accident or other harm; they are known to have shown up to heal someone, or sometimes simply to bring emotional comfort. In our modern world, when we need prayer, we just call a prayer line or post a request online, but there was a time when pastors actually went to the home of a sick person to pray for them:

An invalid was passing through severe physical suffering; every nerve in her body was tense with pain. She had obeyed the Word of God and called for the elder who had prayed and she had received a measure of relief, but as the small hours of the night drew on she succumbed to a new attack of the enemy. She felt it would be impossible to send again for prayer, the minister's strength was already overtaxed by so many calls and it would be an imposition to send for him the second time and at so late an hour. But her physical agony was almost beyond endurance, and in great desperation she called on the Lord to come to her rescue. Suddenly the room seemed filled with a heavenly presence and she felt angelic hands laid upon her body from head to foot. As they touched her the pain left immediately, and she was healed. (*The Later Rain Evangel*, Feb., 1915)

An angel is mistaken for a minister in 1923:

> Little Willie B. was very ill with the small pox in the city of Glasgow, Scotland. The pastor, a godly minister in the Pentecostal faith, was sent to pray for him, and he went one afternoon. As he reached the home, the mother of the sick boy said, "Pastor, how did you get in this morning?" The parents were both away.
>
> He answered, "I wasn't here this morning. I just came this afternoon." "Oh," she said, "you came this morning, and Willie was healed. He heard the bell ring and you came up stairs and prayed for him." They both realized as they talked it over, that it was an angelic visitor who came and prayed for the boy. (*The Later Rain Evangel*, Sept., 1923)

Apparently, the angel rang the doorbell, then just walked through the door because he knew no one was home to open the door except the sick boy.

In former times, before the modern *"God wants you happy and prosperous" movement came along, most* Christians believed that God allowed his children to go through times of trials, tribulations, and testing:

> In a time of special testing, a husband and wife were one night awakened by an angelic host singing sweetest strains of heavenly music. Nearer and nearer they came until they filled the room, strains of surpassing sweetness that forever made the music of earth cheap and commonplace. Each listened breathlessly, fearing to speak lest a word might drive away the rapturous melodies. Verse after verse floated out on the midnight stillness, and finally died away as the heavenly messengers winged their way back to the glory world. The memory of that night lingered with them throughout their lives, one of the first of a number of supernatural visitations which came to them as the Lord led them into deeper truths. (*The Later Rain Evangel*, Feb., 1915)

***

A young Christian but recently saved was going through a testing period. Discouraged and disheartened through manifold temptations and persecutions he had gotten into a backslidden state, and was almost ready to give up trying to be a Christian. In this condition he found himself one evening hurrying down the street of a large, crowded city, a conflict within his breast. As he neared the theater the devil said, "What is the use trying anymore; YOU might as well have a good time." He crossed the street and entered the theater, walked up to the ticket window and asked for a ticket.

Just at that moment he felt someone laying a hand upon him. He turned expecting to see a policeman (he was under condemnation) but faced a young man a little older than himself in appearance, who said, "What are you doing here? I want to talk to you." He left off buying the ticket and followed this strange young man, out of the theater and around the corner.

As they walked on the stranger reminded him of all he had received of the Lord, and wherein he had failed to be like Jesus. The young Christian said to him rather roughly. "Who told you all this and what business is it of yours?" The stranger said, "I know all you have done today. I have watched you and seen all of your actions. Now go and make things right and ask for forgiveness and I will be with you."

As he finished speaking a fear took hold of the young Christian and in obedience to orders he turned and ran nearly all the way home. He asked forgiveness of those whom he had wronged, and did just what he was told, and as he obeyed a most blessed joy and peace filled his soul. He was flooded with a love for the Lord Jesus and an intense desire to do His will which has never left him to this day. Other and similar experiences have proved to him that this was an angel sent forth to minister to him in this time of testing and trial. The young brother shortly after received a call to Central America, and is now laboring [as a missionary] in that hard field. (Ibid.)

You may be tempted to say that this could not have been an angel, because angels do not condemn people, but he merely pointed out the things the young man had done wrong and urged him to make things right. It is possible that the angel knew that if the young man had given in to his temptation to follow after worldly entertainment, he would have fully given up his Christian walk: *What is the use of trying anymore.* God already had plans for the young man to become a missionary, but it appears it would not have happened if the young man had yielded to that one temptation. One of the jobs of angels is to help us accomplish our purpose in life.

On a frosty evening in December 1981, Roy Godwin was driving in the UK through a forest with his wife, Daphne, and children when he saw four headlights ahead of him. One car was passing the other. He swerved but was hit head-on.

It was a very serious collision. *"It was quite clear that I was dying,"* he said. The police and ambulance came, but Roy was trapped in the crumpled wreckage. While they were working to free him, he saw a man walking through the dense woods straight to the car; a forest that should have been "impenetrable." He got in next to Roy and put his arm on his shoulder.

> "It felt as though I had been plugged into the mains [electrical supply]. An incredible force and power was just continuously flooding through me. After a while, the ambulance men came over and said they were taking my family off to hospital.

> "And at that point, this person who was sitting by me, climbed out of the car and said with a very strong and clear voice, "Stop! You are to bring his wife over here to him." The medical team did so.

> Then he said, "Man, you are to know that your wife and children, and you as a family, will be together again and you will be whole. And you are to disregard anything else that anyone tells you." Then he walked away.

At the hospital, the doctors wanted to amputate Roy's left foot, but he remembered what the man said, and refused. *"I didn't have my foot amputated, and I have it today and we are doing very well together."*

He was concerned, because of the seriousness of his injuries, that he had actually dreamed it all. But a few weeks later, the police showed up and asked him some questions.

> "They had two questions: Given the extent of the damage to car, they wanted to know whether I had any explanation as to how it was that I was still alive. And then their second question was about the figure who was in the car with me, who had carried such authority, that they had unhesitatingly obeyed it.

> "It seems to me that God sent an angel to help me. I knew I wasn't abandoned; I knew I wasn't on my own, I was clear that God was going to carry me through where I was. And I felt loved."

Roy was a minister who went on to write a book and start a global house prayer movement. He and his wife live in Wales. The book is called, *The Grace Outpouring*. (News interview video on youtube.com)

You might wonder, why didn't the angel prevent the accident? There are many questions about angelic intervention that no one has the answer to; we can only read the accounts and learn from them. Perhaps God wanted Roy to tell his story of how he was saved by an angel even though he had an accident. Perhaps it happened because he had not prayed enough for protection to begin with. We can only speculate at this point.

***

A lady was in the hospital awaiting surgery, so she prayed:

> Just as I concluded my prayer, a beautiful nun, dressed all in white and with the face of an angel, entered my hospital room. She sat beside my bed and asked me if I would like to talk for a little while. I was very happy for the company and I told her that I was frightened, because I knew that I was dying. I asked her why I felt as though God did not answer my prayers. Did He really love and care about me? I will never forget her radiant face as she quietly explained the difference between praying and just plain talking to "Our Father."

> Clasping my hand tightly in hers and leaning back in her chair, she told me to close my eyes and "talk" to her silently. At the same time, she wanted me to feel as though I was holding the hand of God, not her hand. I laid there very quietly, talking to God just as she instructed, with my eyes closed, for what seemed to be a long time. Suddenly, my hand was released, I immediately opened my eyes and was surprised to see that I was completely alone in my room. . . . . She must have been an angel, because I no longer feared the pending surgery, or death.

When she inquired, she learned that the Mother Superior, who was elderly, was the only nun in the hospital who dressed entirely in white. (Roma Lee Collum, *Angel Watch*, Jan/Feb 1999, page 5)

***

My mother was doing her daily prayers in her bedroom one morning in 1982 when an angel appeared to her. He did not say anything; he just looked at her for a few moments and disappeared. But she immediately knew, because the angel must have put it into her mind, that her father had just died. He was in a nursing home about 250 miles away.

This is not the only time an angel has merely appeared to someone and then disappeared. Sometimes just appearing is enough to bring the comfort needed at certain times.

***

This next letter that was sent to an angel publication may seem unbelievable at first, but I will explain why I believe it, after:

> I would like to share a profound experience that I had when I was 19 years old (I'm 35 now). The experience involved the Archangel Michael. Since I was raised in the Catholic religion, I am very aware of angels and their purpose on earth, and in heaven.
>
> During this time in my life, I was living with my fiancé. We had recently broken our engagement because I had discovered that he was unfaithful to me. I felt alone, angry and a little guilty because I disobeyed God by living with a man before marriage.
>
> One night, I was alone and I let all these negative emotions consume me. I decided that it would just be better for me to end my life. I began to pray for forgiveness and told God to deal with me as He wanted. I felt that He would probably send me straight to hell! The thought terrified me so much that I asked for God to help me by sending me an angel, and that I would know this was His angel because the angel would have a yellow rose.
>
> As I ended my prayer, there was a knock at my front door. I answered the door to find a man standing there with strange, piercing blue eyes. He said, "Hello," and just walked in. I asked him who he was and he said, "Why do you ask such questions? You already know who I am." I denied knowing him, and it was then that he handed me a single yellow rose.
>
> I cannot begin to describe how I felt. The one thing that kept going through my mind was that these things just do not happen to me. He told me that his name was Michael and said that I could ask him anything. He answered all of my questions, and told me that he had known me all my life.
>
> Shocked, I sat down on the floor, across from him and we began to talk, Michael and I. After a while, he looked around the room and then stood up. He looked at me again and said, "You really don't want to go, do you?" I said, "No, not really." Then he said,

"I'll be seeing you again, one day," and he walked out the door, and disappeared. The rose stayed fresh for months, until my life was back on track and my faith was stronger. (*Angel Watch* July/ August 1998, Karen Bentzen, page 6)

I believe this story because God uses indirect angel contact whenever possible, but when there is no other alternative, he does allow for direct angel contact. Since there was likely a high chance of suicide and she directly requested angelic help, she got it.

***

Bruce Van Natta was a self-employed diesel mechanic in Wisconsin on Nov. 6, 2006, when he had a horrific accident. He was underneath a Peterbilt diesel rig when the jack gave way; then he was nearly cut in half by the 10-12,000 lbs. rig, as the axle came down on him. He immediately called out, "*Lord help me!*" twice, and instantly, all the pain went away. Five major arteries had been "*completely severed,*" said Bruce (CBN interview).

Bruce was crushed to about 1 inch thick on this left side, but the axle went up at an angle, so he was only crushed down to about 2 inches on his right. He yelled for his shop-mate to call 911. After the call, he grabbed a jack to raise the truck. When Bruce saw how he had been crushed, he thought to himself that he was going to die.

He yelled for the man to pull him out from under the truck, but he refused, afraid to pull on him, so Bruce tried himself; but when he tried, he died. He came out of his body and floated up and saw two huge, shining angels dressed in white robes with long hair, each one on his knees on either side of him with their hands inside of him; they were stopping the bleeding and keeping him alive. If they stood up, they would have been about 8 feet tall.

"They did not have wings," he said. But they had very broad shoulders. "They looked identical." [1]

He knew he had a decision to make, and he decided to live.

"The next thing I knew, my spirit went down into my body." [1]

The angels' robes were woven in such a way as to create a course, patterned material. "The robes were tight enough that I could see muscles bulging out of their shoulders, backs, and arms," he notes. [2]

It took the medics 30-40 minutes to get there because the accident happened in a rural area. The medics then called for a helicopter, which took him to Madison's Trauma Center. He could later identify 10 people who arrived and were working with him while he was dead.

> "In the ceiling I was at perfect peace, but back in my body I realized, 'Oh crap, I'm the guy who was under the truck.'"

> He glanced to the right and the left, but couldn't see the angels anymore. Somehow, he sensed they were still there. [2]

Every time he shut his eyes, he died and started to "rocket" through a tunnel, then would come back with another slap. The medic, Shannon, asked him if he had a wife and kids, and he was determined to stay alive for them. It took two hours before he actually received treatment at the trauma center.

> With his superior mesenteric artery severed in two places, and other arteries and veins cut, he should have bled to death within minutes. What stunned the doctors is that he still registered a weak blood pressure and his heart was still beating. [2]

To make a long story short, he also had a crushed pancreas and spleen, two broken vertebrae, and a smashed small intestine. The doctors were so certain he would die within minutes, that he received surgery to repair the damaged arteries and nothing more. It was another 12 hours before anything else was done, when they saw that he did not die. But he went through five surgeries in the next year, then another 1.5 years in rehab.

Bruce credits his wife's prayers in his miraculous survival.

> "When she first got the news, she got down on her knees and said, 'Lord, I can't deal with this. I need your help. If Bruce can't be the man he wants to be, then take him. But if he can be who he wants to be, then please save him.'" [2]

Even after the first surgeries, they only expected him to live a year because he only had 3-feet of small intestine, while most people have 20, and he had also lost a lot of weight. But a fellow named Bruce Carlson of New York heard about Bruce Van Natta's medical condition and started a prayer chain. Then God told Carlson to fly to Wisconsin and pray for Bruce in-person.

> "He showed up at the hospital and prayed for me," Bruce recalls. Carlson placed his right hand on Bruce's forehead, and then he

prayed a bold prayer:

"Lord, I add my prayers to all the other prayers for Bruce. In the name of Jesus, I command you small intestine to grow back right now."

Instantly, Bruce felt an "electric shock" and heard a snap. "An electricity, the power of God came right out of his hand and went into my intestines. I could feel them rolling around," he says. [2]

Doctors later confirmed the miracle of seven new feet of intestine, which worked perfectly. *"My pancreas rejuvenated by itself, my spline rejuvenated by itself,"* Bruce said.

After his recovery, Bruce formed Sweet Bread Ministries, and wrote a book called, *Saved by Angels.* He now travels to talk about healing.

"I'm in great health now," Bruce says. "God is real and He is still doing miracles today." [2]

Notice that the angels did not prevent the accident, but only prevented him from dying. Was it because he had not prayed for safety until the truck was laying on him? Only God and the angels know the answer.

1] CBN Interview, 2010. "Bruce Van Natta: Saved by Angels - CBN.com", Youtube.com.

2] Ellis, Mark. *Angels rescued mechanic crushed by truck axle.* God Reports. June 6, 2012. https://godreports.com/2012/06/mechanic-crushed-by-truck-axle-rescued-by-angels/

***

A nurse who had been caring for a very ill patient for five weeks, wrote: "One evening a friend came in to set the table. Then a strong, stalwart angel appeared. When my friend and I went to our dear one (she could be left alone for only a short time) the angel went with us. He said, 'I will restore her to health.' He stood upon the foot of the bed for a short time, then spreading out his beautiful wings, vanished through the wall. The woman recovered." (Baker, *Heaven and The Angels*, page 143)

***

It took everything I had to drive to church that December night in 1993. I had been diagnosed with fibromyalgia, a disabling disorder, and felt completely alone. In despair, I'd holed up at home, but when a friend asked me to meet her at church I thought the change of scenery might do me good. My friend hadn't arrived yet when I slid into a pew in the candlelit church. *God, my whole world seems dark*. I lifted my head. Towering over me was a most magnificent creature, with golden hair and blue-tinted wings so bright, broad daylight seemed to have replaced the dimness inside the church. When my friend joined me, the angel vanished. But that vision brought me out of the darkness. I wasn't on my own. My friend was right beside me, and God was all around. (Jean Maguire, *Angels on Earth*, Nov/Dec 1998, page 2)

***

I was out of town for my job and in my hotel room, laying on the bed crying uncontrollably. I had just telephoned the man that I had been dating, and planning to marry in the near future, and broke off our engagement. I had been made aware of the fact that he grossly misrepresented himself to me.

As the feeling of complete devastation enveloped me, I happened to look up and saw seven angels standing around me! There were three on each side of me and one positioned at my feet. They seemed to be standing over me, in their translucent flowing white gowns, brushing over me gently with large ostrich-like feathers.

A feeling of peace and tranquility came over me and for the first time in a very long time, I felt as though everything would work itself out. I like to operate intuitively through "knowing" as much as possible. I know, in my heart, that the angels were responding to God's love for me. I decided I must have been such an emotional wreck that my guardian angel called for back-up angels for additional help!

About two months after this experience, I met the perfect man for me. We have been happily married for almost eight years and I thank my angels every day for helping me . . . [by] providing me with the knowledge that had been presented to me about the man that I was, mistakenly, about to marry. (Marjie Markowski, *Angel Watch*, Jan/Feb 1999, p. 5)

Chapter 9

Angels in Dreams and Visions

A superstition of great beauty prevails in Ireland -- that when a child smiles in its sleep it is talking to angels. (Alfred Fowler) (Fowler, *Our Angel Friends*, page 32)

We have already read several examples of angels appearing in dreams and visions in the Bible, starting with Jacob and his ladder; and the angel that appeared to Joseph to warn him that the life of Jesus was in danger. Later, an angel appeared to Paul in a dream to direct him on his missionary journey. Here are a few more from Christian history.

Increase Mather, in his book, *A Disquisition Concerning Angelical Apparitions*, relates a story from English history about King Edward the Confessor. When he was near death and in a state of not even speaking, he dreamed that two angels stood by his bed and declared that they were angels, and that the bishops and other rulers of England were not the ministers of God that they claimed to be, but of the Devil; therefore, the Kingdom would be delivered into the hands of an enemy.

> The King awaking, sighed and prayed, saying, Lord Almighty, If this be not an Illusion, but a true Vision which I have seen, grant me ability to utter it to them who are here present, else not. Upon which he was perfectly restored to his speech, & told what he had seen and heard. (page 9)

In less than a year, William the Conqueror arrived and conquered the kingdom, then removed many of the clergy from their positions.

During the early 20th century, many people were in the ministry as "gospel workers." They were not pastors, but they worked full or part-time with outreach, witnessing on the streets, handing out gospel tracts, etc. Here is the dream of a gospel worker:

"If any man's work abide, which he hath built thereupon, he shall receive a reward. If any man's work shall be burned, he shall suffer loss; but he himself shall be saved, yet so as by fire." (1 Cor. 3:10-15)

I sat down in an arm chair, wearied with my work. My toil had been severe and protracted. Many were seeking Christ, and many had found Him. As for myself, I was joyous in my work. My brethren were united; my sermons and exhortations were evidently telling on my hearers and my church was crowded.

Tired with my work, I soon lost myself in a sort of half-forgotten state. Suddenly a stranger entered the room, without any preliminary "tap" or "come in." He carried [with him] measures, chemical agents, and implements, which gave him a very strange appearance.

The stranger came toward me, and, extending his hand, said: "How is your zeal?"

I supposed that the query was to be for my health, but was [expecting to be] pleased to hear his final word, for I was quite well pleased with my zeal, and doubted not the stranger would smile when he should know its proportions.

Instantly, I conceived of it as "physical quantity" and putting my hand to my bosom, brought it forth and presented it [??] to him for inspection. He took it, and placing it in his scale, weighed it carefully. I heard him say, "One hundred pounds [in weight]."

I could scarce express an audible not of satisfaction; but I caught his earnest look as he noted down the weight; and I saw at once that he had drawn no final conclusion, but was intent on pushing his investigation. He broke the mass to atoms, put it into his crucible, and put the crucible into the fire. When the mass was fused, he took it out and set it to cool. It congealed in cooling, and when [dumped] out on the hearth exhibited a series of layers or strata, which all, at the touch of the hammer, fell apart, and were severally tested and weighed; the stranger making [detailed] notes as the process went on. When he had finished he presented the notes to me, and he gave me a look of mingled sorrow and compassion, as without a word, except, "May God save you!" [then] he left the room.

The notes read as follows:

ANALYSIS OF THE ZEAL OF JUNIUS: A Candidate for a Crown of Glory.

Total Weight of Zeal: 100 lbs:

Chemical analysis shows:

Bigotry ………………………..11 Parts

Personal Ambitions …………..22 "

Love of Praise ………………..19 "

Pride of Denomination ………..15 "

Pride of Talent ………………..14 "

Love of Authority …………..…12 " = :[All] Wood, Hay, and Stubble, 1 Cor. 3:10-16.

****

Love of God ………………..4 "

Love of Man ……………….3 " ----- Pure Zeal

I had become troubled at the peculiar manner of the stranger, and especially at his parting look; but when I looked at the figures, my heart sank like lead.

I made a mental effort to dispute the correctness of the record. But I was startled into a more honest mood by an audible sigh from the stranger, who had paused in the hall. I cried out, "Lord, save me!" and knelt at my chair, with the paper in my hand, my eyes fixed upon it. At once it became a mirror, and I saw my heart reflected in it. The record was true. I saw it! I felt! I confessed! I deplored it! And besought God to save me from myself, with many tears. With a loud cry of anguish I awoke.

I had once prayed to be saved from hell, but prayer to be saved from myself now was immeasurably more fervent; nor did I rest or pause till the refining fire came down and went through my heart, searching, probing, melting, burning, filling all its chambers with light, and [dedicating] my whole heart to God.

When the toils of my pilgrimage shall be an end, I shall kneel in heaven, at the feet of the Alchemist and bless Him for the revelation of that day. (*The Later Rain Evangel*, May, 1909)

It is sad that so many people today refuse to consider the extent to which God will send his angels to interact with us and instruct us, if we are only open to it.

***

Uncle KOISTBERG is a humble, little man, poor and of no significance in himself, but happy and contented. His face shows purity of heart, a childlike happiness and communion with God. In the meeting he sings from his heart and praises God as few can do. He belongs to those who can say "amen" and "hallelujah" without being ashamed. And why should one be ashamed when one has such a God and Savior as Uncle Koistberg has? Many pitied our poor old brother when he was outside the camp and joined himself with the despised, Pentecostal people, but God met him and baptized him in the Holy Spirit and he got blessedly filled.

No wonder that people said when they saw him walk with tottering steps and a stick in his hand, "There goes the blessed, old hallelujah man." It is true, his steps are tottering as many anothers are at the age of seventy, but not so his faith.

But I was going to tell about Uncle Koistberg's Christmas. His place in the Assembly was empty, and one understood then that he was ill.

I went to his house, and found him, not living in a palace but in a very poor little room in the yard. This little room was reception-room, dining-room, bed-room and kitchen for himself and wife. Christmas in such a poor, little room, with a stove, two chairs, a bed, a table and an old couch; can that be anything worth telling about? A Babe wrapped in swaddling clothes, lying in a manger in a stable-- can that be something worthy of a place in the Bible? Let the reader answer.

"How do you do, Uncle!" I said. "What sort of a Christmas have you had?"

"Glad to see you, dear brother. I have had a glorious Christmas, praise to my God? I have been dead during Christmas, but was raised to life again. It was wonderful!" This was said in Uncle

Koistberg's own calm manner, and I was curious and asked him to tell me about his death and resurrection.

It was the same dear old Uncle Koistberg I saw before me, and how could he have died and been resurrected again? Listen to his own story:

"I lay over there in my bed, very sick and ill. Suddenly it became awfully dark around me. It was the blackness of death. Just as I was enshrouded in this awful darkness, suddenly a glorious light illumined the whole room. I turned my head to one side and saw there beside me an angel in snow-white apparel. He said, "Uncle, I have come for you. You must come with me to heaven."

I answered the angel, "I am unable to do that because I am too old and feeble." Then the angel said, "look at me!" I looked at him and saw then that he had two large, white wings, and suddenly I too had wings. The angel took my hand and up and up we flew toward heaven. As we were flying we soon got to the heavenly border, and the beautiful city, the New Jerusalem, was right in front of me in all its indescribable glory.

"Outside the wall were a multitude of people of all kindred and tongues who swore and cursed God and all that was holy. I asked the angel what kind of people these were outside the wall cursing God. He answered, 'These are the godless people. They are outside the holy city and as they have lived on earth they will continue to live throughout eternity.' We now arrived at one of the pearly gates.

"The angel took hold of a golden handle and rang, and immediately the gate opened of itself and we went into the city. We met there countless hosts of redeemed who welcomed us. Some of these people were large, others were rather small. I asked the angel if there were no small ones here who belonged to me. I had four little children who died and I hoped to meet them there. 'No,' answered the angel, 'they are not yet here. They will come later.'

"The angel took me by the hand and led me thru the golden streets with beautiful buildings on either side; the beauty of them far surpassed all the beauty of earth. In these streets were multitudes of happy people and all wore crowns on their heads, some of which shone with greater brilliancy than others.

"I asked the angel why this difference in brightness, and he answered, 'These whom you see so glorious and bright, whose crowns shine brighter than the others, are they who, while on earth, served God most faithfully and offered themselves wholly to the service of the Lord. The others have not been so faithful, and have not consecrated themselves so entirely in the service of God; therefore is their joy of less magnitude. The reward and the glory in heaven will be according to the life and service on earth.'

"The angel led me from glory to glory, and I saw also the throne of God and Him who sits upon it, with the hosts of saints and angels around it. The fullness of joy was stamped on every face. As we passed through the city we met a glorious Being. He was more beautifully glorious, more majestic than all the others. The angel pointed to Him and said, 'That is the Lamb you see over there.'

"Oh how meek and gentle He looked, this blessed Lamb of God. The most beautiful of all in heaven is the Lamb! After we had walked about in the city and the angel had shown me its glory and many blessed souls who were so happy there, I asked him if I might not too remain, saying I was old and weak and could do nothing more on earth. 'No,' he said, 'you are not yet made ready on earth. You must return and testify of what you have heard and seen. It will be an encouragement to the Christians and a warning to the godless.' Then he led me out through the pearly gate and dropped my hand, when I awoke and found myself lying in my bed in my poor, little room.

"No one ran imagine how disappointed I was when I awoke from my rapture and found myself in our poor home. Oh what a contrast between our little room and the mansions in this Heavenly city.

"Brother," he said with trembling voice, "I long for home now more than ever before. May the Lord come soon and bring not only me, but all His longing children to that glorious home above, which He has allowed me to see in the spirit."

This was Uncle Koistberg's story. I have tried to repeat it as nearly as possible, hoping it may be both comfort and encouragement to some lonely pilgrim on his way homeward. In the spirit we see the border of our Homeland and the glorious City. Our Bridegroom says, "Behold, I come quickly." We answer, "Amen! Come, Lord Jesus." (*The Later Rain Evan.*, Dec, 1922, p. 10-11)

The above reads more like a vision than a near-death-experience, which is why I have included it in this chapter.

Often, I have read in stories about heavenly visits, that Jesus tells people that they need to go back <u>in order to tell people about heaven</u>. The idea that all we need to know is in the Bible is not a reasonable argument for anything. People who do not believe the Bible will not take that as sufficient evidence! *"Oh, the Bible said it, so it must be true,"* is what they say with mockery. They think the Bible is a fable. So it is understandable that God will give us much more evidence than just saying it in the Bible!

This next vision was seen during WW II:

This story, as told to *The News Chronicle* last night, is the strangest yet of the war and is a parallel of the Famous "Angel of Mons" legend of the Last War:

Mr. Fowler of Firle, Lewes, was attending his sheep on the Sussex Downs when he noticed a white line spreading slowly across the sky. Gradually to his eyes it took the shape of Christ crucified on the Cross. Then six angels took form.

The apparition lasted for two minutes, then faded. Mr. Fowler rushed down the hillside to tell the village, but found he was not the only witness. Villagers working on the land said they had also seen it.

A Newhaven evacuee, Mrs. Steer, of The Street, Firle, and her sister, Mrs. Evangs; said: "We could see the nail in the crossed feet of Christ, and one of the angels with arms upstretched appeared to be praying." Similar statements were made by seven other villagers. (*Strangest Story of The War,* (www.cross rhythms.co.uk/articles/life/Miracles__Angels/39906/p1/)

Chapter 10

Angels at Death and After

People have told me countless stories about angels appearing to collect a loved one at the moment of death. Angels escort us into the Kingdom of heaven, where we are met by loved ones who have gone before us-- and finally by the Lord Jesus Himself. (Judith MacNutt, *Angels are for Real*, page 43)

Christians have long believed that angels carry their souls to heaven or hell, and for good reason; the belief likely began with the story of Lazarus. Jesus said that when Lazarus died, he was *"carried by the angels into Abraham's bosom"* (Luke 16:22). But it was not just a story; there are many other witnesses to this fact throughout history, right up to the present-day.

The first Christian martyr, Stephen, was being stoned when he said, *"I see heaven open and the Son of Man standing at the right hand of God"* (Acts 7:56) (MEV).

The early Christian book called the *Revelation of Paul* tells us about how angels take souls who die to heaven or hell and even mentions that judgment occurs right after death, done by our Lord. This judgment has been reported in many modern near-death experiences. Here is a quote from the *Revelation of Paul*:

And the angel says to me: Paul, look down, and see what thou hast asked. And I looked, and saw one of the sons of men falling near death. And the angel says to me: This is a righteous man, and, behold, all his works stand beside him in the hour of his necessity. And there were beside him good angels, and along with them also evil angels. And the evil angels indeed found no place in him, but the good took possession of the soul of the righteous man, and said to it: Take note of the body whence thou art coming out [of]; for it is necessary for thee again to return to it in the day of the resurrection, that thou mayst receive what God hath promised to the righteous. And the good angels who had received the soul of the righteous man, saluted it, as being well known to them. And it went with them; and the Spirit came forth to meet them . . .

And the angel said to me: Look down to the earth, and behold the soul of the impious, how <u>it goes forth from its tabernacle</u>, which has provoked God to anger, saying, Let us eat and drink; for who is it that has gone down to Hades, and come up and announced that there is judgment and retribution? <u>And take heed, and see all his works which he has done standing before him.</u> And the evil angels came and the good. The good therefore found no place of rest in it, but <u>the evil [angels] took possession of it,</u> saying: O wretched soul, pay heed to thy flesh; take note of that whence thou art coming forth, for thou must return into thy flesh in the day of the resurrection, that thou mayst receive the recompense of thy sins. . . .

[Jesus spoke to a soul after death] Knowest thou not that whensoever anyone dies, his deeds run before him, whether they are good or evil?

Gregory the Great wrote about a man named Stephen who was upon his bed about to die, *"and standing about his bed, some of them beheld Angels coming in, but yet were not able to tell it unto others then present: others there were that saw nothing"* (*Dialogues*, Book 4, chapter 19).

A dying Christian soldier requested the nurse to bring two cups of water, one for himself and another for his friend, who, he said, had come a long distance, and must be tired. The startled nurse said: "I do not see anybody here." "Don't you see him?" said the soldier, pointing into the vacant air. "There is someone standing by the bedside." Soon the soldier's freed spirit and its angel escort sped towards the deathless land. (Bishop Foster) (Fowler, *Our Angel Friends*, page 157)

A fellow named Lord Henry was set to die for his Christian beliefs, and while he was standing on the scaffold, he lifted his eyes to heaven and said:

> Behold I see the heavens open, pointing with his hand to the place, where others also observed a certain brightness which dazzled their eyes. And so he received the stroke of the sword. (Ambrose, *War With Devils,* page 310)

I am sure the angels had come to escort him home. At another time, there was a father and son both on the scaffold about to die for Christ, when the father said:

> Behold I see the heavens open, and millions of angels ready to receive us. (Ibid..)

People who have died normal deaths in centuries past have also seen angels. In those years, most people died at home, surrounded by relatives and friends, rather than in hospitals connected to machines and tubes. Dying at home allowed for many stories of people who said that the angels were there to escort them to heaven.

Romula fell sick and called for her teacher, Redempta, who came to her side with another student. Then they suddenly heard two choirs singing outside the door, one with male voices and one of female:

> . . . the holy soul departed this life, and was carried in that manner up into heaven; and the higher these two choirs did asend, the less did they hear that celestial music, until at length they heard it no more. (Ibid., page 311)

Philip de Mornay was lying on his deathbed and saying his prayers when he spoke about already traveling toward heaven:

> I fly to heaven; the angels of heaven are carrying me to the bosom of my Saviour. (Ibid.)

Mrs. Katherine Stubs was on her deathbed and said:

> Oh would God, you saw what I see. For behold I see millions of glorious angels stand about me, with fiery chariots ready to defend me. These holy angels, these ministering spirits, are appointed of God to carry my soul into the kingdom of heaven. (Ibid., p. 312)

A fellow named Servulus, also on his deathbed, called everyone that was in his house and asked them to sing hymns with him. As they were singing, he suddenly said loudly, *"Do ye not hear the wonderful music which is in heaven?"* (Ibid., page 313) And then he immediately died. Those by his side said there was a *"most pleasant and fragrant smell*." Another fellow named Guthlake also died, and his student by his side said he could hear the angels singing (Ibid., page 314).

Daisy Irene Dryden died in 1864 at age ten. Her desire in life was to become a missionary, her father being a minister with the Methodist Episcopal Church to the Pacific Coast. She was very sick, and during the final three days of her life, she communed with departed loved ones and spoke about it. She did not see them with her physical eyes, but with her spiritual ones. Her mother wrote her story and tells us that Daisy did not receive any education related to *"mysticism or modern spiritualism,"* (*Daisy Dryden: A Memoir*, Mrs.S. H. Dryden., Colonial Press, Boston, 1909, page 5).

> Instances of the opening of the spiritual senses, just before death, are by no means unheard of. In almost every neighborhood may be found some one who, at the bedside of the dying, has witnessed on the countenance unmistakable signs of recognition of departed ones. (page 10)

In Daisy's case, her dying took longer than most, so she was able to describe what she saw with her spiritual eyes. It began when her father was sitting by her bed and noticed an expression of both pleasure and amazement on her face. He inquired, and she replied,

> "It is a spirit, it is Jesus. And He says I am going to be one of His little lambs. . . . I am going to heaven, to Him" (Ibid., page 33).

Daisy spoke about what she saw in heaven:

> "And if I do [have an actual home in heaven], the heavenly flowers and trees that I love so much here-- for I do see them, and they are more beautiful than anything you could imagine-- they will be there." (Ibid., page 39)

A neighbor lady named Mrs. B. did not believe in life after death and was in a state of *"deep distress"* because she had lost both her husband and her 12-year-old son, Bateman. She came to visit Daisy, and Daisy told her:

> "Bateman is here, and says he is alive and well, and is in such a good place, he would not come home for anything. He says he is learning how to be good." Mrs. B. then said: "Ask him if he has seen his father." Daisy replied: "He says he has not, he is not here, and says to you, 'Mother, don't fret about me, it is better I did not grow up.'" (Ibid., page 40)

Bateman had been a very misbehaving boy, swearing, stealing, and breaking things. Because of this encounter, Mrs. B. became a firm believer in life after death. Daisy's Sunday School teacher also came to visit her. Her two children had died many years before, so Daisy had never heard of them. Daisy said to her, "*Your two children are here*" (p. 41) and described them as being fully grown, to which Mrs. H. said, "*How can that be? They were children when they died*" (p. 42).

> Daisy answered, "Allie [Daisy's dead brother] says, 'Children do not stay children; they grow up as they do in this life.'" Mrs. H. then said, "But my little daughter Mary fell, and was so injured that she could not stand straight." To this Daisy replied, "She is all right now; she is straight and beautiful; and your son is looking so noble and happy." (p. 42)

Another lady, Mrs. W., had lost her father and asked Daisy if she had seen him in heaven. Daisy asked her brother; he did not know but would inquire about him, and she shortly reported that, yes, her father was there.

> Mrs. W. then said, "Daisy, why did not Allie know at once about my father?" "Because," replied she, "those who die go into different states or places and do not see each other all the time, but all the good are in the state of the blest." (page 44)

One day Daisy told her mother that Allie, her dead son, was standing right beside her:

> Involuntarily I looked around, but Daisy thereupon continued, "He says you cannot see him because your spirit eyes are closed, but that I can, because my body only holds my spirit, as it were, by a thread of life." (page 47)

Daisy saw angels and heard them singing, but reported that they did not have wings. She was told the very time in which she would die, and it happened as she said.

The idea that a dead child grows up in heaven is supported by a more recent trip to heaven by a child who was having an operation, Colton Burpo, but did not actually die; as mentioned in chapter 5. He saw his dead sister in heaven, whom he had never been told about, because she died before he was born. He later reported that she had grown to a certain age. (Burpo, *Heaven is for Real*)

In 1916, a letter was published in *The Weekly Evangel, a Pentecostal newspaper, saying* that before the wife of A. P. Dennis died, an angel stood at the foot of her bed and said, "*I am sent for thy wife.*" But before she died, she "*asked many questions about the 'bright ones' who were standing around her.*"

Georgia E. Dickerson, of Schoolfield, Virginia was sixteen years old when she died after a long illness in 1923:

> She was a good girl, and said she wanted to get well and join the Pentecostal Holiness Church. Although she said she was ready to go, and prayed for the Lord to take her. She told her mother the day she died, she saw children around her bed, and told her mother [there] was going to be an angel in heaven awaiting for her. (*The International Pentecostal Holiness Church Advocate*, Aug. 23, 1923)

The following letter was sent to a newsletter about angels:

> My grandfather died when I was a child of six. I remember very clearly, a discussion with my aunt. My aunt said that my grandfather sat up straight in his bed and asked if anyone there could see the mountain of angels and hear their beautiful singing.
>
> When my stepfather died several years later, only my mother and my stepbrother, Paul, were in the room. My stepbrother was a college professor, and unsure whether he believed in anything supernatural. As his father breathed his last breath, Paul looked at the foot of the bed. He saw his father standing there, dressed in his best suit and tie! He looked much younger, and relaxed. He had all his dark hair, which had come out due to the chemotherapy. He also had a great big smile on his face, as he disappeared from view.
>
> My husband's mother died of Hodgkin's Disease, which is a form of cancer. She had been in and out of a coma for several weeks. One night, she was so seriously ill that my husband and his aunt sat up all night, she sat straight up in bed and started talking to Jesus. She said, "But you died a horrible death, too . . . Mother, I didn't know whether I would recognize you! (her mother died when she was only six years old) . . . And Dad, what are you doing here?" (We buried her father only three days before and she was not aware of his death, because she was so very ill herself.) She laid back down on her pillow.

An elderly nurse was standing in the doorway. My husband, his aunt and the nurse all had tears in their eyes. The nurse replied, "Every so often, God allows me to see the good as they cross over." (*Angel Watch* July/August 1998, Polly, Gainesville, TX page 14)   ***

This story, published in 1919, is very similar:

I saw an Angel descending from above clothed in a beautiful white garment, girded with black. Her countenance was radiant and her expression very friendly. She announced that she had come to fetch me, and a little later another beautiful Angel arrived, who, beckoning to me sounding a trumpet, announced that my time was short.

A still small voice then whispered to me to say good-bye to my loved ones, which I did. Then a terrible conflict with Satan began, but the Angel, who was always near at hand, continued to encourage me until after I had passed through the dark and deep River of Death. When I arrived at the other side the Angel again sounded a trumpet, and thereupon several other Angels arrived, who rejoiced, saying, Hallelujah, Hallelujah, glory, honour and praise unto the Lamb.

Then I came to Heaven's gate and beheld another most beautiful Angel guarding it. Before I was allowed to enter, Hell or the Place of Destruction was shown [to] me. Words fail me as I recall the horror and awfulness of it, and the anguish of the countless thousands which it had engulfed. Then I was allowed to pass into Heaven, and oh, the brightness and splendor and the glory of the place. It exceeded the brightness of the sun or anything else I had ever seen. We were all so glad and rejoiced and spake in strange tongues [languages].

Going higher and higher, I at last arrived at a place where I beheld the Lord Jesus who was surrounded by thousands and thousands of Angels, and before whose majesty and glory I could not stand. Putting up His hand He kindly and tenderly said to me: "Go back, go back, and work in my Vineyard; many souls are calling. Hearken, hearken, still, still voices calling, calling for you." He then showed me a multitude of people who were still in darkness and had not the Light of Life. I felt so grieved at having to go back, but Jesus smiling kindly said, "Just a little while and I will deliver you all."

Then the Angel took me up and carried me back, saying unto me before she left me, "Trust in the Lord and love one another with brotherly love." I then found myself back again in this world. (Sister R. I. Stevens, *The Pentecostal Evangel*, Dec. 13, 1919, p. 8)

This is another account that reported a female angel, so they must exist.

***

Judith MacNutt, a Christian psychotherapist, co-founded Christian Healing Ministries with her husband, Francis MacNutt. She reported this story of a mother's heavenly escort at death. Emmy Cerveny's mother was near death with emphysema, so Emmy and her husband, an Episcopal bishop, moved into her home to be near her during her final days:

> Because of her deep faith, the MacNutts and many of the community of the faithful, my mother experienced a very holy death. She was not afraid to die. In fact, she looked forward to joining my daddy and others who had gone before here. . . .

> Frank gave her Communion and prayed with her. A few hours later, Mother called me into her room and said, "Emmy, do you see those angels in the corner of my room? There's a path of beautiful flowers on either side, and the street is lined with many, many angels."

> The picture was so vivid to her. As I sat quietly by her bed, she said, "Emmy, the angels -- do you see them now? They want me to come and go with them. I believe I am ready to go; please come hold my hand and help me join them. Wait! Honey, call your brother to be with us." As we stood on either side of her bed, she said, "I am ready to join them." She quietly departed with the angels. (*Angels are for Real*, page 43-44)

Sue Saint Sing saw a vision of four beautiful and tall angels one winter day several years ago, tending to her friend Archabbot Leopold, who was far away in the Latrobe Abbey in Pennsylvania:

> Leopold had been my spiritual director for years, but we now live in different parts of the country. The angels were two by two in formation around Leopold's resting body -- two at his head and two at his feet, as if they were preparing him for something. Then, only moments later, the vision was gone. I called the ab-

bey, and they said that Leopold had just passed away. (Ibid., page 62-63)

Billy Graham reported in his book about angels that his own grandmother said she saw her deceased husband, Ben, and angels immediately before she died:

> . . . the room seemed to fill with a heavenly light. She sat up in bed and almost laughingly said, "I see Jesus. He has His arms outstretched toward me. I see Ben and I see the angels." She slumped over, absent from the body but present with the Lord. (*God's Secret Agents*, chapter 13)

Dying is very different for those who do not have the promise and expectation of heaven. In this, Christians die better than any other people on earth. The writer of the great Bible commentary, *Barnes Notes on the Bible*, said:

> Angels are sent to be man's attendants. They come to minister to him here and to conduct him home to glory! Kings and princes are surrounded by armed men, or sages called to be their counselors; but the most humble saint may be encompassed by a retinue of beings of far greater power and more elevated rank. Then angels of light and glory feel a deep interest in the salvation of men. They come to attend the redeemed; they wait on their steps; they sustain them in trial; they accompany them when departing to heaven. (Rev. Albert Barnes) (Fowler, *Our Angel Friends*, page 30)

Chapter 11

Near Death Experiences

"The most unpleasant truth is a safer companion than a pleasant falsehood." (Theodore Roosevelt)

Even though angels are the main subject of this book and I have already included some Near Death Experiences, I feel it is necessary to include a chapter on heaven and hell and their connection to NDEs because many people do not understand that Satan's deception is not limited to this human life, but continues into the afterlife. The information in this chapter is not intended to be all-inclusive, since whole books have been written on the subject of heaven alone, but I include information that ties in with the rest of this book and provides needed answers to the New Age after-life enigma.

Just as we have many witnesses to the reality and ministry of angels here on Earth, we also have many eyewitnesses of the reality of heaven and hell. Many people have actually died and been escorted to heaven, only to be told that they must return because their work on earth is not finished. They usually beg to stay in heaven but are required to return. Sometimes they are brought back to life by doctors or paramedics, but sometimes they are healed supernaturally by God.

Some testimonies come from people who have died and come back to life, while other testimony comes from people who saw heaven while on the operating table but did not actually die, but were in a coma, which people in the 19th century called a trance.

However, some people who claim to have seen heaven without dying or being on an operating table, are actually lying. Don't believe every person who claims to have visited heaven. One fellow said heaven is 3 trillion miles away and it takes 6 hours to get there.

It is strange that most people get there in only a few seconds or minutes!

The first NDE on record was written down by Plato in *The Republic*, about a soldier who died on the battlefield and came back to life days later on his funeral pyre. And so there have been similar experiences down through history; but nothing like the volume of NDEs we have today because of modern medical techniques of resuscitation.

> In Western culture, return-from-death stories developed within and alongside traditions of late antiquity, flourished in the Middle Ages, declined during the Reformation, and reappeared in connection with some of the evangelical, separatist, and spiritualist movements of the nineteenth century. (Zaleski, *Otherworld Journeys*, page 5)

It is sad that even many Christians refuse to believe in Near-Death-Experiences (NDEs), because they are not in the Bible, <u>but that is not true</u>. The Apostle Paul died by stoning (Acts 14:19) and went to the third heaven (2 Cor. 12:2), but he was not allowed to tell what he saw. And as time went by, other people had NDEs and were told they needed to go back <u>so they could tell people what they saw in heaven</u>.

For some reason, it was not time to reveal the details about heaven during the Apostle Age, but now we have a much larger population and mass media to get the word out. So God is now revealing more details about heaven in order that people will believe and be converted, but also to give hope and expectation to those Christians alive now as we approach the end of the age, but especially to counter the false NDEs that proclaim that we are all going to a beautiful place.

Knowing the truth of heaven and hell is actually important, because many NDEs do not involve either, but the person merely interacts with a wise and loving *"being of light."* But I will provide evidence for the identity of this being who claims to be God, the Creator, the Source, etc.

It is highly likely that the next NDE *on record* after the Apostle Paul happened in the year 584 A.D., when Salvius died. He had spent many years in a monastery and eventually became the abbot, but he left the office for solitude. He was lying on his bed with a high fever when he died. His body was taken out of his room and placed on a table, while the monks and his mother mourned and sang psalms. The next morning, people were present when the body began to move:

And behold his cheeks regained color and, as if roused from a deep sleep, he stirred and opened his eyes and lifted his hands and said: "Merciful God, why hast Thou allowed me to return to this gloomy place of life on earth, since Thy mercy in heaven would be better for me than vile life in this world." His people were wonderstruck and asked what such a prodigy could mean, but he made no answer to their questions. He rose from the bier, feeling no harm from the painful experience he had suffered, and continued for three days without the support of food or drink. On the third day he called the monks and his mother and said:

"Listen, dear ones, and understand that what you look upon in this world is nothing but it is like the prophet Solomon's song, 'All is vanity.' Happy is he who can live in the world so as to deserve to see the glory of God in heaven." Having said this he began to doubt whether to say more or be silent. When he said no more he was beset by the entreaties of his brethren to tell what he had seen, and he went on: "Four days ago when my cell quivered and you saw me lifeless, I was seized by two angels and carried up to the high heavens, so that I thought I had under my feet not only this filthy world but the sun also, and the moon, the clouds and the stars.

"Then I was taken through a door brighter than this light into that dwelling in which all the pavement was like shining gold and silver, a brightness and spaciousness beyond description, and such a multitude of both sexes was there that the length and breadth of the throng could not be seen. A way was made for me through the press by the angels who guided me, and we came to a place which I had already seen from a distance; a cloud hung over it brighter than any light, in which no sun or moon or star could be seen, but excelling all these it gleamed more brightly than the light of nature, and a voice came out of the cloud like a voice of many waters. Then I, a sinner, was humbly greeted by men in priestly and worldly dress who, my guides told me, were martyrs and confessors whom we worship here with the greatest reverence. I stood where I was bidden and a very sweet odor enveloped me so that I was refreshed by this sweetness and up to the present have wanted no food or drink. And I heard a voice saying:

"'Let him return to the world since he is necessary to our churches.' It was only the voice that was heard, for it could not be seen who spoke. And I threw myself on the pavement and said with loud weeping: 'Alas, Alas, Lord, why didst Thou show me this if I was to be deprived of it. Behold today Thou wilt cast me out from Thy face to return to the sinful world and never be able to return here again. I beseech Thee, Lord, not to take Thy mercy from me but permit me to stay here and not fall thither and perish.' And the voice which spoke to me said: 'Go in peace, for I am your keeper until I bring you back to this place.' Then I was left alone by my companions and departed weeping by the gate by which I entered and returned here."

When he had said this and all present were wonderstruck, . . . Now as I write this I am afraid that some reader may not believe it, according to what Sallust the historian says: "When you speak of the virtue and fame of good men each calmly believes what he thinks it easy for himself to do; beyond that he considers it falsely invented." For I call all-powerful God to witness that I learned from his [Salvius] own lips all that I have told. (Gregory of Tours, *History of the Franks*, page 170-171)

This report greatly resembles many others that have come to us in recent years. But though many are similar, they are not exactly the same. Most NDEs have similarities, yet many have differences. It seems that the afterlife is not so totally regimented that everyone experiences the exact same things. There is a lot of variation.

In the 18th century, the Hasidic Jews of Eastern Europe wrote a collection of anecdotes, *In Praise of the Baal Shem Tov*, that says, *"In earlier days when people revived after lying in a coma close to death, they used to tell about the awesome things they had seen in the upper world"* (Ben-Amos, page 4). So NDEs are certainly not a new phenomenon, but with a larger world population and better methods of getting the stories out to the public, it stands to reason that there are many more NDEs being reported today.

The great evangelist, D. L. Moody, was on his deathbed in 1899 when those around him heard him say:

"Earth recedes, heaven opens before me! This is no dream, Will [his son]. It is beautiful. It is like a trance. If this is death, it is sweet. . . . God is calling me and I must go. Don't call me back!"

Then he died, and the doctor present revived him, and Moody said:

> "I went to the gate of heaven. Why, it was so wonderful, and I saw the children! I saw Irene and Dwight." (Rawlings, *Beyond Death's Door*, page 71-72)

I have noticed in reading many NDEs that some of them are not literal; that is, God knows that they will be returning to Earth, so what the person sees is more like a vision than reality. This next NDE is like that; more of a vision.

In 1943, George Ritchie was a private in the army who became sick with double-lobar pneumonia and died of a heart attack. He was dead for nine minutes until he was brought back by an injection of adrenaline. However, his NDE is closer to *Pilgrim's Progress* than to reality. He tells how he left his body and proceeded toward Richmond, Virginia, to keep an appointment, but was upset about his ethereal, nonphysical body because he was only a spirit. So he went back to the hospital to get his body. When he arrived back in the room, it filled with light, and he knew he was in the presence of Jesus, who gave him a life review.

(Most people have a life review after they get to heaven, though some have it before they leave here, or even during a stop along the way.)

Then Jesus took him around the earth, where he saw dead people living in a form of hell among the living. He saw alcoholic spirits in bars trying to pick up shot glasses, but were unable to do so because they were only spirits. And they continued repeatedly doing this forever. He was then taken to another spiritual plain above ground level that was filled only with spirits who were angry and yelling at each other and attempting to fight each other but were unable to touch the other person with their fists, being only spirits.

Then he saw another dimension, which had great buildings and was filled with people. In one building, he saw *"technological machinery"* that was engaged in something beyond his understanding. There was a library filled with books, and people were engaged in some kind of research or study. But this level was not heaven; it was merely filled with people who had spent their lives searching for knowledge. *"They grew, and they have kept on growing."*

But like the other levels, they were just dead people without the light and love of God found in heaven. He and Jesus finally traveled toward heaven, and he saw it off in the distance, but then suddenly they were rushing back to earth and to the hospital room. (Return From Tomorrow, George G. Ritchie, and Elizabeth Sherrill.)

I do not believe that George Ritchie told his story for money or recognition because, after his recovery, he became a psychiatrist and college instructor. Telling the story could have actually hurt his career back then.

In all likelihood, what he was shown was not literal but metaphorical. It likely indicates that how you live on Earth will directly affect your afterlife. Have you ever said or done something you considered a mistake and kept going over it repeatedly in your mind for hours or even days later?

I suspect that this story shows that people will relive their lives in their minds, obsessing about the things they did, going over them and over them, perhaps for eternity. Except for those who make it to heaven, who go through a washing to cleanse them of the issues and painful memories they had while on earth. This washing has been reported numerous times, such as in the next NDE, which has some elements that appear literal, while other elements appear symbolical or figurative, like a dream or vision.

***

In 1966, Gary Wood (1949-2017) was an eighteen-year-old freshman at Wayland Baptist College, preparing to become a preacher, when he was killed in a car accident:

> There I was, looking down at my body, seeing my life go by like a re-run. Everything, in just an instant, flashed before me. I had no fear, and there was no sorrow or confusion. I truly believed that I would never return from this experience. . . . (page 10)

While he was going through the tunnel, he heard angels singing in English, so they must have been singing for him. David saw a wall and gate so tall that he could not see the top of them. An angel, who was 40 feet tall, let him go through the gate, and he was met by his childhood friend, John, who showed him around heaven.

> A beautiful, crystal clear river of water flowed directly in front of me. My eyes followed the river that flowed from the throne of God! It was an awesome sight to see the source of the river was

the throne of Almighty God! . . . Stepping in, I discovered, it was only ankle deep, then it began to rise. It covered my thighs and my shoulders until my entire being was eventually submerged. . . . . . The beautiful water was actually cleansing me of any debris that may have clung to me in my transition from earth to glory. . . . (*I Died And Went To Heaven*, page 11, PDF version)

The streets are crystal clear, yet they are pure gold. I had an atheist approach me not too long ago, who told me, if I was going to go around making up silly stories about Heaven that I needed to get my facts straight, and that any fool knew that gold was yellow and not transparent. It is a proven fact that there is an impurity in gold that makes it yellow. Nothing in Heaven is impure. . . . It seems so strange to me that so many people relate to heaven as just a place where we're going to be floating around on a cloud strumming a harp and looking down on the earth. That's so far from the truth. There will be many new adventures for us as we do what God asks us to do. There is more life in heaven than there will ever be here on earth. Even the flowers sing praises to Jesus and rejoice in His wonderful name!(page 13)

I saw so many angels. All magnificent in beauty, some had wings, while others did not. They each had their own personality and identity. Each angel had a great countenance. God has given them a great intelligence. . . . Each angel was working diligently at whatever task he was assigned. All were joyfully serving God. (page 14)

He also saw a large room with legs and arms hanging in it, even eyeballs. This part was like a dream or vision:

Before my eyes, from my heavenly vantage point, I could see the prayers of the saints below shooting up like arrows towards Heaven. Angels would receive the prayers and bring them into the throne room of God. God would grant the prayer request, and the angel would be dispatched from that room to deliver the miracle. . . . (page 15)

I once believed that reports like this were fabricated nonsense because they do not sound reasonable, but I now understand that many NDEs contain non-literal elements.

> [Jesus] said that there would be three things that would mark his soon return: A Spirit of Restoration, A Spirit of Prayer, and An Outburst of Miracles. (page 17) . . .
>
> Then Jesus showed me that when a child of God got down on their knees before Him, praying in the Name of Jesus, with faith, their prayers would shoot into the Heavens like barbed arrows. An army of angelic forces would appear prepared for battle to destroy the demons' effectiveness. The more prayers of faith there were, the demons would retreat. But if doubt and unbelief were spoken, the demons would begin to overcome. The Lord told me that as time grows closer to his return, demon activity will become more rampant. (page 20)

Gary was dead for approximately twenty minutes until the paramedics were able to revive him. His sister was in the car with him and was praying very hard for him. So he was sent back to Earth with a commission to *"make heaven real to this generation"* (Youtube video).

He came back to life even though he was severely injured. The doctors said he would never be able to speak again because of his crushed larynx, but Jesus appeared in his hospital room, put his hand on his throat, and smiled at him, then walked out. He was speaking moments later and eventually became an evangelist.

I will be quoting a lot from a book written by H.A. Baker, *Plains of Glory and Gloom*, which relates personal testimonies of people who died and went to heaven and returned, and some saw hell (he was the 20th century missionary to China):

> I have the authentic account of almost a score of persons who were raised from the dead. So far as I have been able to secure the personal testimony of these persons as regards their experience while they were out of their dead bodies, all who reached the gates of the New Jerusalem or were permitted to enter therein, saw in their real experience exactly what others saw in vision as realities. . . . We have, then, the testimony of eye-witnesses by those who have died and gone to heaven to corroborate what others in the Spirit have also seen in vision. I know of no better or stronger proof possible, save for you and me to die and go to Paradise ourselves. (*Plains of Glory and Gloom*, by H. A Baker, page 11)

There is no doubt that hell exists, because if hell does not exist for those who reject Christ, then heaven does not exist for believers.

Take the case of Miss D.; she was a Wesleyan Lady who was in what can best be described as a coma for nearly a week. Baker quotes from a published account that is no longer available, "*A Vision of a Wesleyan Lady*," recorded by Robert Young, and originally published by the Free Tract Society of Los Angeles:

> "she opened her eyes and said: 'Mr. C. is dead.' "Her attendants thinking she was delirious, replied that she was mistaken, as Mr. C. was not only alive but well.

> "'Oh, no,' said she. 'He is dead, for a short time ago, as I passed the gates of hell, I saw him descend into the pit and the blue flame cover him. Mr. B. is also dead, for he arrived in heaven just as I was leaving that happy place, and I saw the beautiful gates thrown wide open to receive him; and I heard the host of heaven shout, 'Welcome, weary pilgrim!'

> "Mr. C. was a neighbor and a very wicked person; Mr. B., who lived at no great distance, was a good old man for many years a consistent and useful member of the Church of God. The parties who heard Miss D's startling and confident statement immediately sent to make inquiries about the two individuals alluded to, and found to their utter astonishment that the former had dropped dead about a half hour before while in the act of tying his shoe, and at about the same time the latter had suddenly passed into the eternal world. For the truth of this I do solemnly vouch." This is quoted from the account of Robert Young, a young missionary in India who visited this lady just prior to her trance, and many times during the trance and immediately after she came out of the trance. I know of similar instances that cannot be given for lack of space. The fact that the men who died were seen thus entering realms seen in vision at that exact time is evidence that the other things simultaneously seen were also realities. (Baker, *Plains of Gloom and Glory*, page 10)

There is a similar well-documented case that occurred in 1848, when a 25-year-old woman named Marietta Davis fell into what people of the time described as a trance for nine days. When she came out of it, she described heaven, and she died seven months later, which occurred on the exact day and time she said it would. Her account of an apparent trip to heaven was written down and published by her Baptist pastor.

The book that gives her words, *Scenes Beyond the Grave*, by J. L. Scott and herself, was a very high-selling book in the 19th century, as it went through at least 27 printings. However, though what she saw relates to truth, she is not a first-person literal witness of heaven and hell, which is made clear as the book progresses, because she saw spirits speaking and doing things, and then an angel tells her at one point, *"the spirit addressing him, represents the spirit of those who, in any sphere of existence, had trusted [in] false teachers."* This means that what she saw was more like a dream or vision which is not literal, but must be interpreted to understand the truth it contains. So she did see a spiritual vision of heaven, but she did not literally travel to heaven and see it for real.

Baker said, based on his knowledge of the Bible and the testimonies, that people who hear the Gospel and reject it go directly to hell when they die, but people who were inclined toward good, even though they never heard the Gospel, go to the third heaven. The Apostle Paul mentions three heavens, and the Book of Enoch mentions seven heavens.

Baker said that when a person dies, even though he or she was inclined toward good, they still cannot enter heaven, so they are instructed and allowed to accept Salvation, at which time they are allowed into the higher heavens. Rather than calling it Purgatory, as the Catholics do, Baker called it no-man's land:

> I will now give in summary, as seen by some, what takes place at the death of those dying in "no man's land" on earth and entering "no-man's land" in the lower plains of the First Heaven. These witnesses say that when this majority of men die, they enter as spirits (the body being discarded at death) into the realm of spirits on the intermediate plains of the First Heaven. This place where spirits enter, though earth-like, is more beautiful than the earth. Here these new arrivals are surrounded by angels and by devils and evil spirits. As on the earth-side of the grave so it is on the spirit-side of the grave. Angels are present to influence the spirits heavenward, and devils are there to entice them hellward. In the physical body on the earth-side or free from the body on the spirit-side of the grave the SOUL is in "no-man's land." In both cases it decides whether it will go heavenward or hellward,

whether it will listen to angels or devils, whether it wants light or darkness. The man himself chooses, and in the last analysis, he alone is master of his own soul.

These spirits, coming out of their physical bodies at death, have spiritual bodies much like their former earthly bodies. After entering these spiritual plains, they are attracted by their own class of spirits or people, so that soon there is a separation. Those hating light on earth, reveling in darkness and wallowing in sin, soon go off with evil spirits into lower plains of darkness. At first they enter plains of considerable light and paradise-like conditions, but this they cannot endure. The heaven-light there, though dim and subdued in glory [compared to the upper heavens], is like fire burning these lovers of darkness. The heavenly light, Holy-Spirit-light, like the Holy Spirit on earth, reveals to them and to others all their sins and secret motives as though they were transparent. Hence, though the plains of Paradise are about them, and higher plains of grandeur just above them, and angels wait upon them, these unregenerated souls *"neither come to the light lest their deeds be reproved"* [John 3:20]. Because the light of heaven disturbs them, and because their sins are "naked and opened unto the eyes" [Heb. 4:13] of themselves and everyone else, this class of people hurry to hide themselves in lower plains of gloom and darkness. Jesus does not condemn them. They condemn themselves. (page 23)

You may be surprised to learn that the above information actually agrees with statements in the Bible. Jesus said, *"This is the condemnation, that light is come into the world, and men loved darkness rather than light, because their deeds were evil"* (John 3:9). Speaking of his time as a missionary, Baker said:

In our mission outpost on this front line against forces of evil, we live among the heathen. God has worked among them with signs and wonders, and many have found the way of life. On the other hand, in spite of mighty outpourings of the Holy Spirit and many unmistakable displays of God's love and saving power, many hate the light. The clearer the light the deeper is their hatred. Yet everywhere the gospel goes we find open hearts inclined toward the light. (*Plains of Glory*, page 31)

Young women by the thousands are in the numerous tribes in these mountains, who would make as good Christians as these, and gladly, had they opportunity. Will not a loving God give them a chance hereafter, if not here? Why not? Justice demands it. Surely [the] Lord of all the earth will do right and always be no respecter of persons, but give all equal opportunity on this earth or in the First heaven. (Ibid., page 32)

This information about different levels within the spirit-world, where some people will be able to accept the Gospel and enter heaven while others reject it, will be completely rejected by most Christian theologians, but I believe it is true. (More information on this subject can be found in my next book, which goes much deeper into this subject; *The Fallen Ones: Angels, Humans, and Aliens*; coming out in 2024.)

Baker refers to different levels of the first heaven. I believe it is possible that heaven is made of at least three levels, and hell could also have multiple levels. (The Apostle Paul referred to three heavens, and there are seven heavens in 1 Enoch.) But, like the Apostle Paul said, on this Earth we cannot see what goes on after death clearly, as if looking through a dark glass.

Baker said:

> There are innumerable plains between the glory and light of highest heaven and the dimness and darkness of lowest hell." This is the intermediate realm, which we have called the First Heaven, or "no-man's plains." "In these plains," Sundar Singh says, "angels especially appointed for this work instruct the new arrivals for a time, that may be long or short, before they go to join the society of those spirits — good spirits in the greater light, or evil spirits in the greater darkness — that are alike in nature and mind to themselves. (page 27)

> According to revelations given to those caught up to heaven, the glorified Christians who have preceded us share also, to some extent, with the angels in ministering to the saints still on earth. . . those who have preceded us to glory are, at times, in unusual circumstances, permitted to return on short visits to the earth and in invisible ways like the angels, minister to the spiritual comfort and encouragement of relatives and friends.(Ibid., page 40)

It looks like there is, in fact, evidence that people do work with angels in heaven. We are not just sitting around playing harps. Is this where the belief that good people become angels comes from?

Christians who die go directly into the upper heaven. Mrs. Neer died May 10, 1908, in Colorado Springs, Colorado, but she is one of the rare ones who begged to return:

> "The end came quickly, [people] say there was no struggle, and to me there was none, only a misty, shadowy dampness which was soon passed over, and I was out into a beautiful light.

> "Such a change from death into life! Oh, that I could tell of the abundant life into which I entered, the boundlessness of life in Jesus. There was an intensity, an open vision which made true the words of Paul, 'Now we see through a glass darkly -- but then shall I know even as also I am known.' My life unraveled as a scroll before me from the time when I was about nine years old until the present time of sickness and death.

> "It was all there, except the sins, and though there had been many, yet true to God's precious Word, they were all blotted out.

> "This was what I saw: The works of righteousness which I had done -- the words I had spoken; the prayers offered; the testimonies given -- there they were before me. But how shallow and worthless they were. The intents and purposes of my heart were written plainly, and I found I had done them not alone -- as I supposed -- for Jesus' sake, but also as a work of my righteousness. I tried to turn from it, but I could not. I saw my life, which I had thought so full, was barren and empty. When it should have been yielded through the Spirit to work the works of Him that sent me, I had wrought my own way. With shame I turned from all to Jesus; and what a revelation! In contrast I beheld His life as He had come to me; His life so full, His hands overflowing, bringing me forgiveness and peace -- this was the Christ to whom I yielded so little of the life He had redeemed. Then to my wondering vision opened the possibilities of that abounding life through me for others.

> "With what shame and sorrow I saw the bruised, burdened lives of those He would have loosed through me -- the bowed heads, the broken hearts! Then I knew, 'No man liveth to himself and no man dieth to himself.' Sorrow wrapped itself around me. As I turned with bursting heart to Jesus, an agony which I cannot describe came over me. I could not, I must not pass on so empty. With strong crying and tears I pled to return to earth and continued to plead until I saw my prayer was answered.

"Then in a new way I gave myself to Him, and as I felt those wonderful eyes piercing the shallowness of the past, so I felt the eyes of love looking through the unseen of the future, and putting within the depths of my spirit a great yieldedness into His sweet will. Then with a look of love that brings tears of joy, as I recall it, a nail-pierced hand gently motioned me back. As my gladdened spirit turned earthward I could not but pause for one more look at my dear Redeemer. Through the love that surrounded me and filled my spirit I heard the command, 'Be thou faithful.' Then I quickly returned to earth and into my body amidst the rejoicing of those who had watched me pass out a short time before. And I was well. The same Living Word that had sent me back had spoken soundness into my body, and it was well, every whit.

"And how changed is my life since that day! He has given me the Holy Spirit to reveal the Christ and to teach me to do His perfect will. Could I speak a word more it would be, 'Yield yourselves unto God.'" (Baker, page 47-48)

Notice that she did not have her sins brought before her, yet she still suffered from shame and sorrow because of her lack of having lived as a truly Good Christian. She had been selfish and shallow. No doubt, wasting time and money on frivolous pursuits. How many years of a Christian's life do they spend watching TV? We are all guilty. Baker rightly observed:

It does appear however, that in heaven, as on earth, we shall keenly feel our unworthiness and we shall regret our failures in not having done as much for Jesus as we might have done. Who will escape some such regret? (Ibid., page 49)

However, it also appears that we will not live with the regret of our mistakes for all eternity; Sundar Sing said that shortly after arriving in heaven, we get washed from this. Baker quotes Sundar Sing:

"[We] bathe in the impalpable air-like waters within which they can move about as in open air and neither be drowned nor wet by them. By these waters the saved are cleansed and fully purified to enter the world of glory-light. These particular waters in which every new arrival in heaven must bathe <u>take away from the 'earth -life' the unlovely things that remain of earth -- bad memories,</u>

<u>harrowing remorse, goading regrets</u> for past sins and all the tendencies of the fallen nature, soul and spirit that would hinder perfect happiness and perfect love and development in heaven." (Baker, page 50)

Mrs. Spencer saw in heaven one remorseful man, who had not long before come from earth to one of the lower heavenly plains. This man had fallen into drunkenness and deep sin. Under the influence of drink and a bad woman, he had murdered his mother.

He repented and was saved. After his death when the angels took him to Paradise he was overwhelmed by a sense of utter unworthiness that a man, so sinful as he had been, who had never done anything for Jesus, should be allowed to enter this Paradise of indescribable glories. Saints and angels, who deal with those just arriving from earth, tried in vain to induce this man to bathe in the river of living waters that would enable him to cast off his "earth-life" remorse and advance to higher plains. He left too unworthy to advance, or even to live, in the glorious mansion to which he had been conducted. He declared utter unwillingness to meet Jesus, for he was so unworthy. Only when his murdered mother came from a higher plain to assure her son of her forgiveness did he consent to go with her to bathe in the waters that took away all his remorse and fully initiated him into the heavenly life. (Ibid., page 51)

One question that many people, Christians and nonChristians, desire to know is whether hell is eternal or not. Baker examined the Greek meaning of every word in the Bible that refers to hell and came to this conclusion:

I am aware of the various original words translated "hell." I have carefully and prayerfully considered every word in the Bible that means "Sheol", "Hades", "Gehenna", "Havernas", "grave" and "the pit." I have also studied all the passages in the Bible where the word, "season", meaning "age", occurs, and I am aware of the fact that the word translated "eternal" literally means "ages of ages." I have probably read about all that can be said on the "pros" and "cons" of the question as to whether or not the Bible teaches that hell is eternal.

After comparing scripture with scripture, my conviction is that hell is not absolutely eternal. The words in the Bible translated "eternal", "everlasting", "forever and forever", etc., mean "ages", or "ages of ages", as all know now who read a literal translation of the Word of God. Ages are said to have a beginning and there is the "end of the ages." Ages relate to time. The word does not actually mean "eternity." The blessings of the redeemed are usually expressed in measures of time; that is, in terms of "ages" or "ages of ages." The life of the redeemed is "eternal"; nevertheless, because the saved have become partakers of the divine nature through union with Jesus, who is eternal, they are in the eternal life of God which is His Holy Spirit who indwells all of the saved. The Bible view, however, is usually that of "time", both in relation to the lost and to the saved.

In that case, how long will "time" last? How long in terms of years is "ages of ages?" I do not know. In fact, I have hardly a guess. Some say an "age" is one thousand years. Some say "ages of ages" is twenty thousand years. Others say it might be a million years. Some think all this figuring is only guessing and theorizing without sufficient evidence to furnish real proof as to the length of "ages of ages." I agree with the latter. (Ibid., p. 65)

Here are a few more informative quotes from Baker's book:

In earth the sins of the body make impressions on the spiritual body within like carbon copies from external impressions. Thus when the spiritual body is released from the physical it carries into the regions below the impressions of the sin-distorted body, a witness saw.

In heaven spiritual bodies are clothed with a hundred aurora colors and hues of light. Where heaven and the angels are absent, everybody is an unlovely dark-colored specter or a mocking glitter of elusive phantoms. (Baker, page 73)

In China the idea of different plains in hell is taught in the well-known Chinese expression, "Shih bah tsen dy di iuh", "eighteen plains in hell." All over China the "hell temples" depict in gruesome horror what the wicked in hell suffer, tormented by devils, each in accord with his own misdeeds. . . .

Every Chinese who knows about these hell temples will tell you that the idols in the temples are images of what a certain emperor saw when led in spirit to see the realities of the underworld. The heathen and pagan from prehistoric times believed in hell, not because they imagined it, but because they had been allowed to see it. (Ibid., page 77) . . .

As I have written in my former book, Visions Beyond The Veil, the Lord so poured out the Holy Spirit on the children of our Chinese orphanage and gave such repeated and unmistakable God-sent visions of hell that I could as easily doubt my own existence as doubt the reality of hell as revealed in the Bible and seen by these present day witnesses. The children saw their acquaintances in hell. (Ibid., page 77)

Sundar Singh confirms what others have seen in visions, and repeats what we find in the Word of God about hell being a place of "weeping and wailing and gnashing of teeth." He says that: "from the lowest and darkest parts of the world of spirits a black and evil-smelling smoke rises, and in their effort to hide themselves from the light, these sons of darkness rush down and cast themselves headlong into it, and from it their bitter wails of remorse and anguish are heard constantly to rise." (Ibid., page 83)

Betty Malz was pronounced dead in the hospital in 1959. She described heaven as,

> . . . a bright and glorious place under a deep blue sky. There was no fear, only peacefulness and beauty. I was immediately aware of <u>majestic music, filled with exquisite harmonies from countless choirs</u>. Around my feet, living waves of flowers splashed the velvet green meadows with color. (Malz, *Angels by My Side* (p. 14-15). Kindle Edition.)

Others also describe heaven the same way. It seems that in heaven, music is everywhere, like the soundtrack in a movie, but it is not dramatic or heart-pounding, but always wonderful.

> I recognized people around the throne who had died during my lifetime, and they knew me. (Ibid., p. 16).

> I have since learned of many children from a variety of locations and backgrounds who have seen Jesus or an angel like Him. I have gathered stories of equal intensity from adults of all ages. . . . I discovered that <u>angelic intervention seems to happen when we face challenges that we are powerless to meet, such as when we are in danger and need safety, when we are helpless and need to</u>

be rescued, when we struggle with temptation and need strength. These are the kinds of instances when angels are on duty to obey God's commands for our deliverance. (Ibid., p. 35-36).

She said that her guardian angel was the same one who escorted her to heaven, was by her side from the time she converted to Christianity, and had saved her from several dangerous situations. The question I have is: was that statement said as an actual fact or just her opinion? It was not clear to me in the book. At least she was not claiming that all people everywhere have a guardian angel, like those in the New Age Movement. She said that all Christians have a guardian angel that will protect us from harm unless we behave recklessly, such as by flying a plane below power lines and buzzing cars on the highway, as one Christian man did and died in a plane crash. But I have already given examples of Christians who needed help but did not get it or would not have gotten it had not many prayers been said.

Even with those statements about angelic protection, her angel did not even warn her to seek medical help soon enough to avoid dying from a ruptured appendix that created gangrene and destroyed her internal organs. Why wouldn't the angel have stopped that from happening? I believe it was allowed to happen because she needed to go through all the suffering she went through: being in a coma for 44 days and dying in the hospital was part of her spiritual growth and development.

She gave many speeches about her death, trip to heaven, and recovery, and she said before this happened she had not been sick a day in her life, not even a headache, and she had a "disdain" for people with disabilities. It is strange that a Christian can have such a view of other people, but she changed and became a much more loving and caring person after her ordeal.

> "It was the greatest learning experience of my life. . . . I had to die to learn how to live. I cannot tell you how I suffered. The pain, the horrible pain . . . I never liked people until after this experience." (Youtube video, *My Glimpse of Eternity*)

She had a disdain for people with disabilities because, "*I had no understanding of suffering because I had never been sic.*" (Ibid.). This is just one example of how suffering can bring about great spiritual benefits. It is not Satan who wants people to grow into better people, but God. Do not listen to the false teachers who claim that a true Christian will not suffer cancer or go through other difficulties in this life.

Dale Black was a young man who was a real go-getter. He was a full-time college student and on his way to becoming a pilot. In July 1969, he was the only survivor of a small plane crash piloted by someone else. He was in a coma for three days with massive injuries. Slowly, during recovery, the memory of a trip to heaven came back to him. Like many other people, he had a life review, which occurred after he left his body but was still in the hospital. Only then did he travel through space to get to heaven. But it was not a tunnel, as others describe, but a path of light, as he tells in his book, *Flight to Heaven*:

> Outside of this pathway was total darkness. But in the darkness millions of tiny spheres of light zoomed past as I traveled through what looked like deep space, almost as if a jet were flying through a snowstorm at night, its light reflecting off the flakes as they blurred past.

He traveled "*at enormous speed*," and realized that there were two angels by his side, escorting him to heaven. They wore--

> . . . seamless white garments woven with silver threads. . . . Their skin tone was light golden brown and their hair fairly short. I could see their emotions, clearly delighted to be ushering me through this wonderland. . . . (page 98)

> I was fast approaching a magnificent city, golden and gleaming among a myriad of resplendent colors. The light I saw was the purest I had ever seen. And the <u>music was the most majestic, enchanting, and glorious</u> I had ever heard. . . .

> Somehow I knew I was made for this place and this place was made for me. . . . The colors seemed to be alive, dancing in the air. I had never seen so many different colors. . . . (page 99)

He knew that the light and love of heaven were somehow connected:

> It was as if the very heart of God lay open for everyone in heaven to bask in its glory, to warm themselves in its presence, to <u>bathe in its almost liquid properties so they could be restored, renewed, and refreshed</u>.

Remarkably, the light didn't shine on things but through them. . . . There was a huge gathering of angels and people, millions, countless millions. . . . Holiness hovered over them . . . During priceless moments of worship you are so enraptured by it that you don't miss the moment before or long for the moment after. Somehow the music in heaven calibrated everything . . . (page 100)

He saw a group of people wearing white robes who had come to welcome him, which he did not recognize and had not known on earth, but knew that they were--

my family — my spiritual family, my brothers, my sisters, spanning generations. . . . (page 107)

I did not notice racial differences, but I was aware that they had come from many tribes and nations. . . . (page 108)

Upon his return to Earth, he spent weeks in a wheelchair but eventually recovered and became an airline pilot and businessman with a Ph.D. in business and an M.A. in theology. What he saw was literal; this was not like a dream or vision, but reality. This is where we are going, and some people say this is where we came from. Notice that he called those people his "spiritual family." More on this later.

In another book on the same subject of his plane crash and trip to heaven, Dale wrote:

God is real – I know that for sure. But Satan is also real. And there is an eternal battle raging for every soul on planet earth, including yours. (Black, *Visiting Heaven,* page 146) . . .

In Heaven, light has substance. It does not dissipate at the end of its journey. Instead, it is absorbed gratefully by everyone and everything it touches. And it touches everything. With its touch, the light fills, satisfies, and rejuvenates with life, energy, and love. It has within it life – God's life. Light has within it love – perfect, complete love. This love is pure and true. (Ibid., page 166)

After he died but before going to heaven, he saw one of the other pilots who died but was being taken to hell; *"this soul was taken against its will, kicking and screaming, trying to get free"* (Ibid., page 143).

RaNelle Wallace also went to heaven because of a plane crash in 1984. She ignored many warnings from God about a future plane crash, and as a consequence, she was badly burned, died, and went to heaven. She was told she had to return even though she very much did not want to because of her serious burns, including having most of her face burned, and her lips and eyelids burned off.

One of the warnings she received was when she went with her husband, Terry, to look at a used V-tail Bonanza airplane:

> I went up to it and laid my hand on the wing, and a sudden chill ran from the top of my head to my toes. . . . Somehow I knew at that moment that this plane was a beautiful, immaculate death machine, that somehow it would become our tomb. I said, "We're going to die in this plane." (*The Burning Within*, Wallace, page 22)

But she let her husband repeatedly talk her out of following her premonitions, dreams, and the pleadings of others. At one point on the trip, she prayed, *"Let angels be on our wing tips. Let angels be on our wing tips. Please, Heavenly Father, let angels lift our wings and guide us down"* (Ibid., page 47). But they crashed anyway. Why didn't God send angels? Likely because he had already sent many warnings, which she ignored.

I will not give the entire story as it is much too long, but after the crash, she died in the ambulance. At first her spirit stayed in the ambulance, sitting next to her husband, who only had his hands burned. But then everything went dark, followed by being surrounded by lights. She could see that her body was now completely whole with no burns, which confused her. She thought she was experiencing the effects of morphine the paramedics had given her, then she began flying through a narrow tube that became very tight, which frightened her, and she traveled at "tremendous" speed.

> It felt as if I were whizzing past galaxies, but the colors and lights were right next to me, almost brushing against me . . . (page 92)

RaNelle then heard voices and realized that two men were traveling beside her and were talking about her. They paused the trip, and it was then that she had her life review. About her life-review, she said:

> It flashed before me with incredible rapidity, and I understood it completely and learned from it. (Ibid., page 91)

But she did not merely see the events in her life; she relived them:

> I was that person again, doing those things to my mother, or saying those words to my father or brothers or sisters, and I knew why, for the first time, I had done them or said them. . . . And I also understood the impact I had on others. (Ibid., page 92)

She realized that many bad things she had done were not shown to her because she had repented of them and had been forgiven.

> But then I saw other scenes that I hadn't anticipated, things that were just as awful. . . . I saw that I had let many people down in my life. I had made commitments to friends and family that . . . [were] unfulfilled. . . . (Ibid., page 92)

> Until that moment I had never realized that ignoring responsibilities was a sin. (page 93).

She not only experienced the pain she caused others, but she also saw the good that she did and how it affected people:

> I found myself wanting. Nobody was there to judge me. . . . I wanted to melt in the agony of self-indictment. (Ibid., page 94)

Notice that this is similar to the case above, where the lady begged to return because of her remorse. RaNelle then continued her journey, and as she approached heaven, she saw a speck of light in the distance that grew larger as she approached. The light became brighter than the sun, and then she was in the light, which changed her and was *"made pure"* by it. So, in effect, it washed her, as mentioned in other accounts above:

> "I basked in its sweetness, and the traumas of the past were far behind me, forgotten and transformed by peace." (Ibid., page 95)

She then met her grandmother, who appeared to be in her 20s and spoke without moving her lips, which has been reported by many others. In the spirit-world, people communicate telepathically. All you have to do is think of someone, and they are instantly transported to you to converse with, or you to them.

It was only after realizing that her grandmother was dead that she finally realized that she was also dead. Her grandmother became her guide and showed her around heaven (read her book for more details). In short, she saw the same things that many others have also reported about heaven, but she also saw and learned things that others have not reported.

She tells about a fellow named Jim who died in a car accident. She saw him in the distance but was not allowed to embrace him. There was some kind of gulf between them, even though he was only 10-12 feet away. She was told that Jim had lived a wrong life on Earth. So he had been given a choice and chose to stay, even at that lower level of light:

> He smiled, and I could feel his happiness. Although he didn't possess the same kind of light or power that my grandmother did, he seemed content. . . . (Ibid., page 97)

Jim chose to reject the truth and follow the wrong path by using and selling drugs. RaNelle said,

> And now, to the degree that he became spiritually dark, he is consigned to a similar degree of darkness — or lack of light — here in the spirit. (Ibid., page 98)

She said he can still grow and find some joy, but it is nothing like people who have "*more light.*"

> This is part of damnation, because his progress is limited. But he is choosing to grow. And he is happy. (Ibid., page 98)

RaNelle questioned her grandmother, who explained to her that no one forces truth upon us, and that we are self-governed and self-judged. It seems, based on many accounts, that even the life-review is not a judgment from God. However, how is it that people can know that the actions they took were evil if they did not believe they were evil when they did them? And yet God is not judging us? Clearly, when we are having the life review, we know just what is evil and what is not, more so than when we are on earth. Therefore, I believe, more to the point, that God does not condemn us. Only by God providing the total picture to us are we able to see and know the truth of our lives. So why isn't all of this in the Bible? Because it is absurd to expect the Bible to be 100,000 pages long!

Now, you may ask, why did he not go into total darkness and a burning hell, as we would expect, given that he was a drug dealer who harmed people? She said he did have some light; therefore, I can only surmise that since he was an acquaintance of RaNelle, who was a Christian, and he lived in the USA, where there are many

Christians, he likely attended church as a child or at least saw Billy Graham on TV several times. He may have even prayed the sinner's prayer, but he chose to live in sin. And because he did not live a Christian life, he would never be able to go into the upper heavens with real Christians.

So, it appears that he was consigned to the upper regions of hell, which do not contain torment or fire. If he were merely in the lower regions of heaven, it seems that there should not have been a gulf. It also appears he is able to grow as a spirit-being while in that region.

Theologians will have fits with this information because, to them, you are either going to burn in hell for eternity or be in heaven; with no place in between. They ignore any thought of lower levels of heaven or several levels of hell.

Here is an account of spiritual Paradise. In 1972, Dr. Richard Eby fell off a balcony when the railing came loose, landed on concrete, and busted his head open; then was instantly in Paradise. You do not need to travel through space to get to Paradise, which is not heaven. He describes it in detail, including the spiritual grass and flowers and the wonderful music. He said that Jesus told him that Paradise was now a holding place for dead Christians until the Rapture. If this is the case, then the people who have died and gone to heaven, went there only because God knew they would be coming back to earth; otherwise, they would have gone to Paradise. However, they saw their dead relatives. This is the only issue with his story that, otherwise, rings true.

Five years later, he was practicing medicine in Pomona Valley, California. When the churches there heard about the accident and how he had been to Paradise and came back to life, they told him not to attend their churches because he might disturb their doctrines.

Then he went on a tour in Israel and was inside the tomb of Lazarus when the light bulb went out. At that point, Jesus took him out of his body and told him he was going to hell for only two minutes. He saw many tiny demons that taunted him for being foolish enough to end up in hell, and the smell was beyond horrible. Then Jesus told him that after he (Jesus) returns to earth, hell will be thrown into the Lake of Fire and will no longer exist. The book of Revelation says:

> Then Death and Hades were cast into the lake of fire. This is the second death. (Rev. 20:14)

Dr. Eby eventually told his story many times on TV and video and wrote a book called, *Caught Up to Paradise.* I saw him on TBN and read the book.

In 1991, Mike Crotts of Conyers, Georgia, was a real estate millionaire and running for the state senate when he walked outside of his press secretary's office and collapsed on the sidewalk. Medics and a nurse saw him fall and immediately began medical treatment. He was taken to the hospital and revived, but eventually died five days later.

> As my lifeless body was laying on the sidewalk, my spirit had crossed over into another dimension. I was clinically dead in my flesh, but alive in my spirit. Surprisingly, this death transition was as easy as walking through a door from one room to another, with no pain whatsoever. I can totally relate to the scripture, "O death, where is thy sting? O grave, where is thy victory?" (1 Cor. 15:55). I suddenly found myself in the most beautiful, magnificent garden with indescribable colors and clarity. The waters flowed in rippling brooks through the adjoining gardens and were crystal clear; the colors of the flowers, grass, trees, and the blue skies were more vivid like none I have ever seen. This place was breathtaking! On the horizon, were hills and mountains that radiated with an almost blinding light behind them, like a sunrise, I could feel it drawing me there. As I floated through the meadow . . . (*Dead For 34 Minutes*, Mike Crotts, page 52)

> There was an overwhelming God-consciousness that enveloped my being and I found myself sitting down by a brook that ran through this beautiful garden. I sat down to talk with Him, my God, my Father, my Creator, in the cool of the day, just as Adam had done and it changed my life. (page 96)

But he did not travel through space, and he shortly learned it was because he did not go to heaven but to the Garden of Eden; likely another name for Paradise. (According to Jewish tradition, there is both an earthly and a heavenly Garden of Eden.) He came back to life after his wife commanded him to come back *in the name of Jesus*! But he was not immediately well when he came back to life, but had to heal, like most people who die and come back.

It seems that many people have similar experiences, but many others have totally different experiences. Freddy Vest, a part-time cowboy and home builder, had finished his calf-roping at a rodeo and was sitting on his horse when he suddenly died of a heart attack. He fell off his horse, hitting the ground with a thud. He believes he was instantly in heaven; however, he did not go to Paradise, and did not travel through space, and did not see any angels or any noticeable parts of heaven; he was merely in the presence of Jesus and was enraptured with his love. Therefore, I believe he was merely out of his body, and Jesus was here with him. Jesus then showed him lights shooting up to heaven like lightning bolts or powerful fireworks and exploding into super bright light. All those shooting lights were prayers that were going up for him!

> If I had imagined the most astounding light show on Earth, and then multiplied it exponentially, it would not have matched the wonder of what I saw. Knowing that the bolts were prayers made the heavenly display even more striking. (Vest, *The Day I Died,* page 68-69)

He had a very large family, with 17 brothers and sisters. With all of their spouses, children, and church families praying, there were probably thousands of people praying for him. After seeing all the prayers going up, he was suddenly back inside his body in the hospital.

How is it that some people go to heaven when they die, but others go to Paradise? It all depends on what God wants to show them during their NDE, since they will be come back to Earth.

***

Maurice S. Rawlings was an emergency room doctor for many years but was only a "social club" Christian until one day he was working on a patient that kept dying and coming back to life as CPR was performed. Charles McKaig died several times as they were attempting to revive him and get him stabilized. Then he yelled out,

> *"Don't stop! I'm in hell! I'm in hell! . . . For God's sake, don't stop! Don't you understand? Every time you let go I'm back in hell!"* (Rawlings, *To Hell and Back,* page 40, 41).

Dr. Rawlings knew enough to lead the patient in a prayer about believing that Jesus is the Son of God and giving his life to him. After that, he no longer went to hell. This not only caused Rawlings to convert to real Christianity, but he also began researching NDEs. He studied all types, including those spiritual experiences where people do not actually die, but are merely near death. He noted the many different types of after-life experiences, and came to understand that spiritual deception can continue even after death. This is an important observation that has also been noted by other researchers.

With the popularity of Youtube, many channels now exist that tell the stories of NDEs, some from published books, others from websites that allow users to post their own personal NDE. And as you might expect, some of them claim there is no God, or that there is no heaven or hell, and that we all go to a nice place, etc. Though some stories could be lies, there is significant evidence that deception continues during NDEs.

He found that the positive experiences are remembered and told, but the hell experiences are usually not remembered or, at least, not admitted to. He found there are indeed hell experiences, but they came mostly from the doctors, nurses, and EMTs who were working on the patient at the time, just as he witnessed. Rawlings said:

> It is my contention after reviewing many cases that Satan could appear as Lucifer, the angel of light, to deny and reject the existence of evil, and thereby show that everything is good and okay out there. (Ibid., page 46)

I had always believed that Apostle Paul was referring to false angelic visits, like those mentioned in previous chapters, when he said that Satan appears *"as an angel of light"* (2 Cor. 11:14); but after what I learned while researching this book, I now believe that Paul likely was speaking of NDEs. Satan appears to people who have died as a being of light and tells them lies, and they return and spread those lies. The experience is so powerful that, after the experience, they are practically immune to being converted to the truth.

One fellow on YouTube, I will call him Joe, told how he was raised in a religious home, but when he got to college, he was drinking heavily, just like his friends. Joe said he walked outside and passed out drunk at a frat party; then he left his body and saw this being of light. Joe asked him who he was, and he said, *"You know me as Jesus,"* so he was claiming to be other religious leaders as well, such as Buddha, Krishna, etc.

Joe said this being told him he was not using his life wisely and offered him two different paths he could take in life, and one path was to become a social worker, which would benefit humanity. Joe returned to his body and became a social worker, but he also left behind his traditional religious beliefs. Notice that there is no evidence that Joe actually died. There was no accident, nor was he in the hospital. Nor did he see any of his dead relatives.

So this appears to be an example of Satan appearing as a being of light to bring about deception. And this also means that this same type of thing was happening during the time of Apostle Paul. This likely happened to Joe because he opened himself up to it by his sinful behavior. Also, he may have only been attending church, but had not actually been converted.

Dr. Rawlings noticed that in the NDEs in which people saw a light being of love and wisdom who told them to love each other and be good people, the dead person did not see any deceased loved ones, angels, or heaven, etc. So this is actually an indication that it is Satan.

God has given Satan to be the *"god of this world,"* (2 Cor. 4:4), but that apparently means more than just having authority over world events and individuals to do evil; it also means he has authority in the spirit world over Fallen souls.

Isaiah 14:12, in the KJV says, *"How art thou fallen from heaven, O Lucifer, son of the morning!"* Because of this verse, many people believe that Satan's name is Lucifer, but that is not the correct translation. Other translations say:

* shining star
* day-star
* shining one
* morning star

This accurately identifies Satan as a being of light, which is often seen during NDEs. Genesis 3:1, says, *"Now the serpent was more crafty than any other beast of the field that the LORD God had made"* (ESV).

> The Hebrew word rendered "serpent" in Genesis 3:1 is Nachash (from the root Nachash, *to shine*, and means a shinning one. (*The Companion Bible*, E. W. Bullinger, Appendix 19)

There must be a reason he is referred to as shining like a star. In John 8:44, Jesus said Satan is a murderer, liar, and deceiver:

> "He was a murderer from the beginning, and <u>does not uphold the truth</u>, because there is <u>no truth in him</u>. Whenever he lies, he speaks according to his own nature, because he is a liar and <u>the father of lies</u>."

Satan not upholding the truth? Speaking lies? Satan and demons can put thoughts into people's minds, but their words have been written down in the teachings of Buddha, Krishna, the Dali Lama, and the New Age channelers, who literally DO IN FACT receive messages from light-beings. But it is NOT TRUTH they receive.

But Satan does not appear to all non-Christians who die. Perhaps he is not able to appear to all of the many souls that die every minute of every day, but he selects certain ones in hopes of preventing them from believing the Gospel after they have had their NDE.

But once someone becomes a true Christian, only then do they actually go to heaven during an NDE. Some people do in fact go to hell during NDEs because they have heard the Gospel but rejected it, or did not have true faith in Christ.

Several videos on YouTube tell the story of Peter Panagore, who was ice climbing in Canada in 1980 and apparently froze to death on a mountain. He saw a "light-being" that sent out love and gave him a life review, but that is as close as it gets to Christian NDEs. He did not see the gates of heaven, his dead relatives, or angels. And when he came back, he did not become a good Christian, but pursued eastern mysticism and meditation. Notice that this is another case of no paramedics, no hospital, etc. He merely came back to life.

This NDE has all the markings of one conducted by the Shining One. Although at one point Peter said he wanted to stay, he chose to return because his death at age 21 would break his parents' hearts. But in another video, he said:

> The voice accompanying me urged me to choose. I yearned for a tangible human experience, to revel in the joys and sorrows, and to channel the divine light in everyday life. I craved a life filled with creativity and fulfillment. Ultimately, I made my choice. I desired to live as an ordinary, flawed human being. I longed to experience life's pleasures, to explore my desires, and to share my love with others. It was a conscious decision to embrace the human experience fully. (His NDE Caused Him To Abandon Religion, https://youtu.be/6PXM5-ZYgvc (Heaven Awaits, channel))

People who actually experience heaven Never, Never, Never, say they want to return to Earth <u>to live out the human experience or "life's pleasures</u>." (Those who experience a genuine NDE and want to return do so because they have seen their failings and want to do better, or because of family.) The New Age light-being is a cheap counterfeit of the real thing. An encounter with genuine Divine Light causes people to do much more than seek peace and harmony with others when they return; it causes them to KNOW for a fact that the only way you will get into heaven is through worship and obedience to Yahweh, and his son Jesus.

> (There is lots of evidence that good Jews go to heaven as well. Jesus said that not one jot or tittle of the Law would pass away until all is fulfilled, and all has not been fulfilled. (Mat. 5:18) Therefore, it means those who follow the Law can get to heaven; perhaps not the top level.)

God has allowed Satan to become a god-like being on this planet; so he appears as this all-knowing light-being and fools people into believing he is the real God of the universe. People encounter this light-being that appears to be truly awe-inspiring; and seems to be full of great wisdom, but it is not God. Ezekiel 28 tells us that Satan had great wisdom, but it became corrupted wisdom: *"you have corrupted your wisdom by reason of your brightness."*

Most Christians believe that there are only two opposite pole categories of spirit-beings: holy angels and God, and the opposites are Satan and demons. But there is another category of spirits that are often called demons but are not, which are *"familiar spirits."*

Demons are vile, ugly, smelly, mean, and nasty, and they want to attack and inhabit humans. The Bible does not tell us the origin of demons, but the Book of Enoch tells us that they are the souls of the giants, the Nephilim, who were killed in Noah's Flood. But *familiar spirits* will not attack you but will actually work with humans. These are the spirit guides, the New Age angels, etc. These spirits work with Satan, and they are like little Shining Ones. They even work with magicians.

During the TV special of well-known magician David Blaine, he went into the home of actor Harrison Ford. He handed Ford a deck of playing cards and asked him to think of a card. Then he said, "That card has just left the deck." Harrison looked through the deck and did not find it. David then asked if he could cut open one of his pieces of fruit that were lying on the kitchen counter. The fruit was cut open, and inside was the rolled-up playing card. The first words out of Harrison Ford's mouth were, *"Get the f--- out of my house."* Ford knew that it was not a mere trick but some sort of real magic, which is done with familiar spirits. This can be seen on YouTube (*Harrison Ford Finds Card in Orange: Real or Magic*).

Now, the experiences that people have when they die are real. They really see a light-being that sends out love and wisdom and claims to be the creator; this is why it is such a powerful deception. <u>The experience is real, but it is not the truth</u>. Likewise, New Age channelers receive messages from these same light beings. The Bible speaks against consulting psychic mediums or the spirits of the dead (Deut. 18:11; Lev. 20:6; 20:27). These spirits have deceived many lukewarm Christians.

***

Dannion Brinkley is well-known for writing a book about his NDE in 1975 called *Saved By The Light*. He has deceived many people with books full of falsehoods. Here are a few quotes from one of his video interviews:

> "Only the best of the best get a chance to come here. There might be a billion beings waiting to be born at that moment, through that female, coming in this earth. And in the last moments, before birth is when who it is that got chosen to come, enters this life. . . . We can procreate, so that makes us gods. God creates; we can create life. . . . (We never Die: What are we doing in this Dimension? - Interview with Dannion Brinkley, Mindalia TV - English. March 26, 2018)

Are chimps God? Are fish God? They can reproduce, so they must be God, LOL. I do not know if he is telling lies to sell books or if he really believes his nonsense, but what he said above is way off-base; the spirit does NOT enter the body at birth. That is totally false; it either enters at conception or at heartbeat. (I won't take the space to present the evidence here, but any thinking person should be able to understand that.) At the very least, the poor man has been deceived by the shining light and is trying to give reasons to accept abortion.

***

Ingrid Honkala is a very nice lady who was born and raised in Bogota, Columbia. When she was almost three years old, she fell into a tank of water and drowned. The family maid was listening to soap operas and did not know what had happened.

During her NDE, Ingrid was able to travel from one place to another just by thinking about it. She was in the air above her mother when her mother suddenly knew that something was wrong at home, and started running back.

Ingrid was then surrounded by a bright light that sent out peace and love. She noticed that her body was just light, the same as the larger being of light, and that she had been in that state before. *"I sensed that I was coming back home."* She also saw other light beings while she was dead, but did not have the full NDE experience of a life review, etc.

Then she saw her mother arrive and begin to resuscitate her. Suddenly, she felt vacuumed back into her body. But she did not want to come back, had trouble adjusting, and did not even feel like a kid, but as an equal with her parents. She badly wanted to return to the light, and began to throw tantrums.

Eventually, she began to see the light beings during out-of-body experiences (astral projection). The gold-colored light beings were shaped like humans, but all the others were just balls of colored light. The beings gave her comfort and guidance, and told her that some day she would help people understand the spirit world; this stopped the tantrums. They told her that some day everyone will be able to see the beings of light like she does. She said,

> Did you see a video, went to a conference, or met someone? This is all the ways in which, actually, we are getting guidance from the universe. We are being guided. We are getting what we need, at the moment when we need it; and depending in how ready we are for it. (*How my NDE gave me access to Beings of Light - Part2*, her Youtube channel)

She asked them if they were angels, and they said, *"if that is what you want us to be."* Even though her family was officially Catholic, her mother could see spirits, but a different kind of spirit (she did not explain further). Her grandmother, who was into mysticism and meditation, taught her how to meditate at age 8, which she continued doing thereafter. Ingrid thinks more of the Dali Lama than she does of Jesus.

Even with all this spiritual "truth," guidance, meditation, etc., she wanted to commit suicide in her late teens. The light beings told Ingrid that she was chosen to be a teacher; that she needed to teach others about the spirits, meditation, and such. At age 19, Ingrid finally told the light beings that she did not want any of it because she wanted to be normal. The light beings told her that, in twenty years, she would return to them.

During those years, she became a marine biologist and worked for the US government, but all the while she had <u>many troubles and sorrows</u>, and so she finally gave up and submitted to the light beings. Then she wrote a book called, *A Brightly Guided Life*, and has a website and YouTube channel to spread the message of the light-beings.

She believed everything she saw because she experienced it, but she had no solid grounding in the teachings of true Christianity. She is not able to see that just because some light being tells you something, it does not make it true. Nor does it mean that they are the creators of the universe.

Satan is the god of this world, and he is very cunning in his deception. He not only has demons and Satan-worshipers who sacrifice children to him, but he also has beautiful light beings who send out love. But they are not Yahweh God or his angels.

Finally, you may be wondering how this happened to her. How did Satan have the authority to do this? How did he choose her to become a teacher when she did not want to do it? Remember, her grandmother and mother were into the spiritualism and Eastern mysticism stuff, so this indicates that they opened the door for it.

Dr. Maurice S. Rawlings rightly summed up the problem of people accepting whatever they happen to experience in the spirit world:

> It's strange that the average person doesn't bother to investigate spiritual forgery. People will gratefully accept bogus spirits although they would be furious if someone tried to pass them bogus money. Probably the spiritual gullibility of man is why God specifically forbade man from contacting ghosts, guides, mediums, enchanters, or fortune-tellers (Deut. 18:10-12).

> The popularity of spirit entities has returned. Most of the original NDE researchers and authors are now routinely calling up the dead and doing business with spirit entities. And they don't even know who these entities are. Anyone can be deceived in any experience unless the source of the spirit has been specifically identified or tested.

> The test is simple enough. No matter how kind and considerate,

evil spirits will invariably avoid or deny that Jesus Christ is the only Son of God. But seldom is the test administered, the victim overcome by glorious surroundings. (*The Hell and Back*, page 242-243)

***

The last story is that of Kat Dunkle, who had a bad childhood back in the 1960s. Her father was an alcoholic and abused her mother. She wanted to get away, so she married at 17 to an alcoholic; the next husband was at 19. So life was not good. She visited several churches but did not get the answers she was looking for, so she became a solid atheist. One day she walked outside and looked up into the sky and said, "*God, if you are really there, just give me one year to know what it's like to really feel loved.*" Then he could take everything from her, even kill her; she did not care. But she believed it would not happen.

She left her husband in Kansas City and drove an old beat-up car to Seattle, Washington, where she had relatives, but that did not turn out well either, so she ended up in government housing. She and her two sons slept in sleeping bags on the floor, but she soon got a job and got married to a handsome and kind man with a good job. Kat had a nice home and an incredible life. She got the great year that she wanted at 23 years old.

Exactly one year later, she and her husband had their first bad argument. Then her father died of a heart attack, and her husband's real estate business was going bankrupt. But worst of all, her middle son, Mark, was hit by a car and killed, which devastated her, causing her to almost commit suicide. Then she and her husband, Don, had a horrible fight and were literally hitting each other. She left the house in the car and began having horrible pain in her chest. Kat managed to get back home, and Don drove her to the hospital.

The medical people said because her blood pressure was dropping, they needed to operate to find out why, because there could be internal bleeding. Not long after being on the table, she died.

At first, she went into a tunnel, then she saw Don and some other people who were standing by a street lamp and crying because she had died. But they could not yet have been told. I am sure the doctors were still busy working on her on the table. Therefore, she was seeing a vision, just like a normal human might see a vision. So, like some other NDEs given above, this was a visionary NDE.

Kat was told that *"they will be just fine."* She saw some other people who had concerned looks on their faces. She then moved on through the tunnel, and the thought came to her, *"There is no God."* But just as suddenly, she knew that God existed. *"I knew, that I knew, that I knew; God does exist."* She then experienced overwhelming peace and happiness.

Then the thought came to her, *"There is no heaven."* And she saw a burst of brilliant light and began moving toward it, knowing she was moving toward heaven. She was willing to leave her husband and children to go to this place, but she never made it there.

Suddenly, she started dropping like the floor had fallen away, and she knew she was falling into hell. Kat felt totally separated from everyone, "especially God." She did not see flames but felt the burning pain of the flames. There was no light, just total darkness that she knew would last forever. She also heard the screams of other people and knew that she had put herself there. But she cried out to God, asking forgiveness, because she now knew that he existed. But she also believed that she would not be released from hell.

But then suddenly, she started going backward through the tunnel and knew that she was about to re-enter her body. *"I was clinging to the feeling of being with God, and wanting that so desperately, but knowing that I was going to go back. And I heard an audible voice saying, 'Bring people to me.'"* Then she was in the operating room, screaming, "GOD IS REAL, GOD IS REAL." And she was not referring to some being of light.

She became a solid Christian and has spoken many times about her experience, and many years later she wrote a book about it titled, *"Is it Safe to Die?: A Memoir of Death-to-Life, Second Chances, and Redemption."*

Now, notice that God did not tell her to join any particular denomination. He did not even tell her to become a Christian. But after this experience, if someone had not known anything about Christianity, but merely investigated the different religions to find one that most reflected the truth she learned in the NDE, then Christianity was the only option. The other religions do not believe in heaven or hell. (www.round tripdeath. com/243-kats-nde-changes-her-from-atheist-to-christian/) (*Kat Dunkle lived as an atheist until she died. Her NDE changed everything ... forever.* YouTube)

***

A very interesting NDE is that of Daniel Ekechukwu, of Nigeria. Daniel was a pastor when he had an automobile accident on November 30th, 2001, and was dead for about 42 hours. He visited Paradise and hell and came back to life when his body was taken into the basement of Grace of God Mission Church in Onitsha, Nigeria, where evangelist Reinhard Bonnke was preaching.

Daniel and his wife, Nneka, had an argument during which she slapped him. This greatly offended him, and he resisted attempts to reconcile the next morning. During that day, he remained angry with her and was planning to tell her a few things when he returned home, but he never made it back.

He and a friend drove from Onitsha to a village outside of Owerri to deliver a Christmas gift, when the brakes on the twenty-year-old car failed while driving down a steep hill. The car crashed into a stone pillar, seriously injuring them both. He was rushed to the closest hospital and put into intensive care, but when his wife arrived, he told her to take him to his personal doctor.

On the way to the other clinic, Daniel told his wife that he was going to die. But before he actually did, he saw two angels arrive in the ambulance. Once they arrived at the clinic, he was pronounced dead by Dr. Josse Annebunwa. Daniel's wife did not know what to do, so she took the body to his father, who took the body and wife to the mortuary, run by Mr. Barlington R. Manu. He also testified that Daniel was dead.

Daniel said one of the angels took him to Paradise, where he saw *"multitudes of people who looked like the one who was with me. Their bodies were pure white and were dressed in white apparel."* He asked the angel if they were angels, and the angel said, no: *"They are the saints who have died."* The saints were singing praises to God. He also heard a lot of musical instruments. The angel then showed him the mansion that Jesus had prepared for them, and even the flowers around the mansion were singing praises to God.

Next, he was taken to hell, where he saw all races:

> "They were shouting and there was a lot of pain, a lot of torment. They didn't act as if they could see the angel, only me, and they were asking me for help. I never saw any fire or flames in hell, but the torment looked as if the people were inside a fire." (www.tampa bay .com/archive/2003 /12/20/ resurrection-story-inspires-crowd/)

Daniel saw a man there who shouted at him, *"I'm a Pastor. I only stole church money, and I'm ready to refund immediately."* He was asking Daniel if he might have another chance and said, *"The request of the rich man in hell had been granted to this generation, for the last warning."* Later, when Daniel came back to life and read that passage again, he realized that the rich man in hell had requested that someone come back from the dead to warn others about hell. (*Raised from the Dead*, "lolchristianvhs" YouTube channel, Jan. 20, 2012)

Retired minister, David Servant, personally interviewed Daniel to get more of his story:

> [Daniel] told me of several specific groups that went through endless cycles of torment, held captive to the same sins they practiced on earth. One group consisted of people who would eat their own flesh and then vomit it out onto the ground, at which time the vomit would fly back onto their bodies and turn back into flesh that they would eat again. The angel told Daniel these people were those who had eaten human flesh as an occult practice. (Such things occur in Africa all the time.) Another group, who had stolen land from others while on earth, endlessly dug rock-hard ground with their bare hands. . . .

> The most surprising thing is what happened next. The escorting angel told pastor Daniel, "<u>If your record is to be called here, you will in no doubt be thrown into hell</u>." Pastor Daniel immediately defended himself saying, "I am a man of God! I serve Him with all my heart!" But a Bible appeared in the angel's hand, and it was opened to Matthew 5 where Jesus warned that if one calls his brother a fool he is guilty enough to go into the hell of fire (see Matt. 5:21-22). Pastor Daniel knew he was guilty for the angry words he had spoken to his wife. The angel also reminded him that Jesus promised that God will not forgive our sins if we do not forgive others (see Matt. 6:14-15), because <u>we will reap what we have sown. Only those who are merciful will obtain mercy</u> (Matt 5:7). The angel told Daniel that the prayers he prayed as he was dying in the hospital were of no effect, because he refused to forgive his wife even when she attempted to reconcile on the morning of his fatal accident. (*Resurrection from the dead of pastor Daniel Ekechukwu*, www.davidservant.com /articles/daniel _main/ resurrection-from-the-dead-pastor-daniel-ekechukwu/)

So Daniel saw that what people suffered in hell was based on their sins while on Earth. This agrees with what other people have reported about hell.

The mortician never completed the embalming process but laid the body aside in the rear of the mortuary. Some hours later, Nneka took the body into the basement of the church pastored by Dr. Paul Nwachkwu Sr., while Reinhard Bonnke was preaching. Nneka believed for a miracle. She knew that God could raise Daniel from the dead.

During the service, Reinhard Bonnke prayed for the sick, but he knew nothing about the dead man in the basement. After some minutes passed, those who were praying around the body noticed the body twitch and begin to breathe. The people in the church were informed about the dead man who had come back to life, and they gave a great shout, at which Daniel suddenly rose up. He was then taken upstairs so people could see him.

After that experience, Daniel said he became more afraid of missing heaven, and made a great effort to not have disagreements with his wife. (*Raised from the Dead*, lolchristianvhs YouTube channel, Jan. 20, 2012)

The really sad part is that modern-day Pharisees have declared this story to be "*deception in the church*"! Sandy Simpson at www.deceptioninthechurch.com/bonnke2.html said, "*I smell a rat!*" Most of them are those who teach that a Christian cannot commit a sin that will keep them out of heaven (*Eternal Security*, or *Once Saved, Always Saved*). They cannot accept any suggestion that God will send a Christian to hell for any reason.

John Calvin hanged a man named Michael in the public square because he disagreed with his doctrines. There are many modern-day Calvinists who are following in Calvin's footsteps and are still hanging people in the public square because of disagreement over doctrines. You can find their many videos on YouTube. (It is good to speak against <u>false</u> doctrine, but these Calvinists speak against doctrines that are clearly taught in the Bible as being genuine, such as miracles, dreams, visions, speaking in tongues, appearances of angels, etc.)

The request of the rich man that someone come back from the dead could refer to more than just the NDE of Daniel, because there have been literally hundreds of NDEs over the past few decades.

***

A more recent NDE took place when Gerald A. Johnson, the lead pastor of *Faith Culture Church* in Austin, Texas woke up in the night with sharp pains in his chest, in February 2016. He started praying, but then died of a heart attack. He floated up out of his body, and believed he was heading toward heaven when he was suddenly pulled into hell.

> "I heard people screaming in agony all around me and then I just landed there in hell. I did not see fire . . . but I could feel heat all around me. And I started thinking to myself, 'How did I end up here?' I knew exactly where I was." (www.the-sun. com/ news/7353318/preacher-near-death-experience-rihanna-hell-superbowl/ *Pastor who 'went to hell' makes major update on his claims that Rihanna's music was 'being sung by a demon'* The U.S. Sun, Feb 17 2023)

Pastor Johnson saw things that agree with the previous NDE. He saw a naked man on his hands and knees with a chain around his neck, being led around by a demon.

> "Nobody said anything but I knew telepathically that the demon holding the man's chain had been assigned to that man's life while he was on Earth. And the demon had an agenda that if he could stay in the man's life while he was on Earth, if he could ride him and keep him bound, the goal was that he'll have the man be his slave in the afterlife -- and that's exactly what that man was." (Ibid.)

He saw another section of hell where music was playing, and he knew that it was the same music that is played here on Earth, but words were being sung by demons.

> "But every lyric, whatever it was meant to do on Earth it did the opposite in hell. If music was meant to get you over a breakup or whatever, then down there it would be used to torment you about that relationship." (Ibid.)

After hearing the demonic music, he returned to his body, and then Jesus spoke to him about his own sins. He had been badly hurt some years back, and had been secretly hoping that God would hurt the people who hurt him. Johnson said his NDE changed him forever. He learned that *"unforgiveness is a big deal."*

Take notice of the last two NDEs; each one had a pastor go to hell, and they were told that if they had fully died, they would be in hell because of unforgiveness. And Pastor Daniel saw another pastor in hell for stealing money. True events such as these make me repent and walk closer to God, which is the very reason God has given them to us.

***

Many books have been written about heaven and hell by people who have died and many who have not. Though some people have indeed gone to heaven without dying, I would stay away from any claims of having gone to heaven without having died, unless the person was in a coma or on the operating table, simply because of the chances of it being false. There are so many liars and deceiving spirits in the world, so you cannot trust those accounts. These FAKE books have probably sold millions of copies. One book claims there is a roller coaster in heaven, LOL. It is strange that it was never seen by anyone who actually died!

What you have read in this book is a little deep, but not extremely deep, and yet many people are not able to accept it because they can only believe what their preacher tells them to believe. Or what is clearly seen in the Bible, or what they see on Christian TV shows. But even people who are able to accept it may find my next book above their heads; *The Fallen Ones: Angels, Humans, and Aliens*. It deals with some really deep stuff, so if you cannot handle it, I understand; don't worry about it. Not believing the truth won't change anything that is true.

Many people are turning away from Christianity because they are critical thinkers who do not believe something just because they are told to believe it. The idea that God is going to send billions of people to burn in hell for eternity merely because they were born on Earth does not make good sense to them. But that is the best doctrinal explanation that theologians have been able to come up with to explain the Fall of Man in the Garden.

In *The Fallen Ones*, I provide a much better explanation of why God sends people to hell, when the Fall took place, why it took place, and how it took place. Even why God created this planet in the first place (and it was not so we could worship him). Like I said, it is really deep, and even includes aliens! Unfortunately, most

Christians still put aliens in the same category as fairies and goblins. There is <u>no other book or video with the explanations that I give</u> in *The Fallen Ones*!

Unlike some Christian teachers, I am not going to say that you must believe this information in order to get into heaven. For example, I don't believe that you must believe in the Rapture of the Bride in order to go in the Rapture; and I don't believe that you must believe in the doctrine of Salvation by Grace in order to be Saved by Grace. Accept what truth you can and move on. Some people grow very wise in this life; others only grow a little. If you think you can handle it, then do read *The Fallen Ones,* which I expect to be published probably by September or October 2024.

Selected Bibliography

Ambrose, Isaac. *War With Devils: Ministration of, and Communion with Angels*, Glasgow, 1769.

Angels on Earth magazine by Guideposts, several different editions.

Baker, H. A. *Plains of Glory and Gloom*. Osterhus Publishing House. (PDF version 2017)

Barrett, Sir William. *Death-Bed Visions*. Methuen & Co. LTD: London, 1926.

Bell, Charles D. *Angelic Beings: Their Nature and Ministry*. The Religious Tract Society: London, 1875.

Ben-Amos, Dan and Jerome R. Mintz; transltors and editors. *In Praise of the Baal Shem Tov, Rowman & Littlefield Publishers, Inc.: New York, 1993*.

Berrow, Capel. *A Lapse of Human Souls in a State of Pre-Existence, The Only Original Sin, And the ground work of the Gospel Dispensation.* London, 1776.

Black, Dale. *Flight to Heaven*. Bethany House: Minneapolis, 2010.

Black, Dale. *Visiting Heaven. Secrets of Life After Death.* Sovereign House: Carlsbad, CA, 2018.

Brewer, E. Cobham. *A Dictionary of Miracles*. Chatto & Windus: London, 1901.

Burnham, Sophy. *Angel Letters.* Wellspring/Ballantine; 1st Edition (October 23, 1991).

Carter, Katherine Pollard. *Hand on the Helm.* Whitaker House: Springdale, PA, 1977.

Clayton, Jr., George. *Angelology*, Henry Kernot: New York, 1851.

Connolly, David. *In Search of Angels*. Pedigree Books: New York, 1993.

Contemporary Cases of Miraculous Help. Translated from Russian by Tatiana Pavlova and Natalia Semyanko. From the book of the Klin parish — the Moscow Eparchy of the Russian Orthodox Church. 'The

Christian Life' fund, 1998. The internet issue of the Web-Center 'Omega', Moscow, 2001. https://father alexander. org/booklets /english/ chudesa_e .htm)

Crotts, Mike. *Dead For 34 Minutes*. Rising Star Publications, McDonough, GA, 2018.

Dennis, Clyde H. Editor. *These Live On*. Good News Publishers: Westchester, IL, 1966.

Dryden, Mrs. S. H. *Daisy Dryden: A Memoir*. Colonial Press: Boston, 1909.

Freeman, Eileen Elias. *Angelic Healing: Working with Your Angel to Heal Your Life*. Warner Books: New York, 1994.

Freeman, Eileen Elias. *Touched by Angels: True Cases of Close Encounters of the Celestial Kind*. Warner Books: New York, 1993.

Gaebelein, A.C. *What The Bible Says About Angels*. Baker Bookhouse: Grand Rapids, 1987.

Garlow, James, and Wall, Keith. *Real Life Real Miracles*, Bethany House: Minneapolis, MN, 2012.

Goforth, Rosalind. *How I Know God Answers Prayer: The Personal Testimony of One Life-Time*. The Sunday School Times Company: Philadelphia, 1921.

Gregory of Tours. Translated by Ernest Brehaut. *History of the Franks. Columbia University Press: New York, 1916.*

Hein, Ellie and Rodney. *Mozambique: The Cross and The Crown*, Christ For All Nations: Dallas, 1989.

Hunter, Charles and Francis. *The Angel Book: Personal Encounters With God's Messengers*. Whitaker House: New Kensington, PA, 1999.

Justice, L.A. *Angel Voices*. Globe Digest, New York, 1999.

Malz, Betty. *Angels by My Side*. Baker Publishing Group: Kindle Edition, 2013.

Mather, Increase. *A Disquisition Concerning Angelical Apparitions, In Answer to a Case of Conscience, shewing that Daemons oft appear like Angels of Light, and what is the best and only way to prevent deception by them.*

Mather, Increase. *Angelographia Or A Discourse Concerning the Nature and Power of the Holy Angels. 1696)*

Mather, Increase. *An Historical Discourse Concerning the Prevalency of Prayer*, 1734.

Moody, Raymond A. *Reflections on Life After Life*. Bantam Book: New York, 1978.

P., L. Editor. *A Book of Angels*. Longmans, Green, and Co.: New York, 1906.

Parker, Mrs. Arthur (Rebecca Jane). *Sadhu Sundar Singh: Called of*

God. Trumpet Press: Lawton, OK, 2013.

Rawlings, Maurice. *Beyond Death's Door*. Thomas Nelson: Nashville, 1978.

Rawlings, Maurice. *To Hell and Back*. Thomas Nelson: Nashville, 1993.

Richey, Stephen W. (2000). "Joan of Arc: A Military Appreciation". *The Saint Joan of Arc Center* online. Accessed July 16, 2021. http:// www.stjoan-center.com /military/ stephenr.html.

Ritchie, George G. and Elizabeth Sherrill. *Return From Tomorrow*. Numerous editions.

"Saved By An Angel," *White County Heritage*, 2001. www.argenweb.net/ white/ wchs/ Lonnie_Glossom_files/ Glosson_Guardian_Angel.html

Shedd, Charlie W. *Brush of an Angel's Wing*. Servant Publications: Ann Arbor, MI, 1994.

Unknown. *A Miracle in the Pacific*. "Weekly Unity." March 10, 1946. Kansas City, MO.

Vest, Freddy. *The Day I Died*. Charisma House: Lake Mary, FL, 2014.

Whitehouse A., *Heroes and Legends of World War I.* Doubleday & Co.: New York, 1964.

Wood, Gary. *I Died And Went To Heaven*. Gary Wood Ministries, Sugarland, Texas, 2002.

Zaleski, Carol. *Otherworld Journey*s; Accounts of Near-Death Experience in Medieval and Modern Times. Oxford University Press: New York, 1987.

www.ingramcontent.com/pod-product-compliance
Lightning Source LLC
Chambersburg PA
CBHW071936150726
47999CB00001B/221